The research methods book that has been missing from architectural practice has finally been written! Here is the first architectural research methods book written with the practitioner and studio student in mind. Illustrated extensively with both highly informative diagrams and illuminating case studies, *Research Methods for the Architectural Profession* clearly and compellingly presents research as it may interact with the design process as found in practice. This book is a must have for those in architecture and interior design who seek guidance on how to engage in meaningful and informative research in the real world and produce better designs as a result.

Keith Diaz Moore, Dean, College of Architecture
and Planning, University of Utah

A comprehensive guide to understanding the why, what, when, how, and who needed to conduct and apply research in architectural practice. This book contains important motivations, definitions, categorizations and examples that demystify the process and make research more broadly relevant and applicable to the profession. It should be useful to students, researchers, and professors, as well as all levels and disciplines of architecture, engineering, construction, and operations, as the industry pivots to a more objective, data-driven approach to the built environment.

John Haymaker, PhD, AIA, Director of Research, Perkins and Will

Research Methods for the Architectural Profession succinctly presents qualitative, quantitative, and experimental methods relevant and useful in the architectural profession, academia, and research organizations. The book refreshingly distinguishes itself by avoiding jargon and providing clear examples of various approaches in the primary subject areas in architecture: architectural history and theory, social and behavioral studies, environmental, technology, building systems, economics, and design process. Readily adoptable for research methods and professional context courses and those in collaborative research practices!

Alison G. Kwok, PhD, LEED AP, CPHC, Professor, University of Oregon

Akšamija's is a unique and energetic voice bridging the architectural profession and the academy. The challenges facing humanity demand innovation on a massive scale; nowhere is this truer than with buildings and urban habitat. There has been little convergence within the profession on the role of research in architectural education and practice. Akšamija provides a broad context for consideration, but most importantly, she accurately ties the future of the architectural profession to an integration of research and practice and conveniently lays out a roadmap for research-based architectural practice.

Mic Patterson, PhD, LEED AP BDC, Ambassador of
Innovation & Collaboration, Façade Tectonics Institute

In today's world we confront unprecedented problems in environments hallmarked by escalating complexity. Architects and designers are increasingly challenged to render potent decisions in a daunting milieu, with expectations to do so with skill, evidence and efficacy. Responding to growing demands for architects to be better equipped to operate in these emerging conditions, Ajla Akšamija's book, *Research Methods for the Architectural Profession*, proves timely, informative and inspiring. Written with clarity and readily accessible to a broad readership, Professor Akšamija presents us with a valuable and comprehensive array of chapters that meaningfully inform architects on research strategy, methods, integration and application.

Dr. Brian R. Sinclair, PhD DrHC FRAIC AIA (Intl),
Professor of Architecture + Environmental Design |
Former Dean, University of Calgary + President of sinclairstudio inc.

Research Methods for the Architectural Profession

Research Methods for the Architectural Profession introduces research as a systematic process, describes how to formulate research questions, provides an in-depth explanation of different research methods (qualitative, quantitative, and experimental), and explains how to select appropriate research methods and execute research studies. It describes the process of documentation, knowledge dissemination, and application of research results in architectural design and practice. Most importantly, it provides guidelines for integrating research into the profession and uses extensive case-studies and practice-relevant examples to illustrate the main concepts, procedures, and applications.

Integrating research into practice is essential for developing new knowledge, solving design and technical problems, overcoming different types of challenges present in the contemporary profession, and improving design outcomes. Innovation requires a much stronger correlation between research and design, and it is pertinent for the future of architectural practice that research becomes an integral part of the architectural profession. This book provides a roadmap for successfully integrating research into architectural design and for establishing innovative practices, regardless of a firm's size.

Written by an architecture professor with an extensive research and professional background—specifically focusing on integrating research into practice—and richly illustrated with over 150 color images, this reference will be useful for both students and practitioners.

Ajla Akšamija, PhD, LEED AP BD+C, CDT is a faculty member in the Department of Architecture at the University of Massachusetts Amherst. Her interdisciplinary research expertise includes performance-based design, building science, building enclosures, emerging building technologies, digital design, and innovations in architecture. Akšamija has authored two previously published books, *Integrating Innovation in Architecture: Design, Methods and Technology for Progressive Practice and Research* (2016) and *Sustainable Facades: Design Methods for High-Performance Building Envelopes* (2013). She has contributed to many other books and numerous research publications. As one of the pioneers of practice-based architectural research, she established the Perkins and Will Building Technology Laboratory ("Tech Lab") in 2008, one of the first practice-driven research laboratories in the architectural profession.

Research Methods for the Architectural Profession

Ajla Akšamija

Routledge
Taylor & Francis Group

NEW YORK AND LONDON

First published 2021
by Routledge
52 Vanderbilt Avenue, New York, NY 10017

and by Routledge
2 Park Square, Milton Park, Abingdon, Oxon, OX14 4RN

Routledge is an imprint of the Taylor & Francis Group, an informa business

Library of Congress Cataloging-in-Publication Data
Names: Akšamija, Ajla, author.
Title: Research methods for the architectural profession / Ajla Akšamija.
Description: New York : Routledge, 2021. | Includes bibliographical
references and index.
Identifiers: LCCN 2020040133 (print) | LCCN 2020040134 (ebook) |
ISBN 9780367433970 (hardback) | ISBN 9780367433963 (paperback) |
ISBN 9781003002932 (ebook)
Subjects: LCSH: Architecture--Research--Methodology. |
Architectural practice.
Classification: LCC NA2500 .A436 2021 (print) | LCC NA2500 (ebook) |
DDC 720.72--dc23
LC record available at https://lccn.loc.gov/2020040133
LC ebook record available at https://lccn.loc.gov/2020040134

ISBN: 978-0-367-43397-0 (hbk)
ISBN: 978-0-367-43396-3 (pbk)
ISBN: 978-1-003-00293-2 (ebk)

Typeset in Univers
by Deanta Global Publishing Services, Chennai, India

Cover design by Ajla Akšamija

Contents

**PART 5
CASE STUDIES**   **145**

PART 1

INTRODUCTION

1   Introduction

1.1 WHAT IS RESEARCH AND HOW DOES IT RELATE TO ARCHITECTURAL DESIGN?

Research is a systematic investigation of a certain topic or a problem, aimed to discover or interpret facts and theories, address specific questions, and determine answers to these questions and find practical applications for discoveries. As such, research creates new knowledge and relies on the scientific method to test hypotheses, execute studies, and document results. There are two types—basic and applied research. Basic research refers to the development of new knowledge, facts, and scientific principles and testing of theories. Applied research refers to the development of new applications, products, and systems.

A typical research process starts with identifying specific research problems and objectives, determining appropriate research methods for addressing these problems, and then proceeds with the execution, documentation of results, and dissemination. The process is identical for many different disciplines, but the nature of research problems and objectives vary according to specific domain. In architectural design, the research problems and questions relate to buildings, their occupants, environment, design and construction methods, building systems and materials, design process, etc. The topics are wide-ranging (and can include both basic and applied research), but essentially relate to buildings, their inhabitants, and their environment, and closely relate to the nature of specific design phases.

Figure 1.1 shows typical architectural design phases, starting with pre-design, conceptual design, schematic design, design development, construction documentation, construction administration, building operation, and post-construction activities. In pre-design, architects gather information from the client about the project's requirements, building program, and site and prepare contractual agreements for the project. During the conceptual design, site analysis is performed to understand the project context (climate, environment, demographics, culture, social and economic aspects, transportation, zoning requirements, etc.), and this information, along with client's requirements and building program, is used to develop basic building form and massing. During the schematic design phase, interior spatial layout and organization are determined, based on building codes and building program, as well as structural systems, horizontal and vertical circulation through the building, and schematic building envelope design, such as location of windows, openings, and opaque areas of the facade. During design

DESIGN PHASES

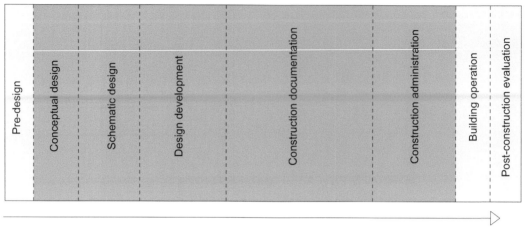

TIME

development, detailed design of building envelope, structural system, selection of materials and building systems, including Heating Ventilation and Air-Conditioning (HVAC), plumbing, electrical, fire safety, and integration of building systems are the primary activities. During construction documentation, technical construction documents (drawings and specifications) are developed, which are used as the basis for construction. Collaboration between architects, engineers, consultants, and the client is important during all stages of the design process but is essential in the construction documentation phase. During construction administration, architects observe the construction process and monitor progress, making sure that the construction follows what is prescribed in the construction documentation (drawings and specifications). Post-construction activities may include preparation of operation manuals, participation in building commissioning, and administering post-occupancy evaluations to assess design outcomes and occupants' satisfaction with the interior environment.

But how does research relate to architectural design? Research and architectural design are both problem-solving processes, but architectural design also requires a creative, subjective approach to finding a solution to a given design problem. On the other hand, research requires an objective approach. These are the main differences between research and architectural design process. However, architectural design relies on research, and Figure 1.2 shows how research relates to different stages of the architectural design process. It is important to note the differences between project-specific research, as shown in Figure 1.2 and broader research that impacts the wider profession. For project-specific research, architects conduct research to solve problems relating to a specific architectural project or to acquire the necessary information for that project (Groat and Wang, 2013; Sarvimaki, 2017). For example, in the pre-design phases, architects conduct interviews with the client to understand project objectives, building program, and requirements. They perform an initial site analysis to understand the location and context, zoning requirements, etc. In some instances, they develop a building program and

Figure 1.1:
Architectural design
phases.

ARCHITECTURAL DESIGN   RESEARCH

DESIGN PHASE	TYPES OF ACTIVITIES	INFORMATION AND DATA		TYPES OF ACTIVITIES
Pre-design	Client interviews Contract Planning and programming Data collection	Client's needs Location and site Program requirements Legal	◁	Interviews with Client Contextual site analysis Building program evaluations
Conceptual design	Site analysis Concept development Massing/building volume studies Programmatic analysis Building form Site development	Climate data Site context data (urban fabric, transportation, history, density, zoning, etc.) Demographics Economic aspects	◁	Full site analysis (climate, site, context, zoning) Building code analysis Program evaluations Building form evaluations Site impact analysis
Schematic design	Spatial layout and organization Schematic building envelope design Circulation Vertical transportation Structural system	Building codes Detailed program Structural loads Economic aspects	◁	Detailed buiding code analysis Analysis of building systems Energy/environmental impacts analysis
Design development	Building envelope design Building systems Integration of building systems Coordination Materials	Building systems properties Peformance data Materials data	◁	Performance analysis (building envelope, building systems, structural, etc.) Materials research
Construction documentation	Technical documentation Technical details Specifications development Coordination	Peformance data Materials/systems specifications Construction methods	◁	Technical research Experimental testing Mock-up testing
Construction administration	Construction process observations Construction progress monitoring	Construction documentation Actual construction progress Specifications	◁	Mock-up testing Observations
Building operation	Review of final construction results	Construction documentation- Operation manuals	◁	Building commissioning
Post-construction evaluation	Evaluation of design outcomes	Construction documentation As-built documentation	◁	Post-occupancy evaluations Observations

Figure 1.2: Research in the architectural design process in relation to different project phases, specific for architectural projects.

perform research to understand spatial requirements, optimal size, and areas of the different types of spaces in the program and the relationships between these spaces. During conceptual design, architects perform building code analysis and detailed site analysis to understand the building codes, climate, environmental factors, demographics, transportation, history, social and economic aspects, culture, etc. because all these factors influence design decision-making. During schematic design, research activities include detailed building code analysis and may include preliminary analysis of building systems and environmental and energy impact. During design development, research activities are mostly associated with integration of building systems, building performance aspects (energy, structural, thermal, daylight, occupants' comfort, building envelope), and building materials. During construction documentation, research is typically conducted to understand specific building components, construction techniques, or application of innovative construction materials and technologies. Since design development and construction documentation are the longest phases of any architectural project, research activities are also proportionally extensive during these two phases. During construction administration, research activities may include mock-up testing, such as experimental evaluation of building envelope mock-ups. During initial stages of the building operation, research activities may include building commissioning tasks, necessary to evaluate operation of building systems and to calibrate their performance. During later stages of building operation, post-occupancy evaluations may be conducted to assess design effectiveness, actual building performance, occupants' satisfaction, and comfort (thermal, visual, acoustic). This process directly applies to the design of new buildings, but is quite similar for building retrofits, renovations, and adaptive reuse projects. The information that is gained through research directly influences decision-making and design outcomes for a specific architectural project; however, the notion of design as a creative activity also has its effect on the final outcomes. Although research conducted for a particular architectural project has the greatest impact on that specific project, the results and lessons learned through the process (or after the building is constructed and occupied) are still applicable to a wider range of design problems, such as similar building types, and can benefit the architectural profession.

CASE STUDY 1.1: EXAMPLE OF PROJECT-SPECIFIC RESEARCH: PERFORMANCE ANALYSIS FOR A COMMERCIAL BUILDING

The purpose of this study was to investigate high-performance design options for a commercial building, located in Boston. The study considered different orientations of the building and different facade design strategies for improving energy efficiency and occupants' comfort, varying the types of materials and glazing, shading options (horizontal shading elements for the south-oriented facade and vertical shades for the east and west facades), and integration of light-shelves for improved daylighting distribution within interior spaces.

Figure 1.3 shows a comparison of incident solar radiation for south-oriented facades, where one of the design options included a series of horizontal shading elements. These results were obtained through simulations, where incident solar radiation was modeled based on the facade design configuration, orientation, and local climatic data. Energy modeling was performed to investigate different design options for each relative orientation, and daylighting simulations were performed to understand the impacts on natural lighting levels for all design options. Annual energy consumption, thermal comfort, and daylight levels were investigated for all options. Figure 1.4 shows summary results for energy consumption for all building

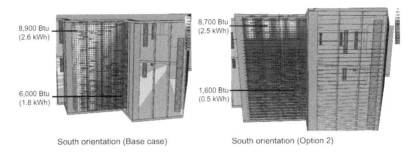

8,900 Btu (2.6 kWh)

8,700 Btu (2.5 kWh)

6,000 Btu (1.8 kWh)

1,600 Btu (0.5 kWh)

South orientation (Base case)   South orientation (Option 2)

Figure 1.3:
Comparison of incident solar radiation for south-oriented facade, showing the impacts of horizontal shading devices.

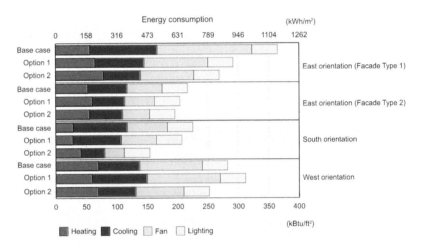

Figure 1.4:
Comparison of energy consumption results for all facade orientations and all design options.

orientations and design options. The best performing option that reduces energy consumption for all orientations was chosen in the final design.

Daylight simulations were performed to investigate availability of natural light reaching the interior space. Since it was found that the best-performing design scenarios for the south and west orientations include horizontal overhang, horizontal shading elements, and a light-shelf for reducing energy consumption, these design options have been used to study availability of natural light. They were compared to two other design options, where one option included a serrated facade without any shading elements or light-shelves, and the second option included a serrated facade with a deep horizontal overhang, series of horizontal shading elements, and an interior light-shelf. Daylight analysis was performed for September 21 at noon, with sunny sky conditions. Since this facade adjoins a two-story interior space, the purpose of the analysis was to compare daylight levels on both levels. Specifically, light redirecting mechanisms for the office space located on the second floor were investigated. These different options are shown in Figure 1.5, as well as the daylight simulation results.

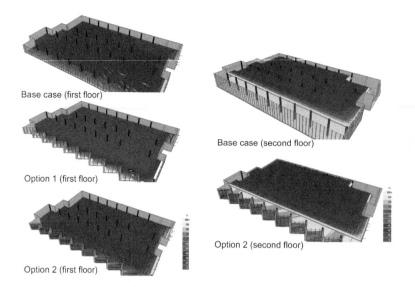

Base case (first floor)

Base case (second floor)

Option 1 (first floor)

Option 2 (first floor)

Option 2 (second floor)

Figure 1.5:
Design options and results of daylight simulations.

Generally, the highest daylighting levels for the first floor would be present for the base case scenario; however, this option is the worst from an energy performance perspective. Comparison between options one and two shows that option two would provide more daylight since the shading elements and a light-shelf would redirect light within the interior space. For the second floor, daylight levels are comparable for both options, although the actual values are higher for the base case scenario. Since option two is the best performing design scenario in terms of energy performance, the addition of light-shelves would balance the effects of shading elements on the availability of natural light.

This case study illustrates how the research process can be beneficial for design decision-making. Having these results and quantifiable data allowed the design team to make informed decisions regarding the facade treatment for this specific project, as well as daylight harvesting strategies. At the same time, documenting results and sharing research processes, objectives and results are beneficial for the design community at large since these results can also be applied to other similar projects or design problems. Besides project-specific research, there is also a need for a broader research spectrum that addresses all the different aspects relating to the design of built environments, which may not necessarily relate to a specific design project. These types of research projects are often long-term and may require substantial involvement from different disciplines, collaboration, and investments.

Now, what are the relationships between research and the architectural profession? How does research influence the architectural profession as a whole? Figure 1.6 indicates different categories of research and relationships to the architectural

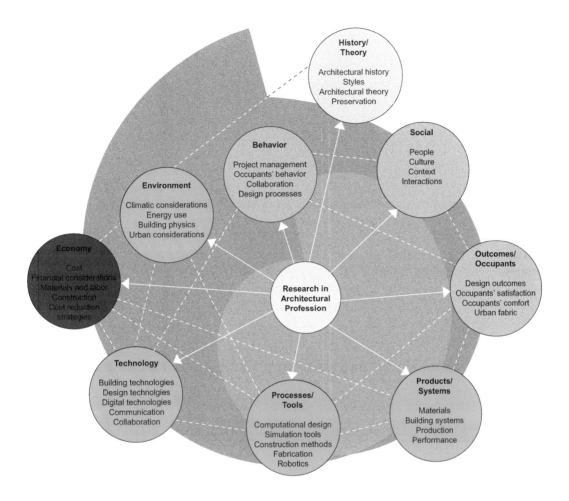

Figure 1.6:
Research in the
architectural profes-
sion, outlining
different areas of
research.

profession. It is important to distinguish between different categories of research in architecture because the nature of research studies, objectives, methods, and results are different. However, all categories influence the architectural profession and are necessary to address various types of inquiries. We can group them according to the primary subject area, such as architectural history research and theory, social and behavioral studies, environmental, technology, building systems and design process research, and economics. For example, architectural history research primarily focuses on historical and archival research, whose focus might be on a specific architectural style, historical building, an architect, or a historic area. This type of research work is closely related to historic preservation. On the other hand, social and behavioral studies primarily relate to people, culture, context, building occupants, and interactions between people and the built environment. These types of studies may also relate to design process, project management, collaboration, and interactions between various stakeholders (project team, architects and their consultants, contractors, clients, manufactures, fabricators, etc.). Specific area of social and behavioral research also deals with design outcomes, design effectiveness, occupants' satisfaction, and occupants' comfort. Environmental research focuses on the physical characteristics of buildings and their environments, environmental effects, energy use and environmental impact of buildings, climatic considerations in design, and building physics. Technology research focuses on building technologies, design technologies, digital processes in architecture, and is closely related to environmental and process research. Process research refers to research studies that investigate design processes, tools, software programs for design and simulation, construction methods, and fabrication. Products and systems research focus on new materials, building systems, production methods, and performance of these systems. These types of studies tend to be closely related to environmental, technology, and process research. Lastly, economic aspects are extremely important in the architectural profession, and these types of studies focus on financial considerations for design, such as cost (initial and life cycle) of materials and building systems, construction costs, cost-effective design strategies, etc. These types of studies often correlate to the environmental, technology, process, or products/systems research. Therefore, research studies may focus on two or more categories of research.

The differences between project-specific research and broader research are often in the scope and objectives of the studies. Project-specific research focuses on a single architectural project, and the primary objectives tend to be associated with that project. For example, a performance analysis of different design options for a building's facade design may require investigation of materials, facade systems, daylight strategies, and thermal and energy performance. The results would be used to optimize facade design for that specific building. The results create new knowledge and may be applicable to similar situations and buildings, but the primary beneficiary of such studies is the project for which the research is conducted. On the other hand, broader research focuses on objectives that are beyond the scope of a single architectural project and addresses a much wider array of problems and issues. For example, a research study may focus on the development of new simulation tools for facade performance analysis, coupling environmental and energy performance analysis, occupants' comfort, and costs. The results would be used to develop a new design decision-making tool, which can be applied during the design process of many different buildings. Results of these broader studies impact the profession as a whole and create new knowledge that is applicable beyond a single building. It is important to note that both types of research are necessary for the architectural profession, but the research processes are different.

CASE STUDY 1.2: EXAMPLE OF BROADER RESEARCH: ENERGY-EFFICIENT RETROFITS OF EXISTING COMMERCIAL BUILDINGS

Retrofitting existing buildings to improve their energy efficiency is one of the critical issues in the built environment. Retrofitting of existing buildings has many challenges and opportunities but is a viable approach for decreasing energy consumption associated with the building stock. Since buildings account for approximately 40% of global energy consumption, focusing on the existing buildings and methods to improve their energy efficiency can greatly benefit environmental impacts and energy performance (Aksamija, 2017). Retrofitted structures reduce the overall demand for new construction materials, and thus also reduce the quantity of new materials required for creating inhabitable space. New building construction requires a higher quantity of new materials, while retrofitted buildings conserve the embodied energy of the original structure. Effective and reliable energy efficiency measures ensure enhanced long-term energy performance and improve occupant comfort through increased natural light, optimized temperature controls, and healthy building operation and maintenance systems (Tobias, 2010).

A specific research study was conducted to analyze the impacts of retrofitting design strategies on existing commercial buildings' energy performance (Aksamija, 2017). The study began with an extensive literature review to determine the current state of knowledge and identified many studies that focused on this topic. The findings of the past studies indicated that the energy and environmental performance of existing commercial office buildings can be improved significantly if retrofit approaches are selected and implemented correctly. However, studies focusing on the effect of climate variation, building form, and building orientation are extremely limited. Therefore, the study proceeded to address this gap in knowledge, with the primary objective to examine existing buildings located in different climate types and the impact of energy-efficiency retrofit strategies on buildings' energy performance. The following research questions were addressed:

- What are the main characteristics of existing commercial buildings in the United States? What is the baseline energy usage for buildings located in different climates? What is the effect of buildings' shape and orientation on energy consumption?
- What are the appropriate strategies for improving energy efficiency for building retrofits located in different climate types? What are the effects of low impact and deep retrofit strategies on energy consumption? How to apply retrofit design strategies to maximize energy savings?

Research methods included data analysis, simulations (energy modeling), and energy consumption calculations. Energy simulations were employed to investigate baseline energy usage, as well as the effects of low-impact and deep retrofit design. These simulations were based on the characteristics and properties of existing commercial buildings located in three different climate zones in the United States.

Chicago (climate zone 5A), Baltimore (climate zone 4A), and Phoenix (climate zone 2B) were selected to represent three different climate zones (cold, mixed, and hot), as seen in Figure 1.7. In order to analyze characteristics of existing commercial buildings and to develop energy models for simulations, data from the 2012 Commercial Building Energy Consumption Survey (CBECS) database was used. The CBECS database provides comprehensive data pertaining to the commercial building sector in the United States, allowing for the accurate analysis of building characteristics. The database includes

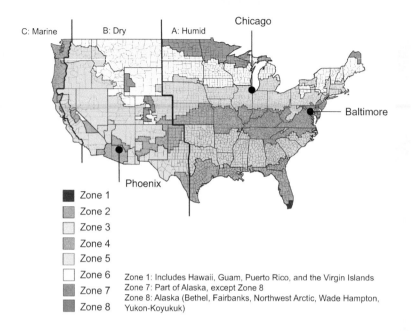

Figure 1.7:
Locations and climate zones considered in the study.

energy-related building characteristics, as well as energy usage data (consumption and expenditures). It focuses on buildings where at least half of the floor space is used for a purpose other than residential, industrial, or agricultural activities. Data is collected through a survey in which respondents supply building characteristics and energy usage data or provide an energy provider account. For the purposes of this study, commercial office buildings were isolated from the CEBCS data and were the focus of the research.

The survey results show that approximately 88% of total commercial buildings are less than 25,000 ft² (2,300 m²), indicating that most commercial buildings are medium to small size. The mean square area for buildings in all regions of the United States fluctuates between 10,000 ft² (930 m²) to 25,000 ft² (2,300 m²), as seen in Figure 1.8. The mean area for buildings located in Chicago is 17,300 ft² (1,608 m²). The mean area for buildings located in Baltimore is 22,300 ft² (2,100 m²). The mean area for buildings located in Phoenix is about 14,500 ft² (1,400 m²). Based on this data collection and analysis, 20,000 ft² (1,850 m²) building prototypes and simulation models were developed to represent the general condition of existing commercial building stock in the United States.

To construct the energy models and set the inputs for building envelope treatment, occupancies, building systems, and construction methods for existing commercial offices, CBECS data was analyzed to determine the details for each building component. Figure 1.9 shows characteristics of exterior walls, Figure 1.10 indicates roofing, and Figure 1.11 shows heating

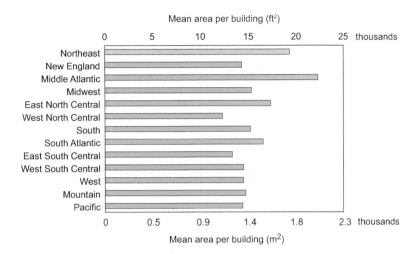

Figure 1.8:
Mean area of commercial buildings in the United States, based on location and region.

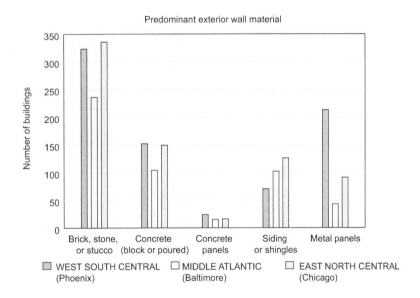

Figure 1.9:
Exterior wall characteristics, based on location and climate.

equipment. HVAC, lighting system control, and efficiency optimization plays an important role in reducing energy consumption during building operation.

The energy simulation software program eQuest was used in the study. Baseline models were created based on the information gathered from the CBECS database, as well as models representing retrofit design strategies. Since the building form and orientations may vary according to specific site constraints, 14 prototypes were created to represent different configurations, forms, and orientations, as shown in Figure 1.12. For each prototype,

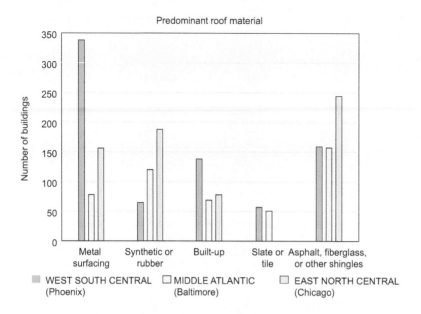

Figure 1.10:
Roofing characteristics, based on location and climate.

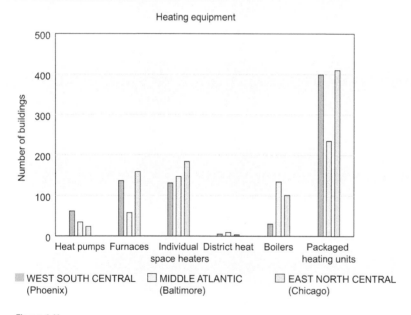

Figure 1.11:
Heating equipment characteristics, based on location and climate.

three different models were created, representing the baseline model, and two alternative runs (low-impact and deep retrofit design options). Energy modeling was performed for all these scenarios and for buildings located in different climate types (Chicago, Baltimore, and Phoenix). In total, 126 different energy models were developed.

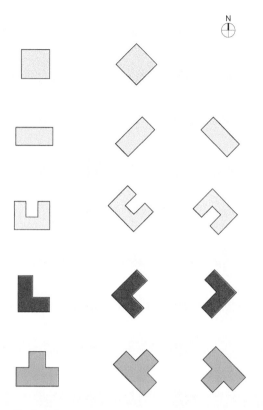

Figure 1.12:
Shapes, forms, and orientations of the modelled buildings.

The first alternative was based on the following retrofit strategies: thermally improved exterior walls, roofs, and windows and lower lighting power density (LPD) for functional rooms, while maintaining the same HVAC system. The results indicated that these strategies would reduce energy consumption by approximately 30% compared to the baseline models. For the building envelope, adding insulation would improve the thermal performance of exterior walls and the roof to better control heat transfer through building envelope. Building envelope upgrades included the consideration of window replacement, exterior shading devices, and interior light shelves. These would contribute to higher energy efficiency and would improve daylight and visual comfort. Retrofitting interior lighting fixtures to reduce lighting power density is an effective way to lower electricity consumption and was included as one of the retrofit design strategies. The installation of occupancy sensors to control interior lighting and the addition of daylight harvesting are feasible strategies which were incorporated into this study. The second alternative considered deep retrofit strategies to achieve significantly lower end uses for heating, cooling, and ventilation. The deep retrofit strategy considered the retrofit of HVAC equipment and the integration of radiant systems, along with improvements to building envelope and lighting system.

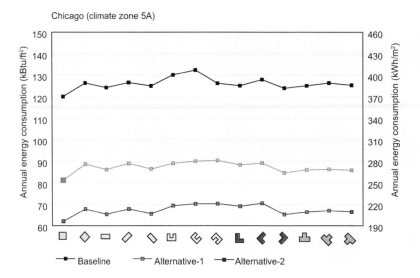

Figure 1.13:
Energy modeling results, showing impacts of low-impact and deep energy retrofit strategies compared to baseline (Chicago).

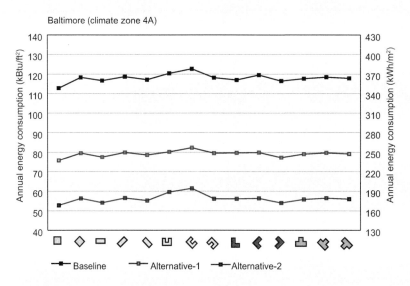

Figure 1.14:
Energy modeling results, showing impacts of low-impact and deep energy retrofit strategies compared to baseline (Baltimore).

Figures 1.13 to 1.15 show results, where energy consumption for baseline, low impact retrofit strategies and deep retrofit strategies is shown for the considered locations. The effects of building shape and orientation on the total energy consumption are also evident in the fluctuations in energy consumption. Detailed analysis of heating, cooling, and lighting loads determined that energy consumption reduces in the heating dominated climate of Chicago with low-impact retrofits, but significantly more with the deep retrofit strategy,

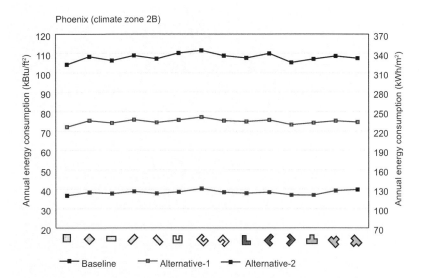

Figure 1.15:
Energy modeling results, showing impacts of low-impact and deep energy retrofit strategies compared to baseline (Phoenix).

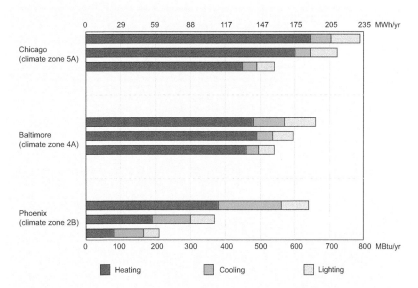

Figure 1.16:
Detailed comparison of heating, cooling, and lighting loads for all investigated climate types.

as shown in Figure 1.16. Improved thermal insulation, as a low impact strategy, reduces heating and cooling loads. However, energy savings are maximized with improvements to HVAC systems, as evident in the results for deep retrofits. Similar trends are evident for Baltimore and Phoenix. Phoenix shows the most significant energy consumption for cooling and the most significant reductions in cooling with more impactful retrofits.

This example shows how broader research, not performed for a specific architectural project but rather within a larger context, creates new knowledge and addresses issues that are important to the architectural profession. Based on comprehensive analysis of existing office buildings in the United States, their current energy use, and the impacts of design retrofit strategies, it is evident that retrofit design can provide significant energy savings. This research analyzed both low impact and deep retrofit strategies and quantified their effect on energy consumption for buildings with various shapes and orientations. Research results show that deep retrofits would significantly reduce energy consumption of existing commercial buildings in analyzed climates. Architects can use this information and detailed results in their work, in discussions with clients, and for selecting appropriate design strategies.

Broad research studies, due to their complexity, scope, and long-term nature, often raise new lines of inquiry and potential research questions that can further our understanding of a specific topic. Relating to the discussed case study, significant barriers still exist in the execution of deep retrofit energy-efficient design. Financial considerations and economic impacts are the most difficult challenges. Property owners may be reluctant to make substantial investments in retrofit analysis, design, and construction. Research and resources are limited when comparing new construction and retrofitted buildings, so it is difficult for most building owners to predict costs during the decision-making process. Further research should be conducted to overcome the barriers relating to economic impacts of commercial retrofits, identifying cost-effective design techniques.

1.2 WHY DO RESEARCH?

Why do we need to perform research in architecture? Research is inherently an integral part of innovation, and as such, it is necessary to discover new knowledge, improve our understanding of the architectural design process and its results, find new methods for design, collaboration, and construction, investigate the impacts of architecture on the environment and people, and ultimately improve the built environment. In academic contexts and higher education institutions, research is an expected activity for many faculty members. Historically, most architectural research came from academic and research institutions, rather than architectural practice (Bayazit, 2004). But this is changing, and many architectural firms are realizing the need to invest in research and the necessity of conducting research (Aksamija, 2016; Samuel, 2017). This is due to many challenges that the contemporary architectural profession is facing, such as climate change, urbanization, depletion of natural resources and environmental concerns, societal transformations, and the changing economy. On the other hand, technological advancements, new materials and building technologies, developments in architectural digital technologies, and new fabrication methods are creating a paradigm shift in architecture and requiring architects to understand how emerging technologies are influencing their work. Therefore, research is essential to understand the effects of these changes and to improve the teaching, learning, and practice of architecture.

Who benefits from research? It has been a long-standing understanding that society benefits from research (Owen et al., 2012). This is the primary driver for investing public funding into research, administered by national organizations and agencies, such as the National Science Foundation (NSF) or National Institutes for Health (NIH) in the United States, and state and local governments. But private industry also invests in research and has drastically increased research spending over the last 50 years. Federal government and private industry have accounted for more than 90% of research funding in the United States since 1953, and federal expenditures peaked in 1964 at 67% (Sargent, 2018). In 2000, private funding accounted for 69% of research expenditures, while the federal government funding fell to 25%, caused by faster growth in industry-funded expenditures. Federal funding grew from $2.8 billion in 1953 to $120.9 billion in 2015, so the reason why the percentage of federal funding is decreasing is not a reduction in actual federal research investments—rather, it is an increase in industry funding (Sargent, 2018). Specific research areas receive different levels of federal funding, and the largest expenditures in the United States are on national defense research and health, followed by space research, general science, energy, agriculture, natural resources and environment, and other types. Where does architectural research fall? Unfortunately, it falls within "other types" (or sometimes "natural resources and environment" or "energy"), and historically has not received wide attention or significant funding from federal funding agencies. Architectural research receives less than 1% of federal research funding (AIA, 2019). This is slowly changing, and specific programs have been developed over the last decade that focus on architectural research topics and the built environment, primarily on energy and environmental impact research, new materials, or advanced building technologies. But it is still not enough to fully sustain the research needs of the architectural profession.

Therefore, it is necessary for the architectural profession to take charge and invest in research that benefits their practices and the entire industry. Studies show that firms which engage in research have higher innovation output and productivity (Crepon et al., 1998). The benefits for individual firms engaging in research also include competitive advantage, new business streams, development of new services, enhanced brand as research-based entities, and staff satisfaction and retention (Dye and Samuel, 2015). However, it is essential that the firms that engage in research share and disseminate research results and obtained knowledge, because only through transparency, discourse, peer review, and sharing, can the entire architectural profession benefit from the research results. The concept of "open innovation", which created a paradigm shift for managing industry research and bringing new technologies to life in other disciplines (mostly technology companies), has been successfully applied for the last 15 years (Chesbrough, 2003; West et al., 2014). The underlying principle for open innovation is the changing role of research from internal discovery to external engagement, where new models for generating and commercializing innovation, collaboration, and sharing are integrated. The architectural profession should adopt some of these principles and apply in our sector.

One of the ways to adopt the open innovation concept in architectural research is to increase collaborations between the architectural industry and academic institutions. However, research in academic and professional contexts is different, and there is still a significant gap between academic and practice-driven research in architecture (Green, 2019). In order to start bridging this gap, it is important to understand these different contexts.

1.3 RESEARCH IN ACADEMIC CONTEXTS

In academic contexts, it is necessary to conduct research to advance our knowledge, to find solutions to pressing societal problems, to discover new technologies, to find applications for these discoveries, and to teach students cutting-edge methods and techniques. Faculty members at higher-education institutions are expected to conduct research, to develop their research agendas, and to publish results and disseminate findings. How does someone initiate a research career in architecture and successfully build a career as an architecture researcher? Best practices for successful academic research careers can be summarized as follows:

- Individuals interested in architectural research and research careers are typically driven by curiosity and aim to answer difficult and complex questions associated with buildings, their occupants, and the built environment. Therefore, the initial step is to determine personal drivers, curiosities, and interests that may spark a research career.
- A successful research career begins with higher education—researchers need to obtain graduate education and training in architectural research. More details are given below, but this is a required step because it exposes future researchers to the research process, research methods, and how research relates to architectural design and profession.
- Researchers need to specialize in a certain area of architectural research, which may include one or more categories of architectural research discussed before (architectural history, theory, environment, technology, social and behavioural aspects, etc.). They build expertise in a certain subject (or intersection of several areas), which typically builds a trajectory for future research careers.
- After formal training, researchers that seek faculty positions in academic institutions need to expand their research agenda, which may include various new research projects related to their expertise, collaborations with other researchers and professionals in the discipline, and collaborations with researchers and professions outside of architecture. It is extremely useful to develop long-term research strategic plans (for example, five-year plans) and short-term ones (relating to a specific long-term plan) that outline research topics, possible projects, possible sources of funding, and expected deliverables. This helps with career development and provides a tangible research agenda. Researchers, once they become faculty members, may also shift the primary focus of their research work, but there is typically a continuity in the types of studies that they conduct. As their careers progress, faculty

members are expected to grow their research outputs (publications, presentations, reports, etc.), apply for and secure research funding, and train and mentor future generations of researchers. Also, as researchers start to build their academic careers, familiarity and involvement with organizations that promote architectural research is very useful.

- In their mid-careers and later, researchers may take leadership roles in their academic institutions or national and international organizations as part of their professional service. This typically results in having less time to conduct research studies but allows individuals to influence the course of education and research agendas for their institution or the future of architectural research.

An academic research career starts with graduate school, where a researcher initially learns about research methods in a specific field, gets exposed to main research literature and resources, and develops their own research project based on personal research interests, in consultation with the primary research advisor and committee. Typically, graduate students develop an interest in a specific category of research, such as architectural history, theory, environmental or technology research, social and behavioral research, design process and methods, or a combination of two or more categories. Learning about research and obtaining necessary research experience is an apprenticeship, where students directly learn from their advisors who specialize in one or more research categories. In some cases, graduate students may serve as research assistants on an advisor's funded research project, in which case this research work may translate into a graduate thesis or dissertation. However, there still must exist personal interest in the subject matter because it is essential to match students' research goals with advisors' research expertise.

In architecture, graduate education begins with a master's degree, which is most often an accredited, professional program. Currently, there is a total of 128 accredited professional master's programs in North America, 82 at public institutions and 46 at private universities (ACSA, 2019). The primary goal of the majority of master's programs is to introduce graduate students to the architectural profession and to teach them about architectural design process, technical areas, professional practice, etc. Typically, research is not the primary objective of professional architecture programs, and the purpose is not to teach students how to conduct research. Rather, the primary objective is to teach students how to independently design architectural projects. But students are typically exposed to some aspects of architectural research so that they can conduct project-specific research work that influences their design projects. Master's programs typically culminate in an independent thesis or a project, where students are expected to produce design projects and to document the resulting designs. In a master's thesis, students are required also to document their work in a written format. The majority of graduate students go into the profession after completing a master's program, without fully being immersed into architectural research (i.e. knowing how to conduct research, select appropriate research methods, execute the study, and document the results). This might be one of the reasons why historically the architectural profession has not been spearheading architectural research efforts—the nature of architectural work and lack of significant research education in professional master's programs created barriers for fully integrating research in practice, beyond project-specific research.

Graduate programs in architecture that fully prepare students for research careers are doctoral programs. In North America, there are currently 39 doctoral programs in architecture, 26 offered at public and 13 offered at private universities (ACSA, 2019a). Doctoral programs offer research-focused graduate degrees, whose primary objective is to teach graduate students how to conduct research, aspects of various research methods and how to select appropriate research methods, and how to execute studies, document results, publish, and disseminate results. Different programs have varying requirements, but one common aspect is that doctoral students are expected to engage in an independent research project, directed by a primary advisor and a committee comprised of several faculty members, focusing on a research problem that has not been addressed before. Therefore, the crucial aspects of a doctoral dissertation are the novelty and originality and the necessity for the dissertation to add new knowledge to the existing body of knowledge associated with the selected research topic. Doctoral programs prepare graduate students for future research careers, in academia or professionally. After completing doctoral dissertations, researchers typically develop expertise within the area that they investigated as part of their doctoral studies. For example, architectural historians focus on research relating to architectural history; researchers focusing on social and behavioral topics primarily work on studies relating to these aspects. Researchers thus develop a research agenda, and may expand their studies beyond the dissertation topic, but they typically remain within the same category of research. It is important to note that most programs prepare students for academic careers, and it is only recently that we have seen the development of a few doctoral programs whose primary objective is to prepare researchers for professional careers.

If a researcher chooses to proceed with an academic career as a faculty member at a higher-education institution, they would most likely expand their research agenda to meet the requirements and standards of that institution, especially for obtaining tenure and promotion throughout their careers. Some universities have very clear guidelines and expectations for obtaining tenure and promotion, while others may have more tacit requirements. Regardless, whether the requirements for tenure and promotion are explicit (such as number and types of research publications, funding, etc.) or implicit, the universal expectation is that faculty members engaging in research must demonstrate the impact of their research work. Some guidelines for assessing value and impact of research for obtaining tenure and promotion are available, which higher-education administration of architecture programs may adopt (ACSA, 2017). Guidelines for assessing the quality of architectural research are currently being developed (ACSA, 2019b).

Research outputs in academic contexts include research publications (journal articles, conference articles, books, book chapters, technical reports, professional

Figure 1.17:
Research outputs in
academic contexts
and their impact.

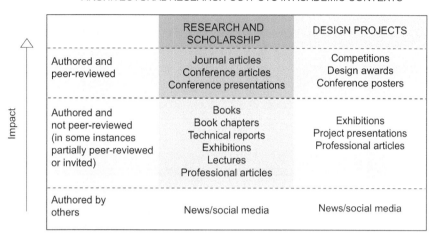

ARCHITECTURAL RESEARCH OUTPUTS IN ACADEMIC CONTEXTS

	RESEARCH AND SCHOLARSHIP	DESIGN PROJECTS
Authored and peer-reviewed	Journal articles Conference articles Conference presentations	Competitions Design awards Conference posters
Authored and not peer-reviewed (in some instances partially peer-reviewed or invited)	Books Book chapters Technical reports Exhibitions Lectures Professional articles	Exhibitions Project presentations Professional articles
Authored by others	News/social media	News/social media

Impact →

articles), presentations, lectures, and exhibitions. Faculty members may also be involved in professional practice and conduct project-specific research for specific architectural design projects. Figure 1.17 shows these two different types of outputs, and their relative impact. An important consideration for evaluating impact of research and design work is the authorship and whether the work has been peer-reviewed by experts in the field.

Architecture schools typically organize their research efforts according to the specialty of faculty members and category of research. The vast majority of programs have representation from all research categories because faculty members also teach relevant courses according to their expertise. In some instances, architectural schools may form centers or labs that focus on a specific area of research, with the aim to increase visibility of their research efforts, attract external research funding, foster collaboration (within the discipline and interdisciplinary collaboration), and engage industry, as well as community.

There are national and international academic organizations whose mission is to promote architectural research. For example, the Architectural Research Centers Consortium (ARCC) is an international association of architectural research centers, founded in 1976. ARCC's primary mission is to support and expand architectural research and to provide research-based infrastructure for architecture and related design disciplines. Historically, ARCC's members have been schools of architecture who have made commitments to architectural research. At the same time, ARCC has sponsored projects, conferences, and other activities involving the broader architectural research community, including industrial laboratories, government agencies, and practitioners engaged in research. The Environmental Design Research Association (EDRA) is one of the oldest international, and interdisciplinary organizations that promotes research relating to the built environment, people, and natural eco-systems. It was founded in 1968 by design professionals, social scientists, students, educators, and facility managers. EDRA's mission is to provide a collaborative, multidisciplinary community to connect theory, research, teaching, and practice. EDRA organizes conferences and workshops and supports dissemination of research. The European Association for Architectural Education (EAAE) is another organization that supports architectural research through its Research Academy. The mission of the EAAE Research Academy is to support various types of architectural research in Europe and globally, to identify concepts and the position of architectural research and how it relates to the changing role and profession of architectural practitioners (especially related to doctoral education), to simulate research activities and foster research networks and collaborations, to identify conditions and challenges faced by institutions and researchers, and to form an open and collegiate community for exchange of research. The ARENA Architectural Research Network is an open, inclusive, and comprehensive network for architectural researchers across Europe. It offers a shared platform to promote, support, develop, and disseminate high-quality research in architecture.

There are also organizations that focus on specific areas of architectural research. For example, the Association for Computer Aided Design in Architecture (ACADIA), founded in 1981, is an international network of digital design researchers and professionals, supporting research into the role of computation in architecture, planning, and building science. It organizes conferences and supports dissemination of research relating to computational design. One of the oldest organizations supporting architectural history research is the Society of Architectural Historians, founded in 1940. It is a membership organization, serving local, national, and international institutions and individuals who focus on the history of the building environment. It promotes research and conservation of architecture, design, landscapes, and urbanism. Architectural Humanities Research Association (AHRA), founded in 2003, is an organization that provides a network for researchers in architectural humanities across the United Kingdom and globally. It promotes and supports research in architectural history, theory, culture, design, and urbanism.

But what is the role of research in professional contexts? How is it different from academic contexts? The next section discusses these aspects in more detail.

1.4 RESEARCH IN PROFESSIONAL CONTEXTS

In professional contexts, researchers may be employed in a variety of organizations, such as architectural firms, national laboratories, private research organizations or consulting firms that provide research services, and non-profit organizations. The types of research work, schedules, timelines, research processes, funding, and knowledge dissemination are different for these varying types of organizations. We will mostly focus on the role of research in architectural firms, but it is important to distinguish and explain major differences between other types of organizations as well.

Private research entities, such as architectural firms that conduct research or consulting firms that provide research services, are internally driven, most of the time privately funded, and work on specific projects that are beneficial to their clients or for their organizations. Most of the time, the research projects are short-term, compared to research conducted at academic institutions. On the other hand, non-profit organizations may be publicly or privately funded, depending on the specific organization's mission, goals, and type of work, and may engage in short-term and long-term studies. National laboratories, in the United States, are funded by the federal government (through public funding mechanisms) to advance science and technology for the public benefit. There is a total of 17 national laboratories, located across the United States, that focus on different areas of research relative to national security, technology, energy, etc. Only five national laboratories have research groups that focus on specific areas relating to architecture and the built environment. For example, Lawrence Berkeley National Laboratory conducts research relating to windows, building envelopes, and daylighting, National Renewable Energy Laboratory focuses on renewable energy systems, Oak Ridge National Laboratory works on building envelope research and testing, Pacific North West Laboratory works on energy efficiency in buildings, and Argonne National Laboratory works on energy production and use. But, since the vast majority of the research work is publicly funded, research studies are typically long-term, and the results need to be widely disseminated and shared.

The number of architectural firms that have active research departments currently is relatively low compared to the number of academic institutions that conduct architectural research, but this is changing (Hensel and Nillson, 2016). There is an increasing demand for architectural firms to invest and conduct research, and some firms are realizing this and actively establishing research departments (Aksamija and Green, 2013). Currently, there is not an established model for integrating research into practice, and different firms are using various approaches. This is discussed in detail in Chapter 4, but three major approaches are: 1) internal research departments within the firm, internally funded by the firm; 2) collaborations with external research organizations, initiated by architectural firms funding research work conducted by external partners; and 3) hybrid methods, where firms partner with external partners, such as academic institutions, or establish non-profit research organizations (funded internally or externally).

Although architects typically conduct project-specific research, and in some instances also broader research (internally, or through collaborations with academic institutions and other research entities), research coming from architectural practices is not greatly visible. This is caused by the fact that the profession does not have a long tradition of documentation and communicating the research work, beyond marketing materials or information about completed buildings. Most architectural publications are not written as research publications and do not give specific details about the design process, methods, or discoveries that often occur during the design and construction of buildings. Moreover, the biased belief that architectural research should be proprietary, due to the competitive nature of architectural business, is the major barrier for wider adoption and implementation of research-based architectural practice. This needs to change, and architectural firms need to look for ways to maintain their competitive advantage, through marketing quality of their services or focusing on a specific market sector, but the firms should accept that sharing high-quality research benefits the entire industry. Professional architectural organizations across the globe, such as the American

Institute of Architects (AIA) or the Royal Institute of British Architects (RIBA), are recognizing the importance of integrating research into their profession and are actively working on establishing guidelines, infrastructure, and knowledge sharing mechanisms and, in some instances, providing research funding through competitive grants.

The AIA Architectural Research Agenda identifies areas of research needs and priorities for the near future (AIA, 2019). It also serves as a call for expanding investment in architectural research, its prioritization within the culture of the architectural profession, and the continued dissemination and exchange of findings. This agenda also provides guidelines that the research coming from the architectural profession should meet:

- There should be clearly identified goals for the research.
- Research results should contribute new knowledge about the research topic, whether augmenting or reinterpreting current knowledge or providing a new inquiry.
- Research must follow a credible, systematic method of inquiry that is objective, reliable, and repeatable.
- Research must be ethical and follow standards for ethical research practice.

AIA has partnered with the National Institute of Building Sciences (NIBS) to create the Building Research Information Knowledgebase (BRIK) database, an interactive online database of peer-reviewed research publications and case studies in all aspects of architectural design, buildings, and the built environment, from pre-design, design, and construction through occupancy and reuse. The aim is to make high-quality architectural research publications openly accessible to practitioners and the public. Knowledge partners that provide publications include academic institutions, non-profit organizations, and architectural firms that engage in research, while AIA and NIBS oversee and manage this database. Moreover, AIA has 21 Knowledge Communities, organized according to the practice area, building type, or special interests (such as building performance, housing and community development, technology in practice, etc.), with the primary mission to share best practices, methods, case studies, and provide a network for practitioners with similar interests.

RIBA also supports and advocates for practice-based research in the architectural profession by providing guidelines, publications, and networks for sharing research results (RIBA, 2014; RIBA, 2017). For example, RIBA conducted a survey to understand the role of research in architectural firms in the United Kingdom, and the findings indicate that architectural practices value research, consider it to be intrinsic to their work, and recognize the potential for research as a separate activity or a diversified service. However, this has not been realized widely or adopted by many firms (RIBA, 2017). Most of the conducted work is project-specific research and technical in nature (environmental impacts and energy-efficiency, precedent analysis, materials and products, and construction techniques research), but post-occupancy evaluations are gradually emerging as an important research activity. Those practices that engage in broader research areas do so to develop expertise in a specific market sector or to enhance credibility and competitive advantage. However, collaborations between architectural firms and academic institutions are not substantial and widely adopted, rather, they are based on individual relationships.

The Architectural Institute of Japan (AIJ) is organized into 16 standing research committees, which promote research activities and conduct studies relevant to the architectural profession. Special research committees also conduct research studies, funded by the municipal governments, public organizations, and the industry. The results are published as reports, technical standards, and books and presented at conferences and symposia. Moreover, several key research journals in architecture, coming from this part of the world are published or supported by the AIJ.

How do we measure the impact of architectural research in professional contexts, specifically architectural firms? While academic institutions have accepted norms and guidelines for measuring impact of research, this does not exist for research that originates in professional contexts. One way to solve this is to adopt methods for evaluating research from academic contexts, primarily putting the largest emphasis on knowledge dissemination and demand for expert evaluation of research process and results through peer review, but also to allow practices to engage in other types of research that may not be subject to peer review, such as development of new tools, software applications, patents, new materials, building systems, etc. Therefore, there should be a balance between internally driven research projects, beneficial only to the firm conducting the research, and disseminated research results through peer-reviewed publications that are beneficial to the wider industry, design community, and general public. Figure 1.18 shows possible research outputs coming from architectural firms and their relative impact.

One of the critical aspects for firms to successfully engage in architectural research is to employ trained researchers who specialize in architectural research. As described in the previous section, architectural research is a specialized skill that requires substantial education and training. Depending on the size of the firm and the research goals and objectives, there are different ways to engage architectural researchers—as full-time or part-time employees of the firm (internal model, internally funded), or by training architectural practitioners to conduct research as part of their work. Another way to engage architectural researchers is to collaborate with academic institutions and fund their research work, but then it becomes more difficult to relate this work to a firm's practice. More detailed discussion is provided in Chapter 4, but to successfully build research culture in professional contexts, it is essential that architectural firms start employing professional researchers.

Best practices for firms to successfully engage in architectural research and integrate research into their work can be summarized as follows:

- The first step is to determine why the firm is doing research, what are the goals and objectives for doing research, and how does it relate to the firm's vision and mission. This can be used to develop a research agenda for the firm, as well as a strategic plan. The research agenda may follow the way

ARCHITECTURAL RESEARCH OUTPUTS IN PROFESSIONAL CONTEXTS

	RESEARCH	DESIGN PROJECTS
Authored and peer-reviewed	Journal articles Conference articles Conference presentations	Competitions Design awards Conference posters
Authored or developed, not peer-reviewed (in some instances partially peer-reviewed)	Books Book chapters Technical reports Software applications Case studies Exhibitions Professional articles	Innovative designs Materials Building systems Patents Exhibitions Project presentations Professional articles
Authored by others	News/social media	News/social media

Impact

Figure 1.18:
Research outputs
in professional
contexts and their
impact.

that the firm is organized, such as different market sectors and building types (residential, commercial, healthcare design, educational buildings, etc.), type of service (architectural, interior design, planning, etc.), or specific area of expertise (building performance, digital technologies, materials, etc.).

- The strategic plan should identify long-term and short-term research objectives, topics, and projects, how research relates to the firm's practice, as well as individuals/researchers/teams responsible for executing these studies. The strategic plan should directly relate to the firm's priorities, business practices, size, operation, and finances. The strategic plan can be used to determine funding mechanisms, number of employees necessary to meet the objectives of the strategic plan (that are already part of the firm or that should be hired), collaborations with external partners, and research methods. The plan should also include an overview of expected outcomes and research deliverables, and how the results will be disseminated. While the strategic plan for research is extremely useful as a planning tool, there should be some room for unforeseen research projects that might be of interest since the nature of architectural work is sometimes difficult to predict. This can be accomplished by annually updating short-term objectives based on the firm's business performance, architectural projects, priorities, etc.

- Firms should distinguish between project-specific research and broad research efforts because this can help with determining funding mechanisms. Project-specific research that applies to a specific architectural project should be included as part of architectural services and funded accordingly from the project's budget. A firm's standard contract language should recognize research as an integral part of architectural services or as an additional service. Broader research efforts that are not project-specific cannot be funded this way, but rather, they must be internally funded by the firm or in some cases through collaborations, partnerships, and external sources.

- Firms that are interested in engaging with academic institutions, or other external partners should determine best practices for collaboration that relate to their research strategic plan.
- It is important to share and disseminate findings of research studies, and firms should determine the best methods for capturing results of their research efforts and sharing them with the wider community. As discussed previously, peer-reviewed publications have the highest impact, because expert evaluations ensure the objectivity and quality of research methods, relationship to current knowledge and novelty, and stature of results. But other forms of dissemination, such as professional publications, presentations, workshops, exhibitions, etc., are also beneficial to the architectural profession because they help to share new knowledge within professional circles. In some instances, research results may be new software applications, tools, materials, or systems, which are typical results of applied research. Firms then also need to determine how to manage intellectual property associated with the results of applied research. For example, software programs can be licensed or publicly available, materials and systems can be commercialized, new technologies can be patented, etc.

Following these guidelines will help to integrate research into architectural practice and wider adoption of research in the profession. Improved collaboration between academic institutions and professional practice is a key component in this effort, and bridging that gap will help improve visibility of architectural research, as well as implementation. The following chapters are a roadmap for understanding the research process, research methods, and mechanisms for architectural research.

1.5 CHAPTER SUMMARY

This chapter introduced research as a systematic investigation of a certain topic or a problem, with the objective to discover or interpret facts and theories, address specific questions, and determine answers to these questions, and find practical applications for discoveries. The important aspect is that research relies on implementation of appropriate research methods to address specific questions, and the rest of this book provides an in-depth guide for conducting architectural research.

The chapter discussed relationships between research and the architectural design process and provided a distinction between research conducted for a specific architectural project (i.e. research conducted during the design process of a single building) vs. broader research that addresses a wide variety of subject areas relevant to architecture, ranging from architectural history and theory, social and behavioral aspects, environmental issues, technology, products and systems, tools and processes, and economy. We have seen how research influences project-specific research during all stages of the design process, starting with the pre-design, conceptual design and the rest of the design phases, construction, and post-construction/occupancy stages, and a specific case study illustrated how research informed the design of a specific commercial building. On the other hand, broader research focuses on objectives beyond the scope of a single architectural project. It addresses a much wider array of problems and issues, and results are beneficial for the entire architectural profession. We have also seen an example of this type of research, focusing on retrofitting design strategies for improving energy efficiency of existing commercial buildings.

Research is an integral part of innovation, and is necessary to discover new knowledge, improve our understanding of the architectural design process and its results, find new methods for design, collaboration, and construction, investigate the impacts of architecture on the environment and people, and improve the built environment.

We have examined differences between research conducted in academic institutions and professional contexts, specifically architectural firms. Historically, the majority of architectural research has been performed within academic contexts, but this aspect is changing. Architectural firms are realizing the benefits of research, as well as the necessity of integrating research in contemporary practice. We explained in detail how individuals interested in becoming architectural researchers start and develop their career, since architectural research requires specific skills and knowledge, obtained through graduate education and research apprenticeship. We also discussed best practices to integrate research into professional contexts and the necessary steps that the firms must take to successfully establish research agendas and maintain research efforts. The future of the architectural profession relies on research.

REFERENCES

ACSA, (2017). "Research and Scholarship for Promotion, Tenure, and Reappointments in Schools of Architecture", Association of Collegiate Schools of Architecture, Retrieved on 9/23/2019 from http://www.acsa-arch.org/docs/default-source/default-document-library/acsa_tenurepromotion_17.pdf?sfvrsn=0.

ACSA, (2019a). "ACSA Institutional Data Report", Association of Collegiate Schools of Architecture, Retrieved on 9/23/2019 from http://www.acsa-arch.org/docs/default-source/resources/acsa_idr_final.pdf?sfvrsn=2.

ACSA, (2019b). "ACSA White Paper on Assessing the Quality of Architectural Research & Scholarship: Working Document", Association of Collegiate Schools of Architecture, Retrieved on 9/23/2019 from http://www.acsa-arch.org/docs/default-source/default-document-library/2019-qualityarchitecturalresearch-whitepaper-workingdoc.pdf?sfvrsn=0.

AIA, (2019). "AIA Architectural Research Agenda, 2019 & 2020", The American Institute of Architects, Retrieved on 9/25/2019 from http://content.aia.org/sites/default/files/2019-05/AIA_Research_Agenda_2019-2020.pdf.

Aksamija, A., (2016). *Integrating Innovation in Architecture: Design, Methods and Technology for Progressive Practice and Research*, Chichester, UK: John Wiley & Sons.

Aksamija, A., (2017). "Impact of Retrofitting Energy-Efficient Design Strategies on Energy Use of Existing Commercial Buildings: Comparative Study of Low-Impact and Deep Retrofit Strategies", *Journal of Green Building*, Vol. 12, No. 4, pp. 70–88.

Aksamija, A., and Green, D., (2013). "Visibility of Research in Design Practice: Current and Emerging Trends", *Proceedings of the Architectural Research Centers Consortium (ARCC) 2013 Conference*, Charlotte, NC, March 27–30, pp. 661–668.

Bayazit, N., (2004). "Investigating Design: A Review of Forty Years of Design Research", *Design Issues*, Vol. 20, No. 1, pp. 16–29.

Chesbrough, H., (2003). *Open Innovation: The New Imperative for Creating and Profiting from Technology*, Boston, MA: Harvard Business School Publishing Corporation.

Crepon, B., Duguet, E., and Mairessec, J., (1998). "Research, Innovation and Productivity: An Econometric Analysis at the Firm Level", *Economics of Innovation and New Technology*, Vol. 7, No. 2, pp. 115–158.

Dye, A., and Samuel, F., eds., (2015). *Demystifying Architectural Research: Adding Value and Winning Business*, London, UK: RIBA Enterprises.

Green, D., (2019). "Less Grey, More Black and White: Architecture Needs a Consistent Platform in Research", *Architectural Design*, Vol. 89, No. 3, pp. 126–133.

Groat, L., and Wang, D., (2013). *Architectural Research Methods*, 2nd ed., Hoboken, NJ: John Wiley & Sons.

Hensel, M., and Nillson, F., eds., (2016). *The Changing Shape of Practice: Integrating Research and Design in Architecture*, New York: Routledge.

Owen, R., Macnaghten, P., and Stilgoe, J., (2012). "Responsible Research and Innovation: From Science in Society to Science for Society, with Society", *Science and Public Policy*, Vol. 39, No. 6, pp. 751–760.

RIBA, (2014). "How Architects Use Research – Case Studies from Practice", The Royal Institute of British Architects, Retrieved on 9/25/2019 from https://www.architec ture.com/-/media/gathercontent/how-architects-use-research/additional-docum ents/howarchitectsuseresearch2014pdf.pdf.

RIBA, (2017). "Knowledge and Research in Practice", The Royal Institute of British Architects, Retrieved on 9/25/2019 from https://www.architecture.com/-/medi a/gathercontent/knowledge-and-research-in-practice/additional-documents/kno wledgeandresearchinpracticepdf.pdf.

Samuel, F., (2017). "Supporting Research in Practice", *The Journal of Architecture*, Vol. 22, No. 1, pp. 4–10.

Sargent, J., (2018). "U.S. Research and Development Funding and Performance: Fact Sheet", Congressional Research Service, Retrieved on 9/18/2019 from https://fas .org/sgp/crs/misc/R44307.pdf.

Sarvimaki, M., (2017). *Case Study Strategies for Architects and Designers*, New York: Routledge.

Tobias, L., (2010). *Retrofitting Buildings to Be Green and Energy-Efficient: Optimizing Building Performance, Tenant Satisfaction, and Financial Return*, Washington, DC: Urban Land Institute.

West, J., Salter, A., Vanhaverbeke, W., and Chesbrough, H., (2014). "Open Innovation: The Next Decade", *Research Policy*, Vol. 43, No. 5, pp. 805–811.

PART 2

RESEARCH PROCESS

2 Research Process

2.1 OVERVIEW OF THE RESEARCH PROCESS

As we discussed in the previous chapter, research is a systematic process, and it is imperative to understand this process before engaging in research activities. Since this book focuses on research methods for the architectural profession, we also need to understand the research process as it relates to architecture, design, and the built environment.

2.1.1 Defining Research Scope and Objectives

Figure 2.1 illustrates the typical research process, which starts with identifying a research topic and specific research problems and objectives that relate to that topic. Figure 2.2 shows the specific tasks that should be addressed to initiate a research study. This helps to frame the research study and to establish the scope of the research. The scope can be wide, narrow, or somewhere in between, but it is not possible to proceed with other steps without identifying the scope of the study. The scope of the study also relates to timeline and specific tasks associated with the study—wider scope research requires more time, effort, and funding for execution, compared to narrower focus research. For example, wide scope research can address pressing, broad issues in architecture, such as development of new simulation tools for investigating building performance aspects during the design or cost-effective design strategies for improving energy efficiency of existing buildings. These types of studies tend to be long-term and require substantial funding and, in some cases, interdisciplinary collaboration. Narrow scope research may relate to a specific architectural project, such as modeling thermal behavior of exterior walls to understand and improve their performance or testing the fire resistance properties of a new material used in construction. Regardless of the type of research, defining the scope is necessary to proceed to the next steps.

2.1.2 Literature Review

The second step is to conduct a literature review, which is essential for any research study. A literature review starts with identifying existing peer-reviewed research studies, publications, and reports associated with the identified topic and research objectives and proceeds by reviewing these prior studies, research methods, and results. Figure 2.3 shows specific procedures for conducting a literature review. The purpose of the literature review is to determine the current

RESEARCH PROCESS

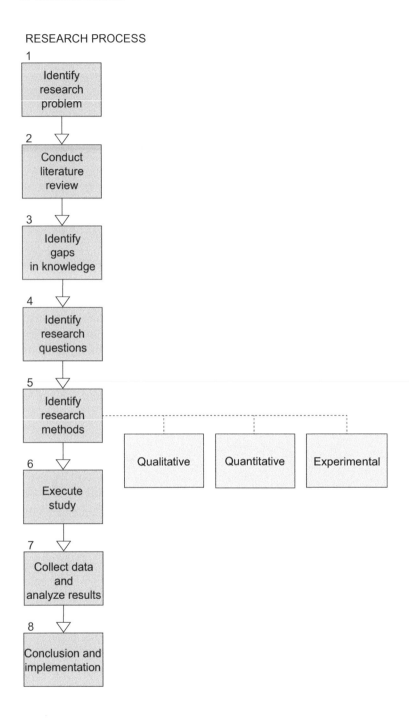

Figure 2.1:
Overview of the
research process
and necessary
steps.

Figure 2.2:
First step of the research process, where specific research problems, objectives and goals, scope, and timeline of the study should be identified.

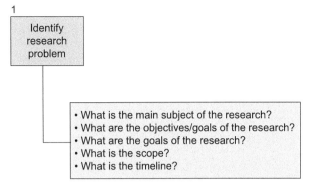

Figure 2.3:
Second step of the research process, indicating literature review procedures.

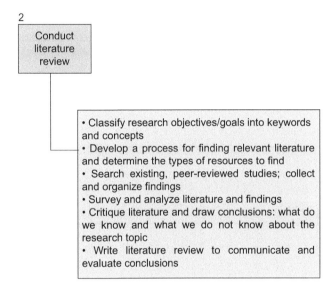

state-of-knowledge associated with a specific research topic and to identify gaps in knowledge. Six steps for conducting a literature review are (Machi and McEvoy, 2016):

- Defining the research problems
- Developing a process for finding relevant literature, determining the types of resources and possible sources of information, and using appropriate search methods (using keywords, concepts, and searching mechanisms) to identify studies that relate to the identified research problems
- Searching for literature, collecting, and organizing the information and relevant sources according to research theme, methodology, chronology, research approach, or another category
- Surveying and analyzing literature, identifying objectives, methods, and find-ings of the previous relevant studies
- Critiquing the literature and drawing conclusions to determine current state-of-knowledge and gaps in research
- Writing the literature review to communicate and evaluate the conclusions

Literature reviews are written by listing studies and sources that were reviewed and providing summaries of the research problems that were addressed in these previous studies, research methods that were used, results, and findings, as well as a critical evaluation of the findings. All the reviewed literature sources must be consistently listed according to one of the standard referencing styles, such as the American Psychological Association (APA) style, Modern Language Association (MLA), Oxford Referencing style, Harvard, or Chicago Manual of Style citation format. Each style has its own rules for properly citing sources, but the common aspect is that author(s), dates, names of publications (books, titles of journals, conference articles, or reports, etc.), place of publication (name of the journal, conference title), publishers and locations (publisher's location, locations of conferences, etc.), and page numbers (for journal articles or conference articles in proceedings) must be included. Dissertation proposals for doctoral studies always must include a literature review, because this establishes the context of the proposed research project. Final dissertations also include an extensive literature review and very often have a dedicated chapter that provides an in-depth analysis of the existing literature. Research publications (articles in research journals or conference articles) must always include a literature review to establish the context of the study, review previous works, and identify gaps that the research addresses. Proposals for funding opportunities must also include a literature review. Therefore, the literature review is an essential step in any research project.

Some research publications provide a comprehensive literature review for a certain topic without presenting new, original research or directly addressing a gap in knowledge with an original study. These indeed are called "literature review" articles and are excellent resources to begin a literature review on a certain topic. These types of articles are still peer-reviewed and evaluated and typically provide a very thorough assessment of past research studies, their findings, and available sources, and may provide an overview of knowledge gaps for a specific subject. For example, a literature review on health care facilities and patient outcomes considered three research areas (patient involvement with health care, the impacts of the ambient environment, and the development of specialized health care facilities for specific patients), as well as relations between architecture and behavioral science (Devlin and Arneill, 2003). The authors reviewed more than a hundred research publications and determined that although health care providers understand that the physical environment of health care facilities can affect patient health, a gap exists between research findings and applications, related to the difficulty in doing this type of research. Since this publication, a number of researchers have tried to address the gaps, and a growing number of research publications on healthcare design have been published (Guenther and Vittori, 2013; Pechacek et al., 2013; van Hoof et al., 2014, Jaychandran et al., 2017). Another example of a literature review concentrated on design principles for traditional residential Islamic architecture, thus falling under the architectural history and theory realm (Othman et al., 2015). The study investigated principles of privacy, modesty, and hospitality in traditional Islamic houses and reviewed nineteen publications and research methods that were used in these previous publications. This literature review concluded that although these three principles are present in all examples of traditional Islamic homes, cultural factors play a big role in shaping architectural styles and use of spaces within residential buildings in different regions. The study also suggests that these differences should be considered by architects, engineers, and builders in contemporary practice. Lastly, an example of a literature review related to environmental factors should be briefly discussed: this literature review focused on outdoor climate around high-rise buildings, particularly wind patterns and the effects on pedestrians (Blocken and Carmeliet, 2004). The buildings impact the environment around their site (especially microclimate), and a specific problem is that high-rise buildings can cause high wind velocities at the pedestrian level, which can be uncomfortable or dangerous. Therefore, the authors reviewed more than two hundred research publications relating to the wind velocity caused by high-rise buildings at the street level and the effects on pedestrians, and in their review also provided an overview of numerical methods, modeling techniques, and an experimental method (wind tunneling) for understanding the impacts of wind around buildings on street level. They also used four practical examples to illustrate the problems and concluded that greater care should be given to this issue during architectural design because the consequences of an unfavorable wind environment near high-rise buildings can have adverse effects on pedestrians. They also provided design guidelines based on previous literature, such as types of building shapes to avoid, an overview of the most common elements that create these problems, recommendations for treating doors and passages through buildings, etc. The authors also specified a gap in knowledge—a lack of and increasing demand for experimental data consisting of many building configurations to be used for Computational Fluid Dynamics (CFD) validation.

2.1.3 Identifying Gaps in Knowledge

The third step of the research process, after conducting an extensive literature review, is to determine gaps in knowledge. Gaps in knowledge are unexplored or underexplored areas that warrant further research to broaden our understanding of a certain topic. Figure 2.4 illustrates what should be addressed in this step of the research process. Original, novel research must address unexplored or underexplored areas; thus, an extensive literature review is necessary to identify what we know and what we do not know. However, in some

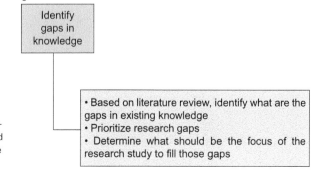

Figure 2.4: Third step of the research process, showing how to identify gaps in current knowledge and set the scope of the study.

instances, we cannot address all aspects that we do not know. Thus, strategizing and prioritizing research gaps helps to set the scope of the original study to be conducted.

2.1.4 Formulating Research Questions

The fourth step, necessary to establish the scope of the study, is to identify and formulate specific research questions that will be addressed by the study, as seen in Figure 2.5. The important aspect is that the research questions should be testable, clear, concise, and focused yet complex enough to require analysis, investigation, and interpretation of data. The research questions also influence the selection of research methods, and this is a key aspect in any research project. If the research methods do not fit or address research questions, it is impossible to continue with the execution of the study.

2.1.5 Selecting Research Methods

The fifth step, after establishing specific research questions, is to select the appropriate research methods to address the research questions, as seen in Figure 2.6. Research methods are mechanisms for testing and evaluating the established research questions. The rest of this book discusses research methods comprehensively, but the three major categories include qualitative, quantitative, and experimental methods. Qualitative methods include non-numerical methods for investigating research questions, including archival research, interviews, focus groups, observations, qualitative surveys, and case study research. Quantitative methods use numerical approaches for investigating research questions, including simulations and modeling, quantitative surveys, and correlational research. Experimental methods use prototyping, testing, and experiments to investigate research questions. Mixed-mode methods, which rely on using more than one research method to address the research questions, can also be used in a specific study, as shown in Figure 2.7. For example, qualitative, quantitative, and experimental, or all three methods can be used to address the research questions. But it is essential that the appropriate methods are selected and determined for the specific questions and scope of the study.

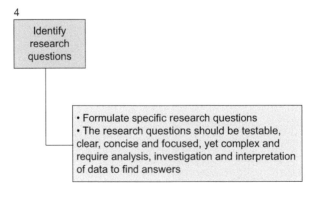

Figure 2.5:
Fourth step of the research process, showing how to determine specific research questions.

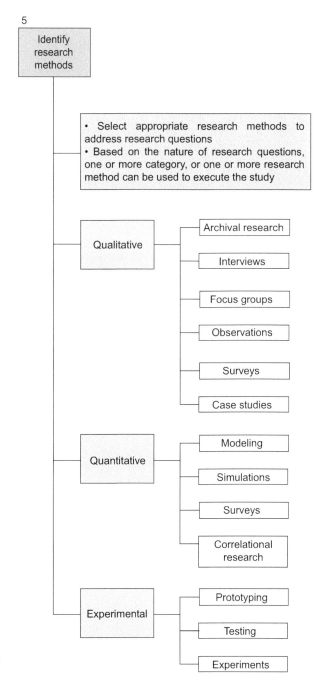

Figure 2.6:
Fifth step of the
research process,
showing differ-
ent categories of
research meth-
ods and how to
select appropriate
methods to address
research questions.

2.1.6 Execution of the Research Study

The sixth step of the research process is to execute the study, which entails
determining activities and tasks necessary to investigate the research questions,
performing these tasks, and detailed documentation of every step, as illustrated in
Figure 2.8. Research execution is also highly dependent on the selected research

MIXED-MODE RESEARCH METHODS

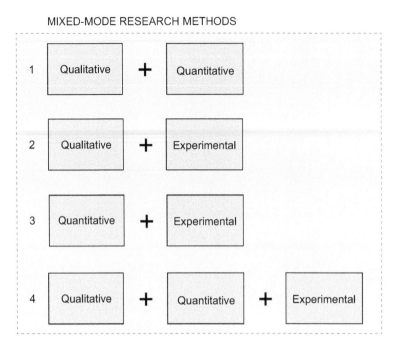

Figure 2.7:
Mixed-mode
research includes
one or more cat-
egory of research
methods.

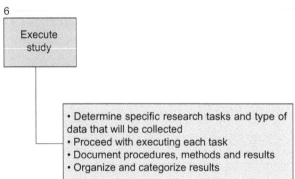

Figure 2.8:
Sixth step of the
research process,
consisting of
research execu-
tion, management,
and documenta-
tion of research
procedures.

methods and scope. It is extremely useful to plan specific research activities and subdivide them into specific tasks, since this can be used to manage the research project, determine how much time is required to complete each task, determine specific deliverables and types of data that will be collected, and, in case of collaborative research projects, decide who is responsible for completing specific tasks.

2.1.7 Data Collection and Analysis

The seventh step is collection and analysis of data, shown in Figure 2.9. Once all the planned research tasks have been completed, the deliverables will include specific data and information that must be evaluated to draw conclusions. The type of data that will be collected is dependent on the selected research methods.

Figure 2.9:
Seventh step of the
research process,
entailing data col-
lection, analysis,
and documentation.

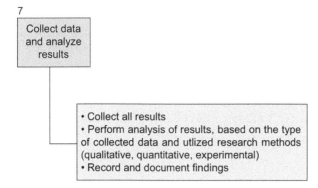

In the case of qualitative research methods, the data might include archival information, survey results (in qualitative format), research notes, graphic information (photos, drawings, and diagrams), etc. In the case of quantitative research
methods, the data might include calculations, simulation results, survey results
(in quantitative format), graphic information (visualization of numeric results), etc.
And for experimental methods, the data might include built prototypes, testing
results, graphic information, etc. Therefore, analysis procedures are dependent on
the type of collected data. Results of qualitative research methods require qualitative interpretation and, in some cases, argumentation to draw the final conclusions. Results of quantitative methods are more explicit and require numeric data
analysis and, in some cases, statistical analysis. Experimental results can include
both numeric and qualitative data; thus, the analysis procedures may include
qualitative interpretation, numeric analysis, and comparison against established
standards. Regardless of the type of data, the results must be synthesized and
analyzed to draw conclusions.

2.1.8 Conclusions and Dissemination of Research Findings

The final, eighth step of the research process is to determine conclusions, disseminate and publish research findings, and in the case of applied research, implement results. Figure 2.10 illustrates the actions associated with the final step.
Dissemination and publishing of research results are extremely important steps,

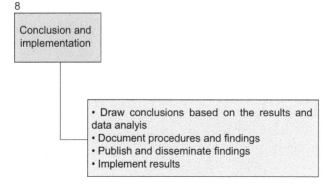

Figure 2.10:
Eighth, last step
of the research
process, consisting
of drawing conclu-
sions, publishing,
and disseminating
findings and imple-
menting results.

especially in the form of peer-reviewed publications. The peer-review process relies on expert evaluations of the research process, methods, results, findings, and conclusions for a specific study—therefore, peer-reviewed articles have the largest impact, especially for basic research. But dissemination can also take place in lectures, presentations, workshops, and development of educational programs. Dissemination of applied research may take the form of publishing or applications, such as releasing newly developed design software tools and accompanying documentation, application of a new material or building system in construction, or implementation of research results on a specific architectural project. Without publishing research findings and disseminating results, we cannot improve our knowledge, add to the body of literature, and create a continuous course of innovation.

2.2 FORMULATION OF RESEARCH QUESTIONS AND SELECTION OF RESEARCH METHODS

Formulating research questions is necessary to determine the scope of the study and the main objectives and to determine what types of research methods are most suitable to investigate those questions. However, sometimes this can be difficult because questions that are too broad may require substantial time and resources to be addressed or may not be addressable at all. On the other hand, questions that are too narrow may not be of interest to wider audiences or may not require substantial research to be addressed. Therefore, there should be a balance, and identifying questions that lie somewhere between these two extremes is recommended.

The best practices for formulating research questions are:

- The posed questions should indeed be written in a question format—this helps to frame the study. As described in the previous section, research questions must be formulated by reviewing relevant research literature and determining knowledge gaps—the questions must directly address these gaps.
- The questions must be testable, clear, concise, and focused, but complex enough to require analysis, investigation, and interpretation of data to be answered.
- The questions can be organized into categories according to their subject area, logical steps (if answers to one question are essential in addressing another question), or relative hierarchical importance (for example, main questions with subset questions).

2.2.1 Selection of Research Methods in an Architectural Context

Research questions directly influence the selection of research methods; thus, the nature of research questions will direct what types of methods are chosen to answer them. In that regard, different categories of architectural research will correspond to different methods. Figure 2.11 shows some examples of research questions relative to various categories of architectural research. Of course, this

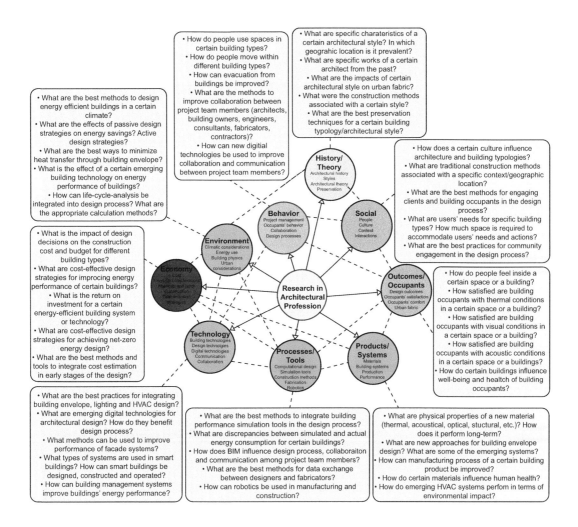

• How do people use spaces in certain building types?
• How do people move within different building types?
• How can evacuation from buildings be improved?
• What are the methods to improve collaboration between project team members (architects, building owners, engineers, consultants, fabricators, contractors)?
• How can new digitial technologies be used to improve collaboration and communication between project team members?

• What are specific charateristics of a certain architectural style? In which geographic location is it prevalent?
• What are specific works of a certain architect from the past?
• What are the impacts of certain architectural style on urban fabric?
• What were the construction methods associated with a certain style?
• What are the best preservation techniques for a certain building typology/architectural style?

• What are the best methods to design energy efficient buildings in a certain climate?
• What are the effects of passive design strategies on energy savings? Active design strategies?
• What are the best ways to minimize heat transfer through building envelope?
• What is the effect of a certain emerging building technology on energy performance of buildings?
• How can life-cycle-analysis be integrated into design process? What are the appropriate calculation methods?

• How does a certain culture influence architecture and building typologies?
• What are traditional construction methods associated with a specific context/geographic location?
• What are the best methods for engaging clients and building occupants in the design process?
• What are users' needs for specific building types? How much space is required to accommodate users' needs and actions?
• What are the best practices for community engagement in the design process?

• What is the impact of design decisions on the construction cost and budget for different building types?
• What are cost-effective design strategies for improcing energy performance of certain buildings?
• What is the return on investment for a certain energy-efficient building system or technology?
• What are cost-effective design strategies for achieving net-zero energy design?
• What are the best methods and tools to integrate cost estimation in early stages of the design?

History/Theory
Architectural history
Styles
Architectural theory
Preservation

Behavior
Project management
Occupants' behavior
Collaboration
Design processes

Social
People
Culture
Context
Interactions

Environment
Climatic considerations
Energy use
Building physics
Urban considerations

Economy
...
...
Materials and labor
Construction
Cost estimation
Strategies

Research in Architectural Profession

Outcomes/Occupants
Design outcomes
Occupants satisfaction
Occupants' comfort
Urban fabric

• How do people feel inside a certain space or a building?
• How satisfied are building occupants with thermal conditions in a certain space or a building?
• How satisfied are building occupants with visual conditions in a certain space or a building?
• How satisfied are building occupants with acoustic conditions in a certain space or a buildings?
• How do certain buildings influence well-being and healtch of building occupants?

Technology
Building technologies
Design technologies
Digital technologies
Communication
Collaboration

Processes/Tools
Computational design
Simulation tools
Construction methods
Fabrication
Robotics

Products/Systems
Materials
Building systems
Production
Performance

• What are the best practices for integrating building envelope, lighting and HVAC design?
• What are emerging digital technologies for architectural design? How do they benefit design process?
• What methods can be used to improve performance of facade systems?
• What types of systems are used in smart buildings? How can smart buildings be designed, constructed and operated?
• How can building management systems improve buildings' energy performance?

• What are the best methods to integrate building performance simulation tools in the design process?
• What are discrepancies between simulated and actual energy consumption for certain buildings?
• How does BIM influence design process, collaboraiton and communication among project team members?
• What are the best methods for data exchange between designers and fabricators?
• How can robotics be used in manufacturing and construction?

• What are physical properties of a new material (thermal, acoustical, optical, stuctural, etc.)? How does it perform long-term?
• What are new approaches for building envelope design? What are some of the emerging systems?
• How can manufacturing process of a certain building product be improved?
• How do certain materials influence human health?
• How do emerging HVAC systems perform in terms of environmental impact?

Figure 2.11: Examples of research questions for different categories of architectural research.

is not an exhaustive list of all the possible research questions that are relevant in the contemporary architectural profession, but rather an illustration of a few questions to show relationships between the type of questions, category of research, and, in some cases, overlap between different categories of research. Figure 2.12 demonstrates different categories of architectural research and typical research methods that are applied. For example, history and theory research studies typically employ qualitative methods, such as archival research, observations, and case studies. Social research primarily utilizes qualitative and quantitative methods, including archival research, interviews, focus groups, observations, qualitative surveys, case studies, quantitative surveys, and correlational research. On the other hand, technology research may use qualitative methods (surveys and case studies), but primarily relies on quantitative (modeling, simulations, quantitative surveys, and correlational research) and experimental (prototyping, testing, and experiments) methods. Mixed-mode methods can be applied to any category of research if research questions require this type of methodology to be employed.

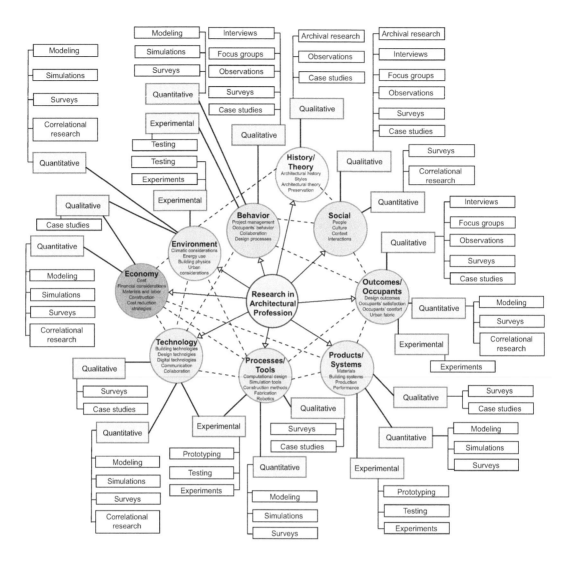

Figure 2.12:
Typical research
methods that are
used for different
categories of archi-
tectural research.

The next chapter discusses the characteristics of all these different methods in much more detail and provides examples, but it is important to understand the relationships between research questions and the selection of research methods in order to design the study, determine specific tasks, and decide how the study will be executed.

Once the research questions have been established and appropriate research methods have been selected, the next step in the research process is to plan precise steps and procedures that will be employed to address the research questions. That might entail developing survey questions for qualitative (or quantitative) data collection, determining what types of software tools will be used for simulation studies and what types of inputs will be necessary for simulations, what types of variables will be investigated through correlational research, how a certain experimental study will be performed and what will be investigated, or what type of information will be collected for case study research. Regardless of the selected research methods, a researcher must determine specific steps, what type of data will be collected and how, and how that data will be analyzed to answer the questions.

2.2.2 Preparation of a Research Proposal

Researchers typically have to prepare research proposals for various reasons. A research proposal is a document that outlines in detail research questions, objectives, and methods that will be conducted in a certain study—it is a roadmap that specifies all the steps and procedures that will be followed. For graduate students working on advanced research degrees, this is one of the crucial steps in their education and training. For doctoral students, this is an essential part of establishing a research topic, determining research questions and research methods, and preparing for dissertation research and writing. Doctoral students typically must defend their proposals before being able to move on to fully engaging in the study and completing the dissertation. And, experienced researchers must prepare research proposals to secure research funding, whether submitted to federal agencies, state or local municipalities, or foundations. Figure 2.13 shows the typical components of a research proposal for a research-based thesis or a dissertation and what must be addressed in the proposal document. For example, a dissertation research proposal always starts with the introduction of a research topic and background, then provides a literature review and states what the current gaps in knowledge are, followed by an explicit statement of research questions, detailed description of research methods, timeline, discussion of expected outcomes, and references for cited literature. Proposals written for funding opportunities are similar, but they also must include financial information, budget, and, in some cases, a research management plan, especially for collaborative research projects that involve several team members. Some funding agencies and programs have specific requirements for proposal preparation and what must be included, and in those instances, researchers should closely follow what is requested. Figure 2.14 shows the typical components of a research proposal for funding opportunities.

After determining research questions, selecting research methods, and determining how the study will be performed, the next step in the research process is to execute the study. The execution is a lot more efficient if the researcher has a clear plan; then, the required steps can be easily followed. The research proposal, as a written document, is an extremely useful tool because it is essentially a planning document for executing research. Of course, there still should be room for discoveries and unplanned work if the direction of the research requires them based on certain findings and results. Nevertheless, the research planning and design of the study will provide necessary steps for conducting the research, gathering data, analysis of results, and dissemination of results.

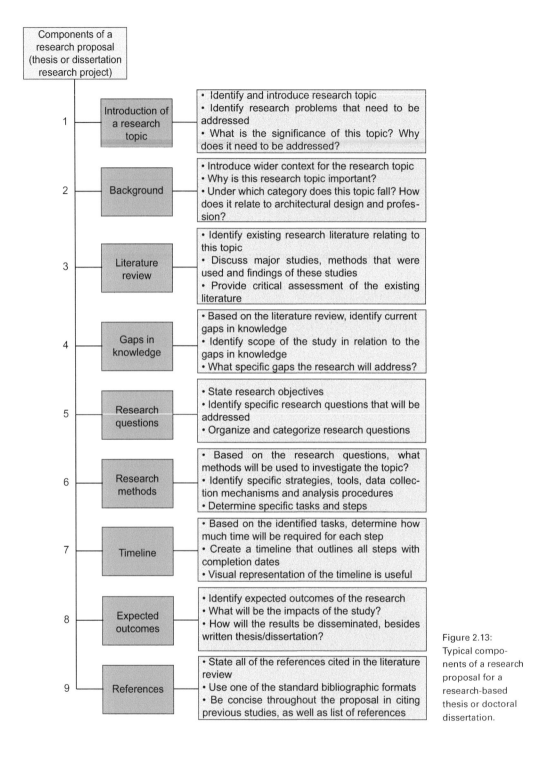

Figure 2.13: Typical components of a research proposal for a research-based thesis or doctoral dissertation.

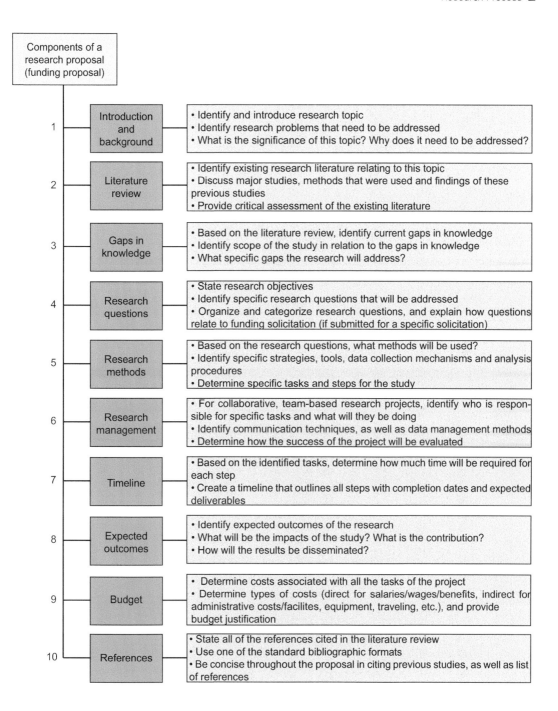

Components of a research proposal (funding proposal)		
1	**Introduction and background**	• Identify and introduce research topic • Identify research problems that need to be addressed • What is the significance of this topic? Why does it need to be addressed?
2	**Literature review**	• Identify existing research literature relating to this topic • Discuss major studies, methods that were used and findings of these previous studies • Provide critical assessment of the existing literature
3	**Gaps in knowledge**	• Based on the literature review, identify current gaps in knowledge • Identify scope of the study in relation to the gaps in knowledge • What specific gaps the research will address?
4	**Research questions**	• State research objectives • Identify specific research questions that will be addressed • Organize and categorize research questions, and explain how questions relate to funding solicitation (if submitted for a specific solicitation)
5	**Research methods**	• Based on the research questions, what methods will be used? • Identify specific strategies, tools, data collection mechanisms and analysis procedures • Determine specific tasks and steps for the study
6	**Research management**	• For collaborative, team-based research projects, identify who is responsible for specific tasks and what will they be doing • Identify communication techniques, as well as data management methods • Determine how the success of the project will be evaluated
7	**Timeline**	• Based on the identified tasks, determine how much time will be required for each step • Create a timeline that outlines all steps with completion dates and expected deliverables
8	**Expected outcomes**	• Identify expected outcomes of the research • What will be the impacts of the study? What is the contribution? • How will the results be disseminated?
9	**Budget**	• Determine costs associated with all the tasks of the project • Determine types of costs (direct for salaries/wages/benefits, indirect for administrative costs/facilites, equipment, traveling, etc.), and provide budget justification
10	**References**	• State all of the references cited in the literature review • Use one of the standard bibliographic formats • Be concise throughout the proposal in citing previous studies, as well as list of references

Figure 2.14:
Typical components of a research project proposal for funding opportunities.

2.3 RESEARCH PROCESSES AND EXECUTION OF RESEARCH STUDIES

Execution of research studies, regardless of the research topic or category of research, always follows similar procedures—determining specific tasks, activities (based on selected research methods), and how the data will be collected; determining types of data and information that will be collected; documenting all the steps, procedures, and results; organizing and categorizing results; conducting detailed analysis of results; documenting research procedures and findings; and disseminating results. Figure 2.15 illustrates specific steps and procedures that must be addressed while executing research studies, which apply to any research process. The type of data and data collection mechanisms are different for different research methods, but the processes are quite similar for all types of research. The next chapter illustrates research processes for different research methods in much more detail.

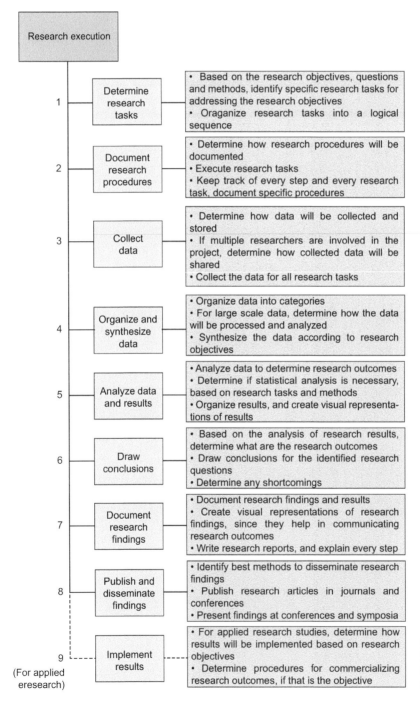

Figure 2.15: Research execution steps and procedures.

Documenting every step, procedure, method, result, and analysis of results is critical in the execution of research studies. The success of any research project lies in not only formulating and designing the research study but more importantly, in documentation of every step in the process. It is extremely helpful to follow the steps outlined in the initial research proposal, determine how to collect, store and archive research results, and periodically check if the goals and objectives of the research have been met.

In the case of individual research projects, such as research conducted for doctoral dissertations, personal databases for relevant literature, research procedures, and results are sufficient, since it is not critical to share every detail of the research process with others. In these types of projects, periodic updates and reports need to be shared with the advisor and doctoral committee; thus, it is helpful to determine the best ways to share and record these updates. For example, online cloud-based document sharing platforms are useful for managing this type of information, comments, and feedback on research progress.

For research projects where multiple individuals and research teams are working on collaborative projects, it must be decided in the beginning how exactly information, research procedures, collected data, and results will be shared among the team members. For example, online cloud-based sharing platforms can be used, but data management plans should be developed that outline specific methods and procedures.

In the case of architectural firms that have active research departments, organizing and structuring research protocols, as well as information exchange mechanisms, must be considered. For example, a firm's network should be used to organize and share information and collected data, while online platforms can be used to share findings, research reports, publications, etc. Firms also must decide what type of information will be shared publicly and how, and how research findings will be disseminated beyond the firm.

2.4 DISSEMINATION OF RESEARCH RESULTS

Documentation of research processes and results is a necessary part of any research project, but dissemination and publishing of research findings are also essential steps. Without disseminating research findings, it is not possible to advance our knowledge about the subject matter nor to add to the existing body of literature. Thus, research writing is a fundamental skill that researchers need to develop and must maintain to advance their research careers. Research writing is different from creative writing and relies on analytical and technical knowledge and skills. Conveying research objectives, questions, methods, and results is the primary goal for writing research publications, and the writing style needs to be direct, succinct, and analytical. Objectivity is critical in documenting and writing about research processes and results; thus, the writing style must also reflect this, and objective discussion of all procedures, results, analysis, and findings should be provided in research publications.

Visualizing research results is important; thus, researchers often need to use effective strategies for graphically representing research processes and findings to easily communicate their work. In the architectural profession, this is even more important than for other disciplines, because architectural design heavily relies on graphics and visual materials for communication. Therefore, effective strategies include mapping, data visualization (two dimensional and three dimensional), diagramming research steps and results, creation of charts and data-flow diagrams, etc. The last chapter of the book provides extensive examples and case studies for visualization of research results.

When writing research reports, research articles, dissertations, etc., researchers need to consider the structure and organization of these documents and how to communicate research processes and findings. Regardless of the type of research publication, structure and organization are quite similar for all different types of research publications, but the length and depth may differ. The structure and organization of research documents typically follows this following sequence:

- Abstract, which summarizes the research topic, questions, methods, results, and conclusion, and provides a succinct overview of the entire research project
- Introduction, which introduces the research topic and research problems and discusses the significance of the specific research topic within the larger context, research goals, and objectives
- Literature review, which reviews the current state-of-knowledge relating to the specific research topic, previous studies, methods and results, and gaps in literature
- Research methodology, which provides a detailed discussion of the research processes, methods, steps, and procedures for collecting data
- Results and discussion, which includes all research results and provides analytical assessment of the results, as well as contextual discussion
- Conclusion, which discusses final research findings, the impact of the research results, recommendations, and any shortcomings or limitations of the study; in some instances, future research may also be discussed
- Acknowledgements, which list funding agencies and specific grants that supported the research or individuals and organizations that helped during the execution of the research study
- References, which list all cited material, organized according to one of the standard referencing styles

In the case of doctoral dissertations, individual chapters follow a similar structure and organization, and multiple chapters may be introduced to document results and discussion. Appendices may also be used to document information that is important for the research project but may not belong into individual chapters (such as full surveys used in qualitative research, computer scripts used for simulations and modeling, overview of focus group questions, etc.). Therefore, the typical structure for doctoral dissertations includes:

- Title page with the dissertation title, doctoral student's name, university/ department, year of publication

- Signature page, which lists the doctoral committee members and their affiliations
- Abstract that summarizes the dissertation topic, research questions, research methods, and major findings
- Acknowledgments to recognize individuals and organizations that assisted in execution of the research
- Table of contents, which lists chapters (headings and subheadings), as well as page numbers
- List of figures and list of tables, which list graphic materials and tables in a consecutive manner, with captions and page numbers
- Individual chapters, which provide the main content of the dissertation. The chapters start with an introductory chapter and then a literature review, methodology chapter, results, discussion and analysis of results, conclusion, and future work
- References
- Appendices, if applicable

Doctoral dissertations are typically the first major research publication for any researcher and require significant time to write and complete. Doctoral students may be required to publish research articles prior to defending the dissertation, which may be incorporated into the final document. These documents are also typically archived by the university where they were completed or might be incorporated into other databases that archive doctoral dissertations. It is always extremely helpful to review other dissertations that deal with similar research topics or areas of research prior to starting to write a dissertation to understand the structure, organization, content, and flow of information.

Content of research articles in journals and conference articles also typically follows the sequence and organization previously described, regardless of the research subject and area. Research articles that are submitted to research journals are often longer and more in depth than conference articles, and the peer review and publication processes last longer. The peer review process is an important step in disseminating research publications because it evaluates research processes and results and relies on objective assessments by experts in relative fields. Therefore, prior to publication, research articles are evaluated by other researchers who are working within the same area of research, who assess whether the manuscripts are suitable for a particular journal (since research journals typically have a specific aim and scope) or conference, novelty of research, quality of literature review (and whether relevant literature has been reviewed), research methods and processes, research execution, results, discussion, conclusion, quality of writing and graphic material, etc. The peer review may include single-blind review, where the names of reviewers are hidden from the author or authors, or double-blind review, where both the reviewers and authors remain anonymous. Double-blind review is more typical, since it ensures objective evaluation of research content without any bias toward authors, institution where research has been conducted, etc.

Academic conferences also employ peer review process for selection of articles that will be presented at these events, and published conference articles are organized into conference proceedings. Therefore, academic conferences typically provide two means for dissemination of research results—presentation and a published conference article. Authors submit manuscripts to conference organizers to be considered for the conference program, and after the peer review process is completed, conference organizers make the decision as to whether the article will be accepted for publication and presentation. The benefits of presenting research work at conferences include networking opportunities to meet researchers working on a similar topic or area of research, opportunities to receive feedback on ongoing research projects, and direct feedback and opportunities for discussions, which are not possible with research journal publications, besides comments and evaluations received from peer reviewers. Nevertheless, research journal articles are regarded as more influential than conference articles, because they have a higher impact compared to proceedings and have more breadth, depth, and present completed research projects.

The impact factor of research journals is one way to measure the relative influence of these types of research publications. It considers citing frequencies of average articles in a specific journal over a certain period. It is calculated by dividing the number of times articles were cited from a particular journal in a specific year by the number of articles that have been published in the prior two years. There are approximately 15,000 research journals on various subjects currently available, and slightly more than 100 of those focus on architectural research. Figure 2.16 illustrates research publications by all subjects and specific journals that focus on architectural research. Architectural research journals typically have specific aims and areas of research that they cover, while a few journals cover wider areas relating to architectural design and the profession. However, it should be noted that not all journals have impact factors assigned, since they must be included in a specific database of citations, and that impact factors vary across disciplines. Therefore, impact factors should not be considered in isolation as the ultimate quality measure of a certain research journal, but should rather be used to identify journals relevant to a certain discipline. Another method to measure influence is h-index, which is determined by the number of publications that have been cited a certain number of times—for example, a journal has an h-index of 10 if there are 10 publications that have been cited at least 10 times in other publications. Figure 2.17 provides an example of impact metrics for one research journal that focuses on architectural research.

Research journals typically require subscriptions for accessing research publications, and university libraries very often provide subscriptions for researchers, faculty members, and students to access research articles. A relatively new trend in research journals is the open access publication model, which ensures public access to research publications without subscriptions. Some research journals in architecture are open access, and the benefit in publishing in these types of journals is wider dissemination of research results since publications are accessible to all. However, researchers should consider the quality of the specific journal and its impact, as well as costs for authors to publish in open access journals (if applicable) before submitting their work for possible publication.

Figure 2.16:
Selected research
journals in archi-
tecture compared
to other subjects,
topics, and number
of publications
(SCImago, n.d.).

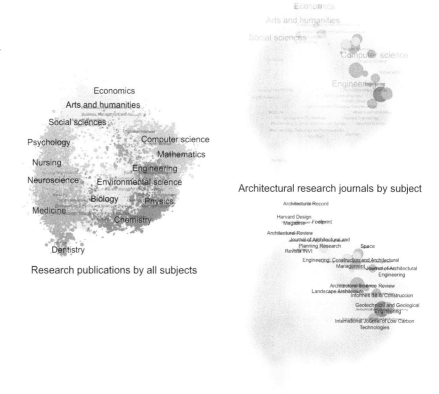

Research publications by all subjects

Architectural research journals by subject

Architectural research journals by title

There are also professional industry magazines that require a peer review process for publishing articles, and this is also a good way to disseminate research results to professional audiences that may not have access to research publications or who typically do not read research journals. However, researchers should keep in mind that the writing style and content of articles published in professional magazines may differ from that of research journals. Industry conferences are also a good way to disseminate research findings to professional audiences, and some industry conferences also employ a peer-review process for selecting presentations.

Some architectural firms publish their own research publications, and these are also of interest to practicing architects. For example, Perkins and Will has initiated the first open access, peer-reviewed research journal coming from the architectural profession in 2008. Over the course of the last decade, this research journal has published over 100 articles in 21 volumes which are relevant to the architectural profession. Gensler has published two volumes of a research catalogue, which also includes studies relevant to the architectural profession. And, as mentioned in the previous chapter, the Building Research Information Knowledgebase (BRIK) database provides peer-reviewed research publications and case studies in an open access format, which is highly valuable to practitioners.

Journal of Architectural Engineering

Country	United States – 🏛 SIR Ranking of United States

Subject Area and Category	Arts and Humanities
	    Visual Arts and Performing Arts
	Engineering
	    Architecture
	    Building and Construction
	    Civil and Structural Engineering

Publisher	American Society of Civil Engineers
Publication type	Journals
ISSN	10760431
Coverage	1995-ongoing
Scope	The Journal of Architectural Engineering is a multidisciplinary forum for dissemination of research-based engineering and technical information related to all aspects of building engineering design in the form of peer-reviewed technical papers, technical notes, and case studies. The scope of the journal's topics include: acoustics; construction; construction management; controls; electrical engineering and systems; indoor environmental quality; lighting and daylighting; mechanical engineering and systems; rehabilitation of existing structures; structural assessment; structural engineering; and sustainable construction/design, in the context of building systems engineering. Innovative and multi-disciplinary studies promoting an integrated approach to planning, design, construction and operation of buildings are especially encouraged. The journal also welcomes papers on the topic of architectural engineering education.

30

H Index

Figure 2.17: Example of a research journal focusing on architectural research, with impact metrics and citation metrics. (SCImago, n.d.).

Regardless of the way that the research is disseminated, without sharing research results it is impossible to advance the current state-of-knowledge and profession. Therefore, it is imperative that the research processes and results are documented and disseminated objectively and transparently, from academia and the profession.

2.5 APPLICATION OF RESEARCH RESULTS

Application of research results can take many different forms, depending on the type of research being conducted. Applications of basic research are typically associated with advancing our knowledge, scientific discoveries, and creation of new information through research publications. Applied research, on the other hand, is associated with practical problems, finding solutions for these problems, developing new technologies and products, software applications, etc., and typically employs experimental research methods.

In architecture, applications of basic research results are used to advance design processes and design services, improve our knowledge, improve educational programs, set standards and guidelines, etc. Applied research can be used to:

- Improve the design process or address technical issues for a specific architectural project (such as methods for improving facade performance or ways to achieve net-zero energy design)
- Create, test, and evaluate new materials used in architectural design and construction
- Test and evaluate new building systems, such as new lighting systems or HVAC systems
- Create, test, and evaluate new building technologies
- Create, test, and evaluate new software applications used for design, simulations, fabrication, and construction
- Test and evaluate new fabrication and construction techniques

Therefore, applied research in architecture is either associated with specific architectural projects or architectural technologies (Emmit, 2013). Results of applied research studies can also be published and disseminated in the traditional way, through research journal articles or conference articles. But results are also applied either for specific architectural projects, series of projects, or specific building products, systems, or technologies.

2.6 CHAPTER SUMMARY

As we have seen in this chapter, research is a systematic process that employs eight steps:

- Step 1: Identification of a research topic, problems, and research objectives to frame the study and to establish the scope
- Step 2: Literature review, which identifies existing peer-reviewed research studies, publications, and reports that relate to the research topic and critically assesses research methods and results of these prior studies
- Step 3: Identification of the gaps in knowledge, based on the literature review
- Step 4: Formulation of specific research questions
- Step 5: Selection of appropriate research methods, based on the identified research questions, and identification of specific tasks, activities, data collection mechanisms, documentation, and analysis procedures
- Step 6: Execution of the study
- Step 7: Data collection and analysis, as well as visualization of results
- Step 8: Determination of conclusions, dissemination, and publishing of research results (and in the case of applied research, implementation, and application of results)

We described every step of the research process in detail and discussed appropriate procedures and considerations that researchers need to address to successfully execute research studies. We also discussed methods for documenting and disseminating research results and how important it is to publish and share research findings. Without dissemination of research results, it is not possible to advance our knowledge or improve design processes. Therefore, transparent and objective dissemination of research results is imperative for the future of the architectural profession.

The next chapter explains different research methods in detail to illustrate research processes and execution of studies using qualitative, quantitative, and experimental methods.

REFERENCES

Blocken, C., and Carmeliet, J., (2004). "Pedestrian Wind Environment around Buildings: Literature Review and Practical Examples", *Journal of Thermal Environment and Building Science*, Vol. 28, No. 2, pp. 107–159.

Devlin, A., and Arneill, A., (2003). "Health Care Environments and Patient Outcomes: A Review of the Literature", *Environment and Behavior*, Vol. 35, No. 3, pp. 665–696.

Emmit, S., ed., (2013). *Architectural Technology: Research and Practice*, Chichester, UK: John Wiley & Sons.

Guenther, R., and Vittori, G., (2013). *Sustainable Healthcare Architecture*, 2nd ed., Hoboken, NJ: John Wiley & Sons.

Jaychandran, C., Ramsey, R., and Roehl, A., (2017). "A protectED ROOM: Design of Responsive and Acuity Adaptable Behavioral Health Room for Emergency Departments", *Perkins and Will Research Journal*, Vol. 9, No. 1, pp. 31–47.

Machi, L., and McEvoy, B., (2016). *The Literature Review: Six Steps to Success*, 3rd ed., Thousand Oaks, CA: Corwin.

Othman, Z., Aird, R., and Buys, L., (2015). "Privacy, Modesty, Hospitality, and the Design of Muslim Homes: A Literature Review", *Frontiers of Architectural Research*, Vol. 4, No. 1, pp. 12–23.

Pechacek, C., Andersen, M., and Lockley, S., (2013). "Preliminary Method for Prospective Analysis of the Circadian Efficacy of (Day)Light with Applications to Healthcare Architecture", *LEUKOS: The Journal of the Illuminating Engineering Society*, Vol. 5, No. 1, pp. 1–26.

SCImago, (n.d.). *SJR — SCImago Journal & Country Rank*, Retrieved on 11/18/2019 from http://www.scimagojr.com.

van Hoof, J., Rutten, G., Struck, C., Huisman, E., and Kort, H., (2014). "The Integrated and Evidence-Based Design of Healthcare Environments", *Architectural Engineering and Design Management*, Vol. 11, No. 4, pp. 243–263.

PART 3

RESEARCH METHODS

3　Research Methods

3.1 OVERVIEW OF RESEARCH METHODS

As we discussed in the previous chapter, research methods are mechanisms that are employed to evaluate the established research questions. Research methods can be categorized into three major categories:

- Qualitative
- Quantitative
- Experimental

Their basic characteristics are shown in Figure 3.1. Qualitative methods use non-numerical strategies, including archival research, interviews, focus groups, observations, qualitative surveys, and case study research. Quantitative methods use numerical approaches for investigating research questions, including simulations and modeling, quantitative surveys, and correlational research. Experimental methods rely on prototyping, testing, and experimental studies. Mixed-mode methods rely on using more than one research method to address specific research questions and can include any category.

The previous chapter provided examples of different categories of architectural research and typical methods that are used for research studies associated with these areas. Qualitative methods are typically used in architectural history, theory, social and behavioral research, etc. Quantitative research methods can also be used for social and behavioral research but are widely employed by researchers investigating building science, building technology topics, building materials and systems, etc. Experimental methods are predominantly used for investigating building materials and systems but also can be used for research addressing design processes, tools, etc.

The following sections explain all these methods in detail.

3.2 QUALITATIVE RESEARCH METHODS

Qualitative research methods are methods used to obtain non-numerical data to investigate specific research questions, typically focusing on human, social, behavioral, cultural, historical, or theoretical aspects of architectural research. Qualitative research methods are used to understand the meaning of certain

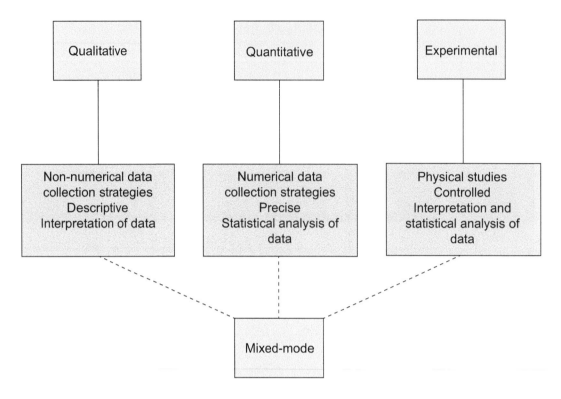

Figure 3.1:
Characteristics of research methods.

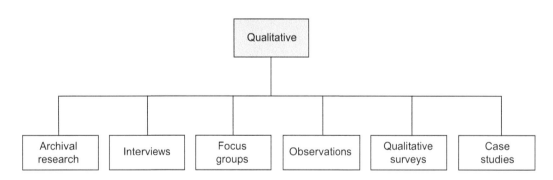

Figure 3.2:
Qualitative research methods in architecture.

phenomena and heavily rely on interpretation of collected data (Merriam and Tisdell, 2016). Figure 3.2 shows different types of qualitative research methods that are used in architecture. The research process is typically inductive, since researchers collect data to build concepts and establish theories, rather than testing hypothesis in a deductive manner. Data collected from observations, archival research, interviews, existing documents, focus groups, etc. is used to describe concepts, theories, design approaches, and design outcomes. Thus, a researcher's analysis and interpretation of data are extremely important in the qualitative research process.

3.2.1 Archival Research

Archival research is research involving primary sources held in archives, special collection libraries, or other repositories of documents. Archival sources include manuscripts (published and unpublished), documents, books, drawings, photographs, letters, newspaper articles, records, objects, sound, and audiovisual materials. These types of sources can include digital and physical artifacts, and institutions are increasingly digitizing archival resources to make them more widely accessible (Armstrong, 2006). Architectural history research and historic preservation research heavily depend on archival research (Wood, 1999; Twombly, 2001; Barbieri et al., 2017; Upadhyay and Sharma, 2018). Figure 3.3 indicates primary characteristics of archival research, data analysis procedures, benefits, and drawbacks.

Architectural records are the principal component of the archival record of architecture. Architectural records include drawings, from initial sketches to presentation drawings and construction documents, photos, correspondence with clients, contractors and builders, manuscripts, etc. Architectural records can serve many different functions, such as documenting design and construction process, providing insight into a specific architectural firm or architect's practice, providing necessary information for historic preservation and restoration projects, or serving as legal records in the case of legal disputes.

In conducting archival research, researchers utilize physical or digital archives to find the relevant documents (drawings, photographs, manuscripts, personal correspondence), read and analyze these documents, interpret collected information, and draw conclusions based on the collected evidence and interpreted results.

	ARCHIVAL RESEARCH
Data sources	• Primary sources from archives (published and unpublished) • Architectural records (drawings, sketches, construction documents, photographs, correspondences) • Other types of sources: books, documents, letters, newspaper articles, records, objects, sound and audiovisual materials
Data analysis procedures	• Review of primary documents • Translation, if documents are written in a foreign language • Documentation and categorization of sources • Interpretation of drawings, documents, published and unpublished materials • Diagramming (for visual data sources), written analysis for other types
Benefits	• Primary sources used in the research process • Essential method for history and theory research, and historic preservation practice
Drawbacks	• Highly relies on interpretation and researcher's perspective • Data might be missing or incomplete

Figure 3.3: Characteristics of archival research.

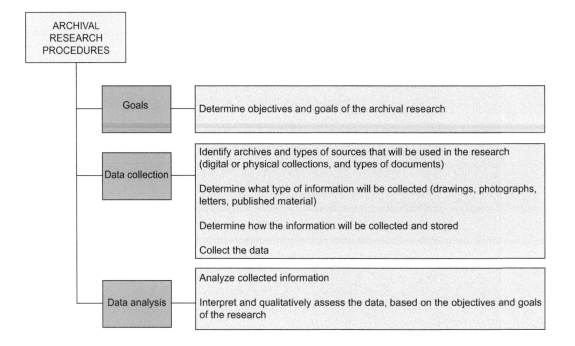

The procedures for conducting archival research typically include these following steps, as shown in Figure 3.4:

Figure 3.4:
Archival research
procedures.

- Determining objectives and goals of the research
- Identifying archives that house the documentation and resources relating to research objectives and deciding whether digital or physical collections will be utilized in the research
- Determining what type of information should be collected from archival research and what types of sources will be utilized (drawings, photographs, letters, published material, etc.)
- Determining how the information will be collected and stored, especially if physical archives or materials and documents that are housed in special collections are used in the research
- Collecting the documentation, analyzing, and interpreting to determine results

In some instances, the original documents may be written in a foreign language, thus requiring translation. In conducting archival research, researchers must become storytellers, piecing together information gathered from primary sources, and, through interpretation, trying to fill in the blanks and construct stories. Thus, researchers' rationales and reasons for their narration and rigorous research paired with the exploratory nature of archival research are critical to producing ethical and transparent scholarship (Gaillet, 2012). Several large architectural archives have created online databases in the last twenty years to facilitate access to the documents. For example, the Society of Architectural Historians maintains a list of archives (at various universities and museums) and digital collections.

3.2.2 Interviews

Interviews are used in qualitative research to explore and understand opinions, preferences, experiences, attitudes, behaviors, feelings, phenomena, etc., and the characteristics of this research method are shown in Figure 3.5. Interviews are always conducted by exploring these aspects for a certain group; thus, the researchers must determine the sample size, characteristics of individuals being interviewed, how these individuals will be selected, and the primary mode for collecting data. Interviews can be conducted in person, by phone, or by videoconferencing. Regardless of the primary mode, it is important to collect the information and discussion in its entirety; therefore, it is useful to record the interview (audio, or both audio and video) so that the data can be transcribed and analyzed as part of the research process. However, researchers must keep in mind that privacy is an important aspect in this type of research, as well as standard practices and protocols for conducting research on human subjects. If interviews are conducted as part of doctoral research or an academic research project, a researcher initially must disclose and file an application for the Institutional Review Board (IRB) with the university's office for human research before engaging in the research. The IRB is a mandated committee that reviews all research involving human subjects and approves research studies and methods, in accordance with established policies on the protection of human subjects, ethical procedures, and federal and state laws and regulations. Researchers also must explain and fully disclose to research participants how the information collected from the interviews will be stored, analyzed, and disseminated.

	INTERVIEWS
Data sources	• People (study participants) • Study participants are asked to express their opinions, preferences, experiences, attitudes, feelings, behaviors • Interviews are conducted as unstructured, semi-structured, or structured conversations • Information should be collected, recorded and transcribed, keeping in mind ethics and privacy
Data analysis procedures	• Detailed analysis of the conversations and transcribed data • Identification of patterns and trends within the collected data • Interpretation of the specific vocabulary used by study participants • Written analysis of qualitative results, visual representation of patterns and trends
Benefits	• Primary sources used in the research process • Possible to explore qualitative aspects relating to many different research topics in architecture
Drawbacks	• Typically limited sample size of participants due to cost and time constraints associated with the research process, thus generalization of results for larger population is difficult • Highly relies on participants' perspectives (and in some cases, bias) • Selection of study participants might influence research results

Figure 3.5: Characteristics of interviews.

There are three types of interviews: unstructured, semi-structured, and structured. Unstructured interviews typically progress with few questions being posed by the researcher. In this type of interview, researchers obtain information from participants in a normal conversation and tend to focus on exploratory topics. Semi-structured interviews rely on a guided conversation between the researchers and participants. Structured interviews strictly follow an established protocol and preidentified questions and tend to focus on a specific topic or evaluative research.

The procedures for conducting interviews typically include the following steps, as shown in Figure 3.6:

- Determining objectives and goals and what type of information should be collected from research participants
- Determining interview type

Figure 3.6: Research procedures for interviews.

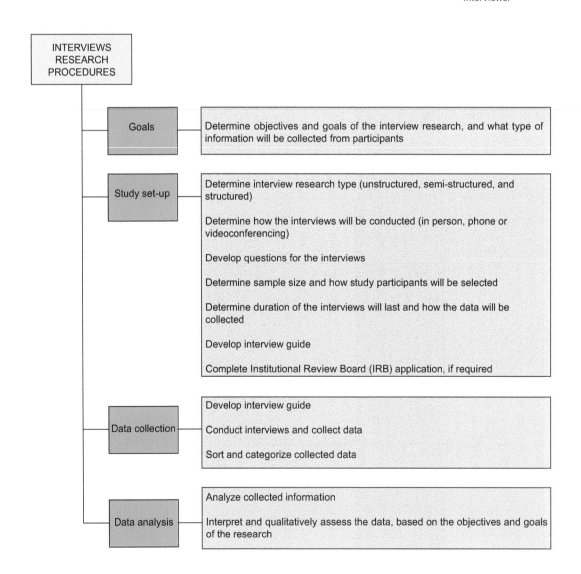

INTERVIEWS RESEARCH PROCEDURES		
Goals		Determine objectives and goals of the interview research, and what type of information will be collected from participants
Study set-up		Determine interview research type (unstructured, semi-structured, and structured)
		Determine how the interviews will be conducted (in person, phone or videoconferencing)
		Develop questions for the interviews
		Determine sample size and how study participants will be selected
		Determine duration of the interviews will last and how the data will be collected
		Develop interview guide
		Complete Institutional Review Board (IRB) application, if required
Data collection		Develop interview guide
		Conduct interviews and collect data
		Sort and categorize collected data
Data analysis		Analyze collected information
		Interpret and qualitatively assess the data, based on the objectives and goals of the research

- Determining interview questions
- Determining the sample size for research participants, how long the interviews should last, how participants will be selected, how interviews will be conducted, and how the information will be collected
- Developing an interview guide
- Conducting the interviews and data collection
- Analyzing collected data and interpretation of results

In architectural research, qualitative research that employs interviews as the primary research method is typically conducted for three different participants' groups: 1) architects, design, engineering, and construction teams; 2) clients; and 3) building occupants. The selection of a specific group is always driven by the research objectives and goals. For example, research studies that focus on qualitative aspects of the design process and modes of practice, such as understating the impacts of novel digital technologies on collaboration or communication between team members, would utilize interviews with architects and design teams (Hochscheid and Halin, 2018). On the other hand, qualitative studies that focus on understanding the effects of specific design outcomes would interview clients and building occupants. For example, interviews with clients can be conducted to understand the client's satisfaction with a certain design project, firm's operation, communication, and project management procedures, etc. (Siva, J., and London, K., 2011). Interviews with clients are also useful for architectural programming, to understand client's requirements and spatial needs for a certain project (Hershberger, R., 2015). Interviews with building occupants are typically conducted to understand occupants' satisfaction with the interior environment, comfort conditions (thermal, visual, acoustic, or indoor air quality), or utilization of space (Day and Gunderson, 2015; Van Steenwinkel et al., 2017).

3.2.3 Focus Groups

Focus groups are similar to interviews, where structured discussions are used to collect qualitative data from a group of people. Characteristics of focus group research are shown in Figure 3.7. The main difference between interviews and focus groups is that interviews are typically conducted individually (based on one-on-one interaction between a researcher and interview participant), while focus groups are conducted collectively. The researcher acts as a moderator and leads the discussion about a specific topic of interest. Therefore, participants in a focus group can also interact and discuss the topic of interest among themselves, as opposed to strictly interacting with the researcher. Typically, focus group interviews involve 8 to 12 participants, and last 1.5 to 2.5 hours (Stewart et al., 2009). The discussions may be structured or unstructured, general or specific, and supported by visual aids and demonstrations. Therefore, focus groups as a qualitative research method are quite flexible and are well suited for exploratory research that addresses broad research questions. Results provide qualitative data about participants' perspectives, ideas, beliefs, opinions, and feelings. Focus groups can also be used as a method to collect data as a supplement to qualitative surveys—in this case, the number of participants for the survey can be much larger

FOCUS GROUPS	
Data sources	• People (study participants) • Study participants are asked to express their opinions, preferences, experiences, attitudes, feelings, behaviors in a group setting • Focus groups are conducted collectively, and the researchers acts as a moderator for the conversations • Information should be collected, recorded and transcribed, keeping in mind ethics and privacy
Data analysis procedures	• Detailed analysis of the conversations and transcribed data • Identification of patterns and trends within the collected data • Interpretation of the conversations between the study participants • Written analysis of qualitative results, visual representation of patterns and trends
Benefits	• Primary sources used in the research process • Can provide insights on multiple and different views • Faster and less costly than individual interviews • Possible to collect data as a supplement to qualitative surveys
Drawbacks	• Difficult to make general conclusions due to limited number of participants • Difficult to obtain a representative sample within study participants • Highly relies on participants' perspectives (and in some cases, bias) • Selection of study participants might influence research results

Figure 3.7: Characteristics of focus group research.

and participants for the focus groups can be selected as a representative sample to collect additional information.

The benefits of focus groups are that data can be collected more quickly and at less cost than for individual interviews. Also, focus groups can provide insight on multiple and different views that may not be possible to obtain through other qualitative research methods, since they provide an ability to collect data based on the interaction within a group context (Ereiba et al., 2004). The main drawback of focus group research is that it may be difficult to make general conclusions based on collected data because of the limited number of participants that are typically involved in these types of studies and the difficulty in obtaining a representative sample within study participants. Analysis of data and interpretation of results can also be difficult, and sometimes it might be difficult to distinguish the views of an individual from those of the group. The third aspect that should be mentioned relates to bias and limitations of focus groups, where participants might be influenced by the researcher's perspectives and questions. The appropriate strategy to limit the possible impacts of bias is to structure and organize focus groups in a way that does not reveal the researchers' perspectives and beliefs.

The procedures for conducting focus groups are shown in Figure 3.8, and include:

• Defining the objectives of the study and the purpose of the focus groups
• Developing the list of main questions and determining the schedule, number of participants, and characteristics of the participants based on the research objectives

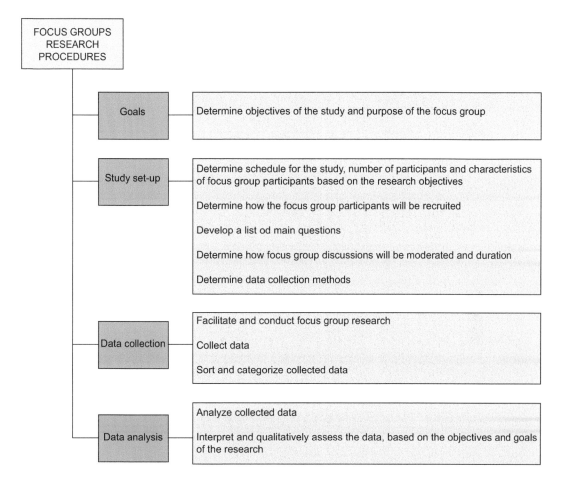

Figure 3.8:
Research proce-
dures for focus
groups.

- Identifying and recruiting focus group participants
- Determining how focus group discussions will be moderated and data collec-
  tion mechanisms
- Facilitating and conducting focus group research and collecting data
- Analyzing collected data and interpreting results

Identifying and recruiting study participants is a crucial step in focus group research. Selecting a representative sample based on specific research objectives is extremely important for the success of the study. For example, research studies that focus on architectural design processes, project management, and construction would utilize architects, designers, project team members, and contractors as participants in focus groups. Research studies that focus on architectural education would utilize faculty members and students as study participants. For example, a specific study used focus group research in an academic setting to investigate experiential learning and universal design principles in architectural education, where all study participants were architecture students (Mulligan et al., 2018). Another study, which investigated the impacts of architectural elements on care in healthcare facilities (specifically, specialized buildings for cancer care), conducted focus group research with different participants—architects who designed buildings that were included the study, staff members and volunteers, and visitors (Martin et al., 2019). The study was conducted over several years, and 12 focus groups with a total of 66 participants were part of the study. Topic guides and questions focused on the utilization of these healthcare facilities and how they compared to other healthcare buildings that the participants knew, and aimed to determine how materials, color, light, shape, and building form influence participants' perspectives.

3.2.4 Observations

Observations rely on observing certain phenomena as the primary data collecting mechanism. Characteristics of observations are presented in Figure 3.9. As a qualitative research method in architecture, observations most often focus on social and behavioral research, understanding space utilization and interactions between people and the built environment, and understanding the physical characteristics of the built environment (Zeisel, 2006). Data collection mechanisms for observations might include digital photography, video, and audio recordings, sketching and drawings, and note-taking. There are two types of observations— structured and unstructured. Structured observations focus on specific variables and utilize a predefined plan for collecting data during the research process. For example, structured observations can be used to investigate utilization of public plazas in an urban environment, where variables can be the number of people that use these spaces, times of day, climatic conditions, or the amount of time that

	OBSERVATIONS
Data sources	• Direct observations (structured or unstructured) of a phenomena or participants • Structured observations focus on specific variables and use a predefined plan for data collection, while unstructured observations collect data organically • Data collection methods include digital photography, video, and audio recordings, sketching, drawings, and note-taking • Controlled, naturalistic and participatory observations as three different types, based on the interaction between researchers and study participants • Researchers must follow ethical procedures for data collection when observing people
Data analysis procedures	• Direct analysis of observations when research focuses on physical phenomena • Interpretation necessary when research focuses on interactions between people and the environment • Written analysis of qualitative results, visual representation of physical phenomena
Benefits	• Ability to directly observe physical phenomena, people's behaviors, and interactions between people and the built environment
Drawbacks	• Time-consuming • When focusing on people, participants may not be representative of a larger population group • Research bias may influence data collection, interpretation and analysis

Figure 3.9: Characteristics of observations as a research method.

people spend in these outdoor spaces. Another example of structured observations is collecting data about physical conditions of an existing building, such as structural systems, materials, construction techniques, etc. Unstructured observations collect data organically and capture people's behaviors and interactions without focusing on specific predetermined variables. For example, unstructured observations of utilization of public plazas would capture all aspects that might be present during the study, including environmental conditions, social and behavioral aspects, design features, etc. Specific variables would then be determined during the data analysis process.

We can also classify observations into three different categories, based on the interaction between researchers and study participants: controlled, naturalistic, and participatory observations. In a controlled observation, study participants are pre-selected, and the research takes place in a predetermined place, typically following a standardized procedure. In architectural research, this method can be used to study interactions between people. Naturalistic observation focuses on observing study participants in a natural setting and typically involves studying the spontaneous behavior of participants. In architectural research, this method can be used to study interactions between people and the built environment, utilization of spaces, design effectiveness, construction methods, etc. In participatory observation, the researcher becomes part of the group that they are studying. In architectural research, participatory observation might focus on investigating team dynamics and collaborative efforts within a design firm, where the researchers would become part of the team to better understand interactions, communication protocols, team dynamics, etc. Regardless of the type of observations, researchers must follow ethical standards and protocols in collecting data through observations, if the research focuses on human subjects and socio-behavioral aspects.

Figure 3.10 shows procedures for conducting observations, which include:

- Defining the objectives of the study
- Determining what type of observations will be conducted and developing the research plan accordingly (i.e. determining place and time for observations, what type of data will be gathered, and how the data will be collected)
- Conducting observations and collecting data
- Analyzing collected data and interpretation of results

The main benefit of using observations as a qualitative research method is an ability to directly examine people's behaviors, characteristics of the built environment, and interactions between people and the built environment. However, there are associated disadvantages with this research method, specifically for social and behavioral research. First, the major disadvantage is that the study participants may not be representative of a larger population group, and characteristics of participants may influence research results. Selecting an appropriate sample size is possible in structured, controlled observations, but not in other types. The second disadvantage is that observational studies are time-consuming since it may take significant time to collect enough data for a specific research

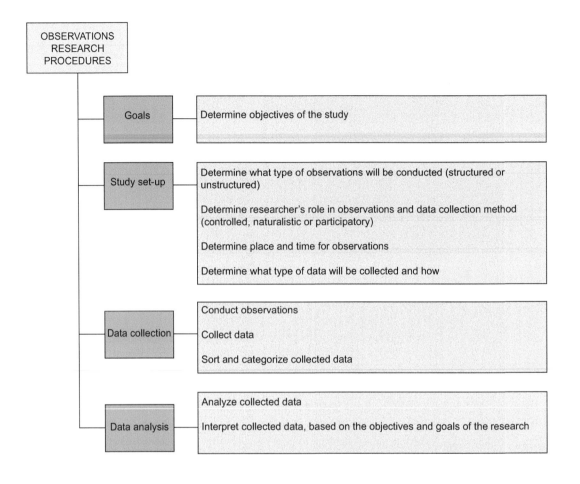

OBSERVATIONS RESEARCH PROCEDURES

Goals — Determine objectives of the study

Study set-up —
Determine what type of observations will be conducted (structured or unstructured)

Determine researcher's role in observations and data collection method (controlled, naturalistic or participatory)

Determine place and time for observations

Determine what type of data will be collected and how

Data collection —
Conduct observations

Collect data

Sort and categorize collected data

Data analysis —
Analyze collected data

Interpret collected data, based on the objectives and goals of the research

study. Third, research bias may influence data collection, interpretation of data, and analysis. For example, participants' behaviors might be affected and altered if they are aware that they are being observed, or the researcher's behavior might be affected in a participatory observation.

Figure 3.10: Research procedures for observations.

3.2.5 Qualitative Surveys

Qualitative surveys utilize questionnaires to ask open-ended questions about a certain phenomenon or a topic. In architectural research, qualitative surveys are used as a research methodology to collect information about people's opinions, perspectives, feelings, thoughts, and experiences as they relate to the built environment, and Figure 3.11 shows characteristics of this research method. Qualitative surveys employ a questionnaire format to obtain written information from participants, but the questions are prepared in such a manner as to allow participants to record their responses in an open-ended format. Figure 3.12 shows how typical questions are formed to gather data from the participants. Therefore, these types of questionnaires allow participants to express their opinions, thoughts, feelings, and reflections regarding a certain topic, and researchers analyze written responses to draw conclusions. The questions are developed, structured, and organized by researchers, based on specific research objectives and the aims of

QUALITATIVE SURVEYS	
Data sources	• Questionnaires with open-ended questions • Questionnaires used to assess people's opinions, perspectives, feelings, thoughts, and experiences relating to the built environment • Questionnaires are developed, structured, and organized by researchers, based on specific research objectives • Questionnaire distribution and data collection can be in-person, by mail or online • Sample size for questionnaire distribution must be determined by researchers
Data analysis procedures	• Qualitative analysis of responses • Interpretation of written words • Identification of patterns and trends in the written responses • Results are described by researcher's analysis of responses
Benefits	• Ability to gather qualitative information • Results can indicate further direction for research and exploration • Can be integrated with quantitative surveys
Drawbacks	• Participants may not represent a larger population group • Time-consuming data analysis process • Research bias may influence interpretation and analysis

Figure 3.11: Characteristics of qualitative surveys as a research method.

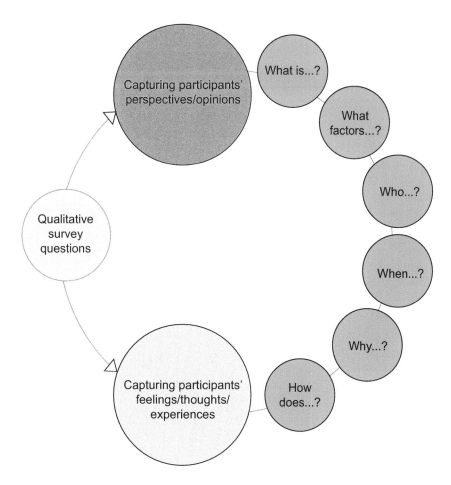

Figure 3.12: Types of questions used in qualitative surveys.

the study. For example, research studies that focus on understanding occupants' thermal comfort in various buildings might utilize qualitative surveys to collect information about occupants' satisfaction with interior conditions and building operation, thermal sensation during different seasons, etc. In this case, survey questions would be written to allow participants to express their opinions about interior conditions and thermal comfort. Another example relates to understanding design effectiveness of an open office floorplan as a planning strategy in commercial buildings. In this case, qualitative surveys can be conducted to gather information about benefits and drawbacks of this design strategy, as they relate to satisfaction with the working environment, collaborations, acoustics, etc.

Questionnaires can be administered in-person, by mail or online, and the mode depends on the sample size. For a smaller sample size, administering in-person questionnaires might work well to collect information from study participants individually or in a small group (for example, as a follow-up method for interviews to collect additional data). However, for larger sample sizes, it is easier and more effective to deliver and collect data in a web-based format, since online surveys can reach wider audiences. Also, online surveys allow participants to respond asynchronously, thus providing more flexibility.

But what are the strategies for determining an appropriate sample size? It is not possible to survey an entire population in a certain community; thus, a representative sample size should be selected that represents that community (Emmel, 2013). The study's objectives should determine ideal characteristics of study participants and which and how many participants to select. Sample sizes should be large enough to obtain enough data to sufficiently address the research questions, considering the point of saturation. Saturation occurs when inclusion of more participants to the study does not result in additional information or perspectives. There are three basic strategies for sampling qualitative surveys—purposive, quota, and snowball sampling (Mack et al., 2005). Purposive sampling is most common, where study participants are selected based on pre-identified criteria, relevant to a particular research question. For example, architectural students and faculty members would be selected for research studies focusing on architectural education. Qualitative research studies that focus on the design effectiveness of healthcare facilities would aim to select patients, healthcare staff, and visitors as study participants. Quota sampling relies on deciding how many participants with which characteristics to include as participants prior to conducting the study. Snowball sampling relies on chain referral, where study participants use their networks to refer the researcher (or survey) to other people who could participate in the study.

The procedures for conducting qualitative surveys, shown in Figure 3.13, are:

- Defining the objectives of the study
- Determining research questions that will be addressed by the study and how the survey will be administered
- Identifying characteristics of participants based on the objectives of the study, sample size, and data collection method
- Developing survey questions

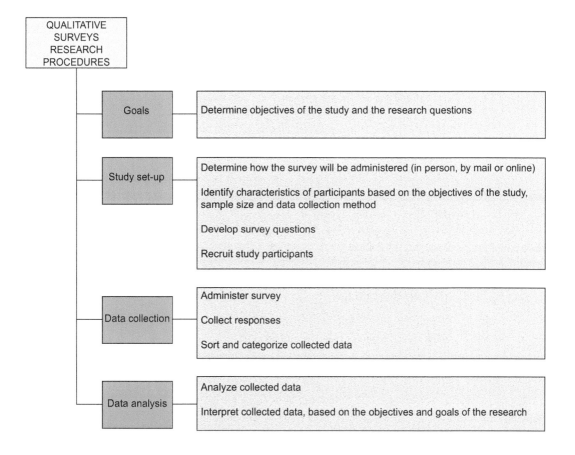

QUALITATIVE
SURVEYS
RESEARCH
PROCEDURES

Goals — Determine objectives of the study and the research questions

Study set-up — Determine how the survey will be administered (in person, by mail or online)

Identify characteristics of participants based on the objectives of the study, sample size and data collection method

Develop survey questions

Recruit study participants

Data collection — Administer survey

Collect responses

Sort and categorize collected data

Data analysis — Analyze collected data

Interpret collected data, based on the objectives and goals of the research

Figure 3.13:
Research proce-
dures for qualitative
surveys.

- Recruiting study participants
- Administering surveys and collecting survey responses
- Analyzing responses and interpreting data

A special type of questionnaire that aims to collect information about specific buildings, after they are designed and constructed, is typically utilized as part of the Post-Occupancy Evaluation (POE) process. POEs aim to understand how well a specific building performs and meets the needs of clients and building occupants. These evaluations are typically conducted at least a year after construction (and after a building has been occupied by users for a prolonged time) in order to assess how a certain building functions, occupants' comfort, and the client's satisfaction. POEs use both qualitative and quantitative surveys, which are discussed in the next section, to assess buildings' energy and water use, environmental conditions, acoustics, occupants' comfort and satisfaction with the interior environment (thermal, visual, acoustic), indoor air quality, lighting levels (natural and artificial), circulation and movement through the building, space utilization, and design effectiveness. Qualitative surveys, when used as part of the POE process, use open-ended questions to inquire about clients' and occupants' perspectives, feelings, opinions, and behaviors.

POEs have both short-term and long-term benefits, and can be used to provide feedback about building operation (for immediate problem solving), troubleshooting during early stages of building operation, fine-tuning buildings' use through continuous feedback, focused studies into specific aspects of building performance, documentation of successes and failures in building performance, and improved knowledge that can benefit the architectural profession (Preiser et al., 2015). POEs have developed rapidly over the past decade and will continue to expand, but they are still not a norm in the building industry (Li et al., 2018). Although some architectural firms offer POEs as part of their standard services, these types of studies are not included in every design project. The barriers for adopting POEs as a standard practice are complex, including broad economic drivers in AEC industry for profit and efficiency rather than long-term benefits to clients and wider society, specific economic impacts of time and resources necessary to conduct POEs (i.e. whose responsibility it is to fund POE studies), insurance and liability issues (i.e. what happens if negative aspects are uncovered about a specific building), and the need for stronger support from professional organizations (Hay et al. 2017). Nevertheless, the future of the architectural profession relies on better integration of research and the design process, and POEs play a critical role in that endeavor.

3.2.6 Case Study Research

Case study research analyzes specific research questions within the boundaries of a distinct environment, group, building, or building type, and focuses on real-life contexts. As a research method, it can be used to explore a single subject in depth or to conduct multiple case studies to compare certain phenomena according to pre-defined research objectives and questions. In architectural research, case study research is a widely used methodology, with many different applications varying in scales (individual buildings to communities and large urban areas), time periods (historical to contemporary aspects), building types (single or multiple case studies based on building function), specific space utilization (according to the functional use), design practices (such as software programs in the utilized design process or project delivery methods), etc.

But what are the primary characteristics of case study research? Figure 3.14 indicates properties of case study research in architecture. There are five particular aspects that characterize this research methodology: 1) specific focus on either a single case or multiple cases, studied in a real-life context; 2) ability to explain casual links between a cause and effect; 3) reliance on theory development as part of the research design phase; 4) reliance on multiple sources of evidence; and 5) ability to generalize the results to form theory (Groat and Wang, 2013). Therefore, a researcher must decide how exactly case study research will be conducted, how the data will be collected, and how it will be analyzed— these steps should be based on the research objectives, research questions, and primary aims. Since a significant amount of collected data for case studies is qualitative, fieldwork is often a necessary part of the research process and protocols (Sarvimaki, 2018). Fieldwork allows researchers to collect qualitative data within the natural context to understand certain phenomena in that setting.

Figure 3.14:
Properties of case
study research.

CASE STUDY RESEARCH	
Data sources	• Distinct environment, group, building or a building type within a real-life context • Single in-depth case study or multiple case studies, purposely chosen based on the research objectives and questions • Information about the characteristics, physical properties, utilization, or practices relating to the investigated case studies
Data analysis procedures	• Interpretation of qualitative data • If multiple case studies are investigated, analysis of similarities/differences should be performed • If quantitative data is collected as part of the case study research, numeric analysis or statistical analysis can be performed • Qualitative results are presented in written format, while visual representation of physical properties and quantitative data can be included (photos, drawings, diagrams, charts, tables, etc.)
Benefits	• Ability to collect detailed information • Widely used in architectural research • Can be easily integrated with other research methods in mixed-mode research
Drawbacks	• Specific case studies cannot necessarily be generalized, but rather be outliers • Difficult to replicate • Research bias may influence data collection process

Before selecting specific case studies for architectural research, researchers first must determine ideal characteristics of potential case studies that are suitable for addressing specific research questions based on the study's objectives. For example, research questions that are associated with environmental impact and sustainable design might focus on investigating distinct high-performance buildings as case studies to understand design processes, design strategies, design outcomes, and environmental impact of these buildings. Research questions that are trying to address relationships between the built environment, infrastructure, and transportation issues might focus on specific cities and urban areas as case studies. Therefore, the selection of case studies is not random. Rather, case studies are purposely chosen based on certain criteria established by the research study. Regardless of the type or scale, case studies should be able to offer new insights into the research topic, support or challenge existing theories, and provide new knowledge.

The procedures for conducting case study research, as shown in Figure 3.15, are:

• Defining the objectives of the study
• Determining research questions that will be addressed by the study
• Identifying ideal characteristics of case studies, based on the research objectives and questions, and how many case studies will be conducted (single or multiple) to address the research questions
• Determining what type of data will be collected and how, and what analysis procedures will be used to analyze the data

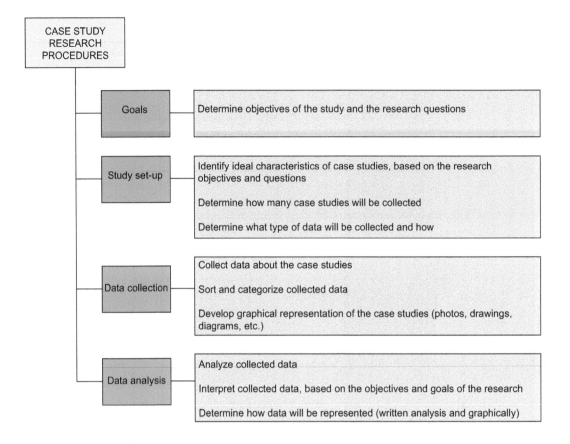

Figure 3.15:
Procedures for case study research.

- Collecting data and organizing it for analysis
- Analyzing and interpreting collected data

Case study research, within the context of the architectural profession, has many advantages. The primary benefit is that a lot of detailed information can be collected about a certain research topic, in greater depth than when using other research methods. Architects rely on case study research in practice to explore many different areas, such as specific design methods, use of innovative technologies, application of specific materials, space planning techniques, energy-efficient design methods, construction techniques, and many other research topics. Case studies are also widely used in architectural education to teach students about the intricacies of architectural design and design principles. Case study research can also be easily integrated with other research methods as part of mixed-mode research studies, discussed in the later sections of this chapter. However, one of the main disadvantages is that the data collected for specific case studies cannot necessarily be generalized—sometimes specific case studies might be outliers and not representative of general principles. Case studies are also very difficult (or impossible) to replicate; therefore, their applicability in scientific research is questionable. The researcher's bias might also affect the data collection process, which then influences research results. Nevertheless, case study research is an important part of architectural research as a qualitative method.

3.3 QUANTITATIVE RESEARCH METHODS

Quantitative research methods are used to obtain numerical data to investigate specific research questions and test hypotheses, typically focusing on environmental, technology, economic, and performance aspects of architectural research. Quantitative methods use some form of measurement to investigate certain phenomena and can be replicated, as opposed to qualitative methods. In architectural research, the most common quantitative methods include simulations and modeling, quantitative surveys, and correlational research, as shown in Figure 3.15. These research methods are objective by their nature. They can be used to investigate the performance of buildings and the built environment, test theories, understand people's behaviors and opinions using precise measurements, and predict future performance. Quantitative methods also rely on statistical techniques for data analysis process, rather than the researcher's interpretation.

3.3.1 *Simulations and Modeling*

Simulations and modeling are the most common types of quantitative research methods used in architectural research, and their characteristics are shown in Figure 3.17. Simulations are representations of real-world phenomena which utilize models of those phenomena to investigate their behavior, interactions, performance, etc. In architectural research, simulations can be used to investigate the performance of building systems, behavior of different materials, effects of energy-efficiency measures on building performance, structural performance, daylight, movement and circulation of people through a building, acoustic behavior, air flow, heat transfer, moisture transport and thermal performance of building envelopes, occupants' thermal comfort, etc., as shown in Figure 3.18. Simulations typically rely on computer-generated models of a system or process under study to predict their behavior. Therefore, a model is a representation of an object or a process, and three general types exist—visual, mathematical, and computational models, as shown in Figure 3.19. Visual models use graphical representation of a system or a process. Mathematical models use equations to represent a certain phenomenon. Computational models use complex algorithms to represent phenomena, systems, and behaviors, and often utilize specific software programs for different types of research studies. Various research-based and commercial

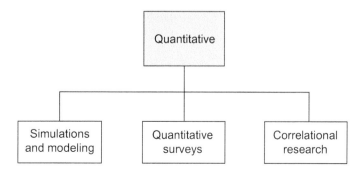

Figure 3.16:
Quantitative
research methods in
architecture.

SIMULATIONS AND MODELING	
Data sources	• Use models of real-world phenomena to investigate performance, behavior, and interactions through simulations • Simulaitons rely on computer-generated models
	• Simulations can be used for a wide variety of research topics in architectural research (building systems, energy efficiency, materials, occupants' behavior, daylight, fire, airflow, etc.) • Scale of simulations wide-ranging (from single building system or a building, to multiple buildings, district or an urban area) • Data depend on the type of simulation study and the utilized simulation tool • Simulation tools are wide-ranging, and include publicly available software programs, commercial programs, and custom modeling tools • Some simulation tools are integrated with BIM tools, or can use data from BIM design software programs for simulations
Data analysis procedures	• Collected data from simulations are always quantitative • Numeric or statistical analysis procedures are used to analyze quantitative data • Results are best presented in graphical format (charts, diagrams, tables) for numerical data, while written analysis should accompany numeric analysis
Benefits	• Ability to understand and explore complex phenomena computationally • Reduced time and costs compared to other research methods • Can be integrated with the design process to investigate design decisions and improve building performance • Advancements in computational tools used in architecture, such as BIM and vast number of available simulation tools, offer opportunities for integration of research with the design process
Drawbacks	• Limitations of simulation tools • Accuracy, uncertainty and validity of simulation tools • Some simulation tools are complex, and most require specialized knowledge

Figure 3.17: Characteristics of simulations and modeling.

simulation software programs are available for architectural research, and the selection of the specific software program should be based on research objectives and questions. There are several hundred available simulation software programs with various capabilities, both as an open-source, publicly available resource and as commercial tools.

Historically, the primary driver for initial growth in building simulation research has been energy research. This area of architectural research began in the 1960s, and it primarily focused on studies in fundamental theory and algorithms of energy loads and estimations until the 1990s (Hong et al., 2000). In the 1990s, this architectural research area significantly advanced with the increase in government funding focusing on energy-efficient buildings and research programs, the release of open-source simulation engines, technological developments in information technologies, wide adoption of personal computers, and increased global concern about environmental challenges. In contemporary research and practice, building performance and energy analysis are an integral part of the design process for energy-efficient and high-performance buildings, since they help investigate design options

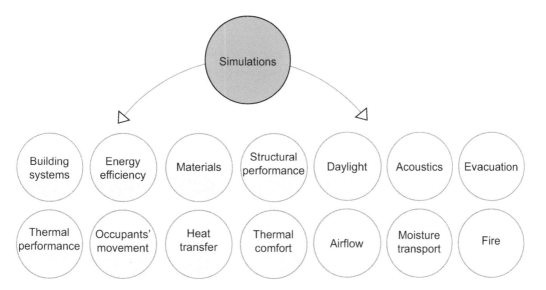

Figure 3.18:
Types of simulations used in architectural research.

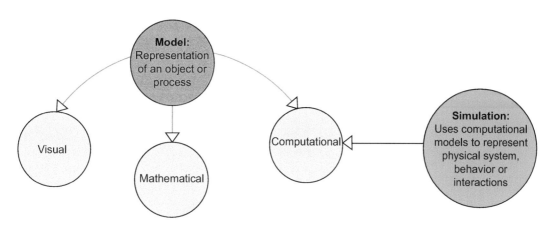

Figure 3.19:
Types of models and relationship to simulations.

and assess the environmental and energy impacts of design decisions (Aksamija, 2010). Energy-efficient buildings aim to reduce the overall energy consumption necessary for their operation. High-performance buildings are designed to improve the overall building performance, besides energy usage, such as improving occupants' thermal, visual, and acoustic comfort. A performance-based design method which relies on different analysis cycles that must be integrated into the design process is used to evaluate and optimize building performance. This performance-based design method challenges the traditional design paradigm, and has the ability to estimate the impact of a design solution since: 1) performance measures are investigated with actual quantifiable data and not rules-of-thumb; 2) it uses detailed building models to simulate, analyze, and predict behavior of the system; and 3) it can produce an evaluation of multiple design alternatives.

Over the last 15 years, the introduction of Building Information Modeling (BIM) has created a paradigm shift in architectural practice. BIM is a three-dimensional, digital representation of buildings and building elements and may also include non-geometric information, such as material properties and quantities, schedules, construction scheduling, facility management information, etc. Simulation tools can be grouped into BIM-based or non-BIM-based software programs, depending how well they are integrated, as seen in Figure 3.20. Benefits of BIM-based simulation programs are that the same design models can be used for different types of simulations, which saves time. Some simulation programs allow data exchange between BIM design and analysis programs. However, there are not that many fully integrated BIM-based simulation programs, and efforts are currently underway to increase the number of applications that are fully integrated within BIM-design modelling software programs. Best practices for data exchange between BIM and simulation software programs depend on the analysis objectives, what type of simulation tool is used, and what type of data is needed. For example, for the determination of building massing that minimizes solar exposure or incident solar exposure on the facade, geometric properties of the building massing or component under analysis (for example, part of the facade with shading devices) are sufficient. For other types of studies, such as daylight or thermal analysis, enriched information about interior spatial organization, material properties, and properties of shading surfaces is needed. Therefore, information stored in "design" BIM needs to be exported as "analysis" BIM (Aksamija, 2015).

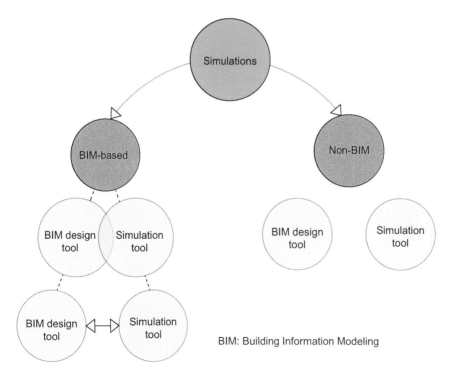

BIM: Building Information Modeling

Figure 3.20:
Basic categories of simulation software programs, based on integration with BIM tools.

There are specific data schemes that have been developed to facilitate the transfer of building properties stored in BIM to different simulation programs.

Selection of the right simulation method is always based on research objectives, research questions, and the scope of the study (Hensen and Lamberts, 2011). For example, in some instances, existing open-source or commercial software programs might be suitable, while for other cases, it might be necessary to develop custom modeling tools. For some studies, several simulations software programs might have to be used to address research questions. Regardless of the type of simulation or modeling tool, researchers need to establish procedures that will be followed, such as how exactly the physical phenomena will be represented, how many simulations will be conducted and for which scenarios, what types of inputs will be used to represent these scenarios, what types of variables will be investigated (and constant values that will be applied for simulation models), what type of data will be generated, and how it will be analyzed.

The procedures for conducting simulation and modeling, shown in Figure 3.21, include:

Figure 3.21:
Procedures for
simulations and
modeling research.

- Defining the objectives of the study
- Determining research questions that will be addressed by the study

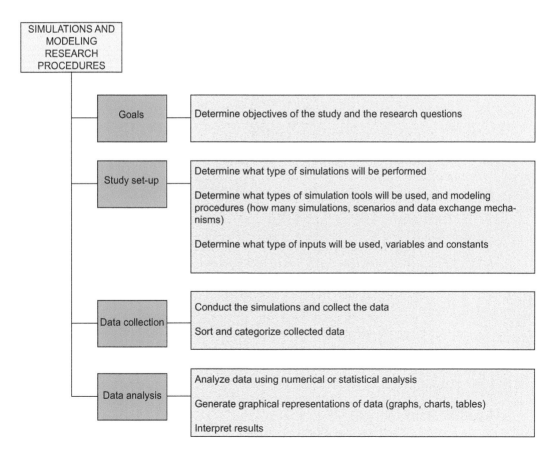

- Determining what type of simulations will be performed, tools that will be used, and modeling procedures
- Determining various types of inputs that might be necessary in a simulation study
- Identifying how the data will be collected and analyzed
- Running the simulations and collecting the data
- Analyzing and interpreting collected data to draw conclusions

The main benefit of using simulations and modeling in architectural research is the ability to understand and explore complex phenomena computationally, which can reduce the time and costs associated with the research study. Moreover, simulations allow investigations of design decisions during the design process, which can improve the design outcomes and building performance. Lastly, new advances in computational design are offering unprecedented opportunities for integration of simulation procedures and research into the design process (Aksamija, 2016). But there are some drawbacks associated with these research methods. Three aspects that researchers should keep in mind when using simulations and modeling are accuracy, uncertainty, and validity of software tools or modeling strategies. Before being widely adopted in the architectural profession, simulation programs must be validated. Generally, validation can be based on three different methods of comparison: analytical solutions, empirical data, and peer models (Ryan and Sanquist, 2012). Researchers should be familiar with validation techniques and cognizant of capabilities and validation for the chosen simulation software programs. Regarding accuracy, researchers should keep in mind that the accuracy of results will be dependent on inputs and how well the inputs are representing the real-world scenarios. Lastly, uncertainty also relates to inputs but primarily to types of inputs that might have large variations or data ranges. Therefore, researchers must understand any limitations of simulations and modeling procedures when utilizing these research methods.

3.3.2 Quantitative Surveys

Quantitative surveys employ questionnaires as the primary research method to obtain numeric data about a certain research topic. These types of questionnaires employ sets of well-defined, focused, close-ended questions where respondents rank their responses, rather than providing open-ended responses as in qualitative surveys. Thus, quantitative questionnaires numerically evaluate people's opinions, experiences, thoughts, feelings, and perspectives. In architectural research, quantitative surveys can be used for a wide variety of research topics, ranging from social, behavioral, environmental, and technological aspects to financial considerations, design processes and tools, and design outcomes. Figure 3.22 indicates characteristics of quantitative surveys as a research method. This method can be used to assess design teams' familiarity or satisfaction with emerging building technologies, materials, or design approaches. For example, a study was conducted to understand the adoption of simulation tools among building energy management professionals, and the primary research method included a quantitative survey that was distributed to almost 450 professionals across the

Figure 3.22:
Characteristics
of quantitative
surveys.

QUANTITATIVE SURVEYS	
Data sources	• Questionnaires with well-defined, focused, close-ended questions where respondents rank their responses • Questionnaires numerically evaluate people's opinions, perspectives, feelings, thoughts, and experiences relating to the built environment • Questionnaires are developed, structured, and organized by researchers, based on specific research objectives • Ranging mechanisms must be determined by researchers, and what types of scales will be used in the questionnaires • Questionnaire distribution and data collection can be in-person, by mail or online • Sample size for questionnaire distribution must be determined by researchers
Data analysis procedures	• Quantitative analysis of responses (numeric or statistical) • Graphical representation of numerical results (graphs, charts and tables), complemented with written analysis and interpretation of results
Benefits	• Ability to gather quantitative data from large samples of population • Wide-application in architectural research • Numerous variables can be investigated • Development and administration require minimal investments • Data collection is simple, especially for online surveys
Drawbacks	• Participants may not represent a larger population group • Sample size influences results

United States (Srivastava et al., 2019). Quantitative surveys can be used to analyze clients' satisfaction with architectural services, and these types of studies are primarily conducted by architectural firms that are interested in understanding client engagement. This research method can be employed to numerically assess occupants' satisfaction with the thermal, visual, and acoustic comfort conditions of certain buildings, satisfaction with the design outcomes, evaluation of spatial qualities and aesthetic features, etc. Thus, they are an essential part of POEs, since they allow researchers to collect a large amount of data from building occupants in a streamlined manner and to measure building performance in terms of occupants' satisfaction.

In quantitative surveys, researchers first must define the objective of the study and determine specific research questions and variables that will be investigated to answer these questions. Researchers must also determine the sample size for study participants, desired response rate, what approach will be employed to recruit participants, and how the survey will be administered (in person, by mail, or online). Then, researchers need to develop survey questions that will be included in the questionnaire to collect the responses and determine what type of scale or rating options will be used by participants to evaluate their responses. The questions must be clear, concise, and easily understood by respondents. The researcher's perspectives should not be indicated in the wording nor order of the questions, and questions should not include any assumptions.

Rating options should be balanced in terms of positive and negative options. Typically, numerical scales, Likert scales, or semantic differential scales are used, because these types of rating methods are easiest for survey respondents to answer and for researchers to analyze the data. Figure 3.23 shows different types of rating options and examples. The numerical scale is the simplest method, and it consists of a series of numbers (for example, 0 to 10) and verbal anchors that describe the possible range—participants choose a specific number that reflects their view. Likert scales are used to determine respondents' levels of agreement or disagreement with specific statements, organized symmetrically around a neutral point. Likert scales typically use 5-point or 7-point ratings but can use up to a 10-point scale. For example, a 5-point Likert scale, associated with a specific

Figure 3.23: Different types of rating options used in quantitative surveys.

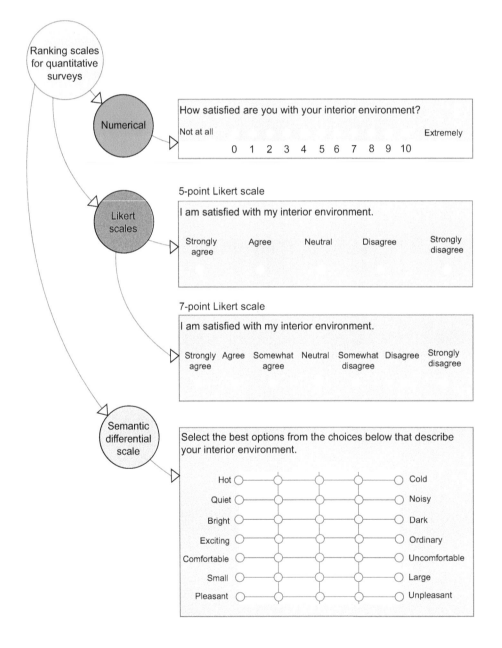

statement, might include the following rating options: 1) strongly disagree; 2) disagree; 3) neutral; 4) agree; and 5) strongly agree. More choices are given to respondents with the increased number of options; thus a 7-point Likert scale might include these following options: 1) strongly disagree; 2) disagree; 3) somewhat disagree; 4) neutral; 5) somewhat agree; 6) agree; and 7) strongly agree. Beyond focusing only on agreement or disagreement, variations of Likert scale can be used to assess respondents' perspectives regarding frequency, quality, intensity, approval, awareness, importance, familiarity, satisfaction, or performance, as shown in Figure 3.24. A semantic differential scale is used to measure

Figure 3.24:
Variations of 5-point
Likert scale.

connotative meanings and respondents' attitudes regarding a certain topic using multi-point rating options. It uses a series of opposite adjectives at each end to describe a certain phenomenon, with intermediate options in between the opposite ends. Respondents then choose values that describe their attitudes.

The procedures for conducting quantitative surveys, shown in Figure 3.25, include:

- Defining the objectives of the study
- Determining the research questions that will be addressed by the study and specific variables that will be investigated to address these questions
- Determining how the survey will be administered
- Identifying characteristics of participants based on the objectives of the study, sample size, and data collection method
- Developing survey questions and determining appropriate rating mechanisms
- Recruiting study participants
- Administering surveys and collecting survey responses
- Analyzing responses and interpreting data

Figure 3.25: Procedures for quantitative survey research.

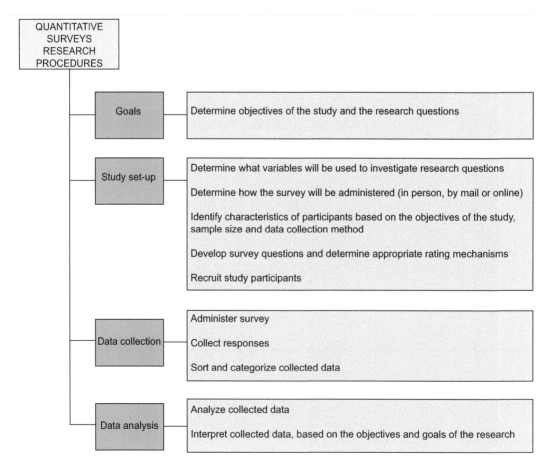

The benefits of quantitative surveys are: 1) the information can be collected from large samples of the population; 2) research topics that can be investigated using this method are wide-ranging; 3) numerous variables can be studied; 4) development and administration of questionnaires require minimal investments (except for longitudinal studies, which focus on shifts and transformations over time and focus on long-term studies); and 5) data collection mechanisms are straightforward, especially with online survey distribution. The drawbacks are that the characteristics of respondents may not necessarily represent the general population, and the sample size influences results.

Often, a combination of qualitative and quantitative surveys is used in architectural research. This allows researchers to collect and analyze numeric data associated with a specific research problem and also gather qualitative information about people's perceptions, beliefs, feelings, and opinions. Therefore, a questionnaire might include both types of questions (i.e. closed-ended with ranking scales and open-ended), but it is up to the researcher or research team to use appropriate analysis methods to analyze qualitative and quantitative results to draw conclusions. For example, POEs typically include both types of surveys (Li et al., 2018). The structure, organization, and types of survey questions are different for various building types—for example, POEs for residential buildings often focus on studying occupants' experience and utilization of space, while for commercial office buildings, POEs focus on understanding occupants' comfort and productivity (and might include physical measurements as well). Therefore, both types of survey methods should be used as part of the POE process, but the questions should be appropriately developed, depending on the building type.

3.3.3 Correlational Research

Correlational research relies on measuring relationships between two variables and can be used to understand related events, conditions, and behaviors. This research method heavily relies on statistical data analysis procedures, with the primary purpose of determining whether and to what degree a statistical relationship exists between two variables. The relationships that are investigated in a correlational study are statistically measured by calculating a correlation coefficient, which measures two aspects of the relationships between variables, the directions of the relationship, and the strength of the relationship (Mertler, 2019). Complex correlational research can be conducted to determine relationships between more than two variables. In this case, a correlational matrix can be used to determine a correlation between every possible pair of variables in the study. In architectural research, the correlational research method can be used for a wide array of research topics, ranging from social, environmental, financial, and technology considerations to design outcomes. Figure 3.26 presents characteristics of correlational research. For example, this research method can be used to analyze relationships between thermal performance of building enclosures and the energy consumption of buildings. It can also be used to study relationships between window sizes, glass types, and available daylight in specific climates. Correlational research can be used to investigate relationships between occupants' comfort and productivity; relationships between climatic conditions, design

CORRELATIONAL RESEARCH	
Data sources	• Measurements of relationships between two variables • Variables can relate to events, conditions and behaviors • Researcher must ensure that collected data is sufficient to determine relationships between investigated variables • Complex correlational research can be conducted to determine relationships between more than two variables, where correlational matrix is used to determine correlation between every possible pair of variables
Data analysis procedures	• Statistical analysis of data • Relationships are statistically measured by calculating a correlation coefficient between variables (direction and strength of the relation-ship) • Graphical representation of numerical results (graphs and charts), complemented with written analysis and interpretation of results
Benefits	• Ability to determine relationships between phenomena • Relatively simple
Drawbacks	• Focuses only on statistical relationship • It cannot be used to determine cause and effect between variables

Figure 3.26: Characteristics of correlational research.

Correlational coefficient

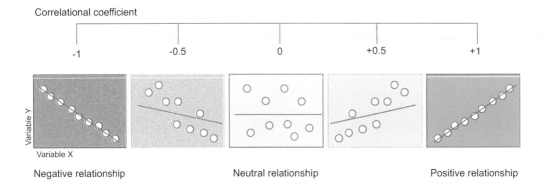

| -1 | -0.5 | 0 | +0.5 | +1 |

Variable Y

Variable X

Negative relationship   Neutral relationship   Positive relationship

Correlational matrix example

Variables	X	Y	Z	Q	W
X	+1	-0.5	0	+0.5	0
Y	+0.5	+1	+0.5	-1	+0.5
Z	0	-0.5	+1	+0.5	-0.5
Q	-1	+0.5	-1	+1	0
W	0	-0.5	+0.5	-0.5	+1

Figure 3.27: Correlation coefficient between variables, indication of relationships and an example of cor-relational matrix.

strategies, and buildings' energy usage; project delivery methods and construction time; and many other types of studies. It should be noted that correlational research does not imply causation between variables but can be used to determine relationships.

The relationships between variables in correlational research can be positive, negative, or neutral, as shown in Figure 3.27. A positive relationship indicates that an increase or decrease in one variable creates a similar change in another variable. Negative correlation indicates that an increase or decrease in one variable creates an opposite change in another variable. Neutral correlation indicates that variables are not statistically connected, and a change in one variable may not influence a corresponding or opposite change in another variable.

The procedures for conducting correlational research, shown in Figure 3.28, are:

- Defining the objectives of the study
- Determining research questions that will be addressed by the study and specific variables that will be investigated
- Identifying the data collection method
- Collecting data
- Statistically analyzing data and calculating the correlation coefficient
- Interpreting data

Figure 3.28: Procedures for correlational research.

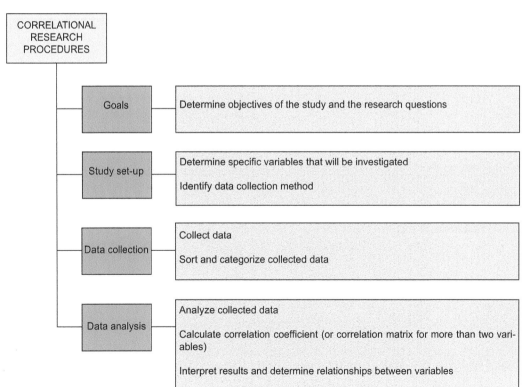

The benefits of correlational research are that it is a relatively simple and straight-forward method and provides an opportunity to discover new relationships between phenomena. However, the researcher must ensure that the collected data is sufficient to determine relationships between variables and draw conclusions. Therefore, the main drawback of correlational research is that it focuses on the statistical relationship between variables—it cannot be used to determine cause and effect between variables, and there might be undiscovered variables that are not part of the study but impact results.

3.4 EXPERIMENTAL RESEARCH METHODS

Experimental research methods are systematic approaches used to investigate physical, real-world phenomena that allow researchers to manipulate one or more variables and control and measure changes in other variables. These research methods are suitable for explanatory research, specifically for studies aiming to determine cause and effect relationships between variables. Experimental research can be conducted in a laboratory setting or in the field. In a laboratory setting, researchers have more control over the research set-up and process. Experimental research conducted in the field utilizes real-world settings. In architecture, experimental research methods are typically used for studies relating to understanding people's behavior, environmental aspects and building performance, technology, design process and tools, products and building systems, and measuring design outcomes. In architectural research, three common experimental research methods include prototyping, testing, and experiments, as shown in Figure 3.29.

3.4.1 Prototyping

Prototyping utilizes prototypes to evaluate certain phenomena and to validate ideas, assumptions, and design approaches before they are fully implemented in architectural design. Prototypes are physical models (scaled or real scale), which are used to investigate specific research questions. They can be simple, representing the geometry, scale, and general features of an object, or complex and fully detailed, utilizing identical materials and construction techniques to the real object.

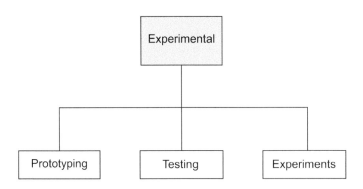

Figure 3.29:
Experimental
research methods in
architecture.

Prototyping can be used be to evaluate a design approach, process, technology, or product. Therefore, possible applications of prototyping in architectural research are broad, ranging from investigations of specific building systems, installations, materials, and construction techniques to evaluations of new design and fabrication processes, tools, software programs, etc. Figure 3.30 shows characteristics of prototyping. As an experimental research method, prototyping is a very useful technique for refinement, communication, exploration, and gaining new knowledge (Camburn et al., 2017). Refinement refers to gradual improvements, and prototyping can be used to validate requirements or discover critical design concerns. As a communication technique, it can be used to share critical information about the qualities and characteristics of a prototype, which might be difficult to communicate in other forms. As an exploration technique, it can be used to develop new design concepts and gain new knowledge about design and construction techniques, materials, building systems, manufacturing, and fabrication techniques, etc. (Burry, 2016).

There are two general types of prototyping—iterative and parallel (Camburn et al., 2017). Iterative prototyping relies on successive refinement of a prototype, where gradual iterations are used to improve characteristics, performance, and outcomes. Parallel prototyping concurrently investigates multiple prototypes and allows comparative evaluations. Evaluation techniques and data collection mechanisms depend on the research objectives and questions but might include data

	PROTOTYPING
Data sources	• Physical prototypes (scale or real scale) • Prototypes can be simple (representing scale and geometry) or complex and fully detailed (using different materials and construction techniques) • Digital fabrication increasingly used for prototyping • Two types of prototyping: iterative (successive refinement to improve characteristics, performance and design outcomes) or parallel (concurrent investigation of multiple prototypes for comparative evaluations) • Collected data might include prototype characteristics (materials, aesthetics, construction methods), performance or implementation
Data analysis procedures	• Observations of properties, evaluations of characteristics, materials, construction techniques • Refinement and iterative process • Graphical representation of results (drawings, diagrams, photographs), and written analysis and interpretation of results
Benefits	• Ability to evaluate design concepts, assumptions and approaches before application in buildings • Flexibility and opportunities for refinement • Possibility for using digital fabrication • Prototyping can also be combined with testing
Drawbacks	• Limited number of possible iterations due to time and cost constraints • Cost and time for conducting research increase with the complexity of prototypes

Figure 3.30: Characteristics of prototyping as a research method.

capture about the prototype characteristics (materials, aesthetic qualities, construction techniques) and the performance characteristics, implementation, etc.

The procedures for implementing prototyping as a research method in architecture, shown in Figure 3.31, include:

- Defining the objectives of the study
- Determining research questions that will be addressed
- Determining what type of prototyping will be used, characteristics of prototypes (scale and complexity), and construction method
- Determining what type of data will be collected and how
- Creating the prototype (or multiple prototypes if parallel prototyping is used)
- Evaluating the prototype and collecting data
- Interpreting data

Computer-aided manufacturing and digital fabrication are increasingly being used for prototyping (Aksamija, 2016). These methods are also useful for evaluating constructability, material properties, form, and geometric properties. By combining computational design tools with prototyping techniques, researchers can generate multiple prototypes and iterate design approaches. The diversity of accessible fabrication processes, such as laser cutting, 3D printing, computer-numeric

Figure 3.31:
Procedures for prototyping research.

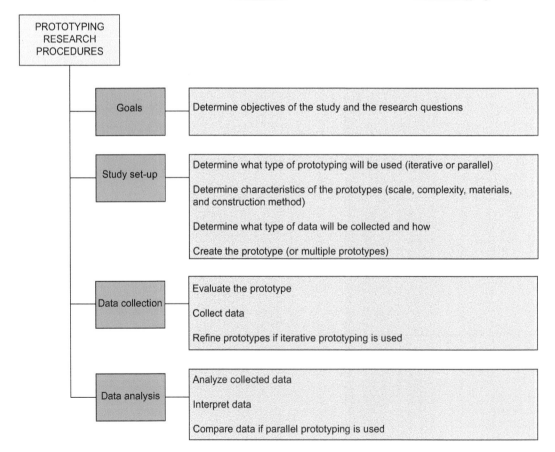

controlled (CNC) milling, and robotic construction, enable the production of prototypes in a variety of forms and materials. The classification of digital fabrication methods can be grouped into three general categories: additive, subtractive, and formative. Additive methods, such as 3D printing, create shapes and forms by depositing certain materials. Subtractive techniques, such as CNC milling or laser cutting, remove parts of a material to form a shape or an object. Within the formative category, techniques such as robotic construction are used to form objects and components. Some of these methods are suitable for planar and 2D fabrication, such as laser cutting and CNC milling, while others are suitable for 3D fabrication, for instance, 3D printing and robotic construction. Regardless of the type of digital fabrication method, researchers must be familiar with the size limitations, production sequence, suitable materials, and data exchange mechanisms to use these techniques for prototyping. Besides digital fabrication techniques, manual fabrication can also be employed for prototyping. This approach is typically used when actual materials need to be used for prototype production, instead of representational materials.

The benefits of prototyping include an ability to evaluate design concepts, assumptions, and approaches before application in actual buildings; flexibility and the opportunity for refinement; the experimental nature of possible investigations; the possibility of using digital fabrication techniques for prototyping; and the ability to conduct performance testing in some cases (discussed in the next section). The limitation of this research method is that the number of possible iterations and prototypes is usually limited, due to time and cost constraints. As the complexity of a prototype increases, such as larger scale or realistic representation of materials, the cost and necessary time for conducting these types of studies also increases.

3.4.2 Testing

The *testing* research method utilizes testing to evaluate characteristics of a specific product, process, or phenomenon according to a specified procedure. Testing, as opposed to experiments, is used to determine properties or physical behavior without necessarily investigating cause and effect relationships. In architectural research, testing can be used for a wide range of topics, but it is mostly applied for environmental, technology, processes and tools, products, and building systems research. Figure 3.32 indicates characteristics of the testing research method. For example, physical testing of materials is typically used to understand their properties and characteristics (structural, thermal, fire-rating, moisture content, acoustic-rating, etc.). Testing of building enclosures is used to determine their physical behavior, such as air infiltration, water penetration, structural stability, fire resistance, condensation risk, etc. For these types of studies, physical mock-ups are required, which include all materials and components of the actual building enclosure system. The mock-ups are used as testing specimens and must be of sufficient scale to adequately represent the entire system. Testing of new design software programs is also relevant for architectural research, but the objectives are different than for building materials and systems—in these types of studies, user evaluations are typically used as a testing procedure to evaluate effectiveness, data exchange mechanisms, or user satisfaction.

TESTING	
Data sources	• Physical tests of materials, products, systems or processes according to a specified procedure • Procedures can follow industry standards, which outline specific testing procedures/equipment/measurements, or use non-standard techniques • Physical mock-up are required for materials, products and systems testing • Testing can be conducted in a controlled, laboratory setting or in the field • User evaluations are used for testing processes, such as implementation of design software programs • Collected data and measurements depend on the objectives of the research and testing type
Data analysis procedures	• Standard testing procedures prescribe data capture and analysis • Non-standard testing requires numeric or statistical analysis • Graphical representation of results (drawings, diagrams, photographs, charts, graphs and tables), and written analysis and interpretation of results
Benefits	• Ability to physically investigate properties and behaviors of materials, products and systems • Ability to evaluate processes and tools in real-world setting • Ability to evaluate long-term performance
Drawbacks	• High costs • Requires testing equipment and space • Physical prototypes or mock-ups required

Figure 3.32: Characteristics of testing as a research method.

There are two types of testing procedures—those following industry standards, and non-standard techniques. Industry standards for testing establish uniform criteria, standard procedures, data collection, and, in some cases, specific minimum performance criteria that need to be met. For example, the ASTM International is an international standards organization that develops and publishes technical standards for a wide range of building materials, products, systems, and services. ASTM standards prescribe testing procedures for air leakage and ventilation performance in buildings, acoustics, durability performance of various systems, structural performance, performance of building enclosures, etc. Similarly, the European Committee for Standardization (CEN) provides testing standards for its member countries. Other industry organizations that develop and publish industry standards for testing includethe American Architectural Manufacturers Association (AAMA), American National Standards Institute (ANSI), American Society of Civil Engineers (ASCE), National Fenestration Rating Council (NFRC), Safety Glazing Certification Council (SGCC), UL, and others. Architectural testing agencies can be employed for research studies that require standardized testing, because these organizations specialize in supporting the architectural profession with laboratory spaces, necessary equipment, and technical knowledge about standardized testing procedures. Field testing can also be performed following industry standards—for example, indoor air

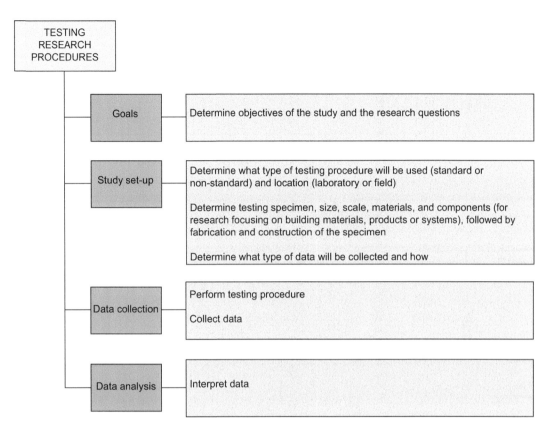

Figure 3.33:
Procedures for
testing.

quality testing is a common procedure used to detect and measure contaminants within interior environments. Another example of field testing is air leakage and water penetration testing of fenestration systems—specific industry standards prescribe the testing methods, but these can be performed at a construction site rather than in a laboratory setting. Non-standard testing procedures are wide-ranging and are determined by researchers according to research objectives and questions, type of study (i.e. focusing on a material, building product or system, tool, or process), type of specimen (physical specimen or non-physical), and scale. For example, non-standard testing procedures can be used to investigate small-scale specimens of a new material before large-scale, standardized testing. Non-standard testing procedures can be also used to investigate fabrication techniques, such as robotic fabrication using concrete composite materials, utilization of design software programs, long-term performance of materials and building systems, etc.

The process for implementing testing as a research method in architecture, shown in Figure 3.33, includes:

- Defining the objectives of the study
- Identifying research questions that will be addressed by the study
- Determining what type of testing procedures (standard or non-standard) and location (laboratory of field) will be used

- Determining testing specimen size, scale, materials, and components (if focusing on building materials, products, or systems), followed by fabrication and construction of the specimen
- Determining what type of data will be collected and how
- Performing testing procedures and collecting data
- Interpreting data

The benefits of testing as a research method include an ability to physically investigate properties and behaviors of building materials, products, and systems (and utilizing standardized testing procedures for research projects where that might be an objective); an ability to evaluate processes and tools in real-world settings and applications; and an ability to evaluate long-term performance. The drawbacks of this research method are that it is a costly process and typically requires specialized testing equipment, which may not be directly available to researchers. Thus, researchers might be forced to utilize established testing agencies to gain access to the testing equipment, which increases the costs of research. Moreover, performance testing of physical mock-ups of building systems requires sophisticated fabrication techniques, and researchers should be aware that collaboration with manufacturers, fabricators, and contractors is a necessary part of these types of studies.

3.4.3 Experiments

Experiments are systematic research processes conducted under controlled conditions in order to test a hypothesis, discover unknown facts, or to determine a cause-effect relationship between variables. In the architectural profession, experiments are used to evaluate people's behavior (in relation to design outcomes or design processes), for environmental research (relating to building performance, buildings' energy use, and building physics), technology (evaluating new building technologies, digital technologies, communication), design processes and tools, products and systems, and to evaluate design outcomes. Therefore, experiments in architecture can focus on physical objects and systems and the design process, as well as understanding relationships between people and the built environment. Regardless of the research objectives, experiments are used to examine the effect of an independent variable on the dependent variables in a specific study, where an independent variable is manipulated by the researcher to measure its impacts on the dependent variables. Figure 3.34 presents characteristics of experiments.

Experiments can be used to determine cause and effect relationships between variables. For example, a study was conducted to evaluate the effects of interior design characteristics, specifically spatial properties, on the physiological stress response of building occupants (Fich et al., 2014). The researchers investigated two different room typologies (closed rooms without views and rooms with views to the outside) in a virtual environment and measured participants' physiological response (saliva cortisol and heart rate variability) to these different spaces. The study participants included 49 people, and the results indicated

Figure 3.34:
Characteristics of
experiments.

EXPERIMENTS	
Data sources	• Physical evaluation conducted under controlled conditions, can be used to determine cause-effects relationships between variables • Possible implementations are wide-ranging, including research relating to products and systems, people's behavior, building performance, technology, design process, and design outcomes • Used to examine the effects of an independent variable, manipulated by the researcher, on the dependent variables • Measurements of impacts of the independent variable
Data analysis procedures	• Numerical or statistical analysis of measurements • Evaluations of non-numerical data • Graphical representation of results (drawings, diagrams, photographs, charts, graphs and tables), and written analysis and interpretation of results
Benefits	• Ability to control independent variables and eliminate irrelevant variables • Possibility to determine cause and effect relationships • Broad applications in architectural research • Possibility to replicate experimental set-up
Drawbacks	• Time consuming and costly • Results may apply to one situation • It may be difficult to generalize findings that apply to many different scenarios

that participants in the closed room responded with more pronounced cortisol reactivity. Another example is a study conducted to evaluate the effects of facade design and window openings on the indoor thermal environment in residential buildings located in a tropical climate (Tong et al., 2019). The authors measured indoor air temperature near residential facades in naturally ventilated buildings in Singapore. Four different residential sites were chosen for the study, including inhabited and vacant units constructed from the 1970s to the 2010s. The authors experimentally investigated the effects of window-to-wall ratio, facade orientation, and shading mechanisms on indoor air temperature. The results indicated that windows greatly impact the indoor thermal environments—lower window-to-wall ratio decreases interior air temperature. The study also found that the interior thermal conditions in the investigated buildings met thermal comfort standards.

Experimental research can be grouped into two broad categories—true experimental research and quasi-experimental research. The main difference between these two categories is that true experimental research relies on random assignment of research subjects, while quasi-experimental does not. In quasi-experimental research, researchers control the assignment based on a certain criterion, primarily applicable to studies where randomization is difficult or impossible. In architectural research, true experiments are typically conducted for research studies relating to environmental research, technology, products, and systems, while quasi-experimental research is typically associated with studies focusing on design processes and evaluation of design outcomes.

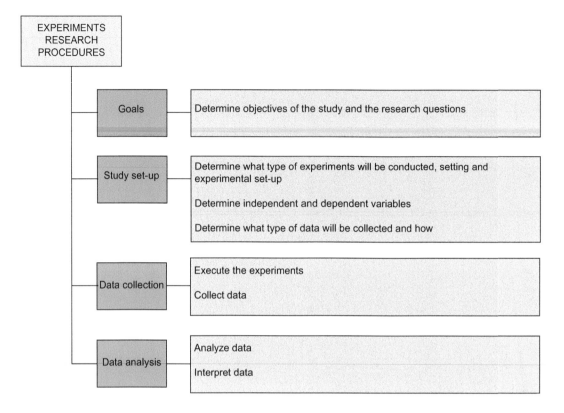

Figure 3.35:
Procedures for
experiments.

The procedures for implementing experiments as a research method in architecture, shown in Figure 3.35, include:

- Defining the objectives of the study
- Determining research questions that will be addressed
- Determining what type of experiments will be conducted, setting, and experimental set-up, as well as independent and dependent variables
- Determining what type of data will be collected and how
- Executing the experiments and collecting data
- Analyzing and interpreting data

The benefits of this research method are an ability to control independent variables and to eliminate irrelevant variables in the experimental set-up, the possibility of determining cause and effect relationships between variables, broad applications in architectural research, and the possibility of replicating the experimental set-up. The drawbacks are that this research method is typically time consuming and costly, results may apply to only one situation, it may be difficult to generalize findings that apply to many different scenarios, and it can raise ethical issues if human subjects are used in the research.

3.5 MIXED-MODE RESEARCH METHODS

Now that we have examined different research methods, it should be noted that mixed-mode research methods are very often applied in architectural research.

Mixed-mode research combines quantitative, qualitative, or experimental research methods in a single study or series of studies relating to the same research topic. Two or more research methods can be integrated in mixed-mode research, and the main benefit is that it provides improved understanding of a specific research problem by combining different approaches for addressing that problem. Figure 3.36 indicates typical combinations of research methods used in architectural research.

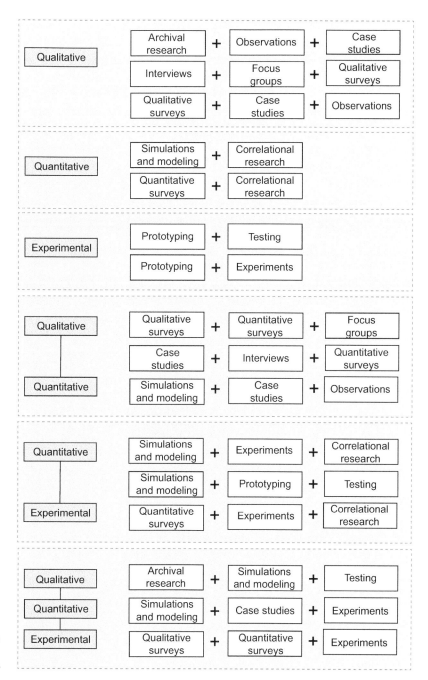

Figure 3.36: Typical combination of mixed-mode research methods used in architecture.

For example, qualitative and quantitative surveys can be combined into one study, as can case study research and simulations, or prototyping and experiments. Therefore, research problems can be analyzed from different perspectives, using different data collection mechanisms and analysis approaches. Considering the complex nature of architecture and its dependency on convoluted social, economic, cultural, environmental, technological, and behavioral interactions between people, systems, and the built environment, it becomes apparent that mixed-mode research methods are often best-suited to investigate these complex interactions. In architectural research, we often must address "how", "what", and "why" relating to the same research problem; thus, a combination of different research methods can be employed to address research questions of different natures. This ensures that research problems are approached from multiple angles, typically referred to as "triangulation". Triangulation entails using more than one method to collect data on the same research problem to increase the credibility and validity of research findings, as seen in Figure 3.37. Moreover, strengths and weaknesses of individual research methods can be considered, and the complementary nature of different approaches can be beneficial for mixed-mode research.

When selecting appropriate research methods for mixed-mode studies, researchers need to determine applicable methods based on the specific topic and research questions, level of interaction, and the point of interface. In terms of interaction, mixed-mode studies can utilize an independent or interactive research process. The independent process relies on using specific methods for the discrete parts of the study, while the interactive process integrates two or more research methods concurrently. The point of interface refers to a specific point in the study where different methods are integrated. The possible points of interface include the data collection step (different types of data are collected at the same time), the data analysis step (data are collected at different times, but analyzed simultaneously), and the interpretation of results (data are collected and

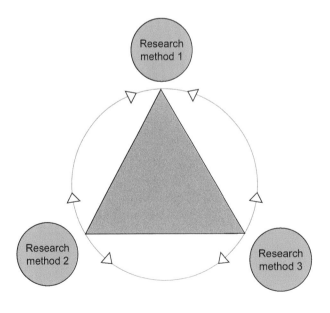

Figure 3.37: Triangulation employs more than one research method for the same research problem to increase credibility and validity of findings.

analyzed at different times, but results are compared or combined to form final conclusions).

The procedures for conducting mixed-mode research studies include:

- Defining the objectives of the study
- Determining research questions that will be addressed
- Determining what types of research methods will be employed
- Determining the level of interaction between the different research methods (independent or interactive)
- Determining the point of interface between the different research methods (for data collection, data analysis, or interpretation of results)
- Executing the study and collecting data
- Analyzing data
- Interpreting results

For example, a study was conducted that investigated the effects of different architectural design features (openness of space, density, presence of windows, daylighting, levels of artificial lighting, symmetry, exposure to nature, ease of access, acoustics, and ambient noise) on peoples' experiences in interior spaces and their preferences using mixed-mode methods (Ergan et al., 2018). The researchers investigated people's perceptions of each individual design feature and the impact of these features on the overall experience. Focus groups, experiments, and a combination of qualitative and quantitative surveys were conducted. Initially, researchers identified architectural design features that impact human experience and conducted focus groups with 18 experienced architects to finalize a list of features that would be used in the experimental study. For the experiment, researchers created image sets that visually represented different configurations of each individual design feature and used an online platform to create a survey, which was used to collect qualitative and quantitative data from study participants. The survey instructed participants to select a preferred image for each design feature from two possible images, where two opposing design techniques would be represented. Participants also rated both images using semantic bipolar scales and were asked to write descriptive words that described their feelings for each image. A total of 356 participants responded to the survey, and collected data included quantitative and qualitative measures. Statistical analysis was conducted for quantitative data. Qualitative data was analyzed by frequency analysis of words that were used by participants to describe their feelings about specific architectural features. Research results indicated that the participants preferred the configuration of the architectural design features that were aligned with the positive end of the bipolar scales. Specifically, participants preferred natural daylight, spaces with large windows and high ceilings, access to nature, open spaces, symmetry, and regular layouts in rooms (Ergan et al., 2018). The results are useful for architectural practitioners in understanding how people experience the space and the relative importance of different design features. Moreover, the mixed-mode research allowed researchers to objectively quantify the impact of architectural design features on human experiences.

3.6 CHAPTER SUMMARY

In this chapter we examined different research methods (qualitative, quantitative, and experimental), their application for different types of studies in architectural research according to specific research areas, and detailed research procedures, benefits, and drawbacks. Qualitative methods rely on non-numerical research strategies and include archival research, interviews, focus groups, observations, qualitative surveys, and case study research. These research methods are typically used in architectural history and theory, qualitative socio-behavioral research, understanding design outcomes, understanding design processes (collaboration, communication, tools), and qualitative studies relating to materials, building systems, and construction. Quantitative methods utilize numerical approaches for data collection and include simulations and modeling, quantitative surveys, and correlational research. These methods are typically used in building technology and environmental research, financial research, quantitative socio-behavioral research, design processes and tools, and quantitative studies relating to design outcomes, building materials, systems, fabrication, and construction. Experimental methods include prototyping, testing, and experimental studies, and rely on physical investigations. Experimental methods are useful for environmental and technology research, experimental socio-behavioral research, design methods and outcomes, building materials and systems, as well as production processes. We also examined mixed-mode research, which combines two or more research methods to address the same topic. Mixed-mode research is very typical in architecture since it allows researchers to approach the research problem from multiple angles.

The next chapter focuses on integration of research within the architectural profession and discusses models, funding mechanisms, implementation of research, and interaction with the architectural design process.

REFERENCES

Aksamija, A., (2010). "Analysis and Computation: Sustainable Design in Practice", *Design Principles and Practices: An International Journal*, Vol. 4, No. 4, pp. 291–314.

Aksamija, A., (2015). "BIM-Based Building Performance Analysis in Architectural Practice: When, Why and How", in *Architecture and Sustainability: Critical Perspectives for Integrated Design*, Khan, A. and Allecker, K., eds., Brussels, Belgium: Sint-Lucas Architecture Press, pp. 221–230.

Aksamija, A., (2016). *Integrating Innovation in Architecture: Design, Methods and Technology for Progressive Practice and Research*, Chichester, UK: John Wiley & Sons.

Armstrong, A., (2006). "Architectural Archives/Archiving Architecture: The Digital Era", *Journal of the Art Libraries Society of North America*, Vol. 25, No. 2, pp. 12–17.

Barbieri, G., Valente, M., Biolzi, L., Togliani, C., Fregonese, L., and Stanga, G., (2017). "An Insight in The Late Baroque Architecture: An Integrated Approach for a Unique Bibiena Church", *Journal of Cultural Heritage*, Vol. 23, No. 55, pp. 58–67.

Burry, J., (2016). *Prototyping for Architects*, London, UK: Thames & Hudson.

Camburn, B., Viswanathan, V., Linsey, J., Anderson, D., Jensen, D., Crawford, R., Otto, K., and Wood, K., (2017). "Design Prototyping Methods: State of the Art in Strategies, Techniques, and Guidelines", *Design Science*, Vol. 3, e13.

Day, J., and Gunderson, D., (2015). "Understanding High Performance Buildings: The Link between Occupant Knowledge of Passive Design Systems, Corresponding

Behaviors, Occupant Comfort and Environmental Satisfaction", *Building and Environment*, Vol. 84, pp. 114–124.

Emmel, N., (2013). *Sampling and Choosing Cases in Qualitative Research: A Realist Approach*, London, UK: SAGE Publications.

Ereiba, Y., Glass, J., and Thorpe, T., (2004). "TBY Using Focus Groups in Construction Management", *Proceedings of the 20th Annual Association of Researchers in Construction Management (ARCOM) Conference*, Heriot-Watt University, UK, September 1–3, pp. 857–865.

Ergan, S., Shi, Z., and Yu, X., (2018). "Towards Quantifying Human Experience in The Built Environment: A Crowdsourcing Based Experiment to Identify Influential Architectural Design Features", *Journal of Building Engineering*, Vol. 20, pp. 51–59.

Fich, L., Jonsson, P., Kirkegaard, P., Wallergard, M., Garde, A., and Hansen, A., (2014). "Can Architectural Design Alter the Physiological Reaction to Psychosocial Stress? A Virtual TSST Experiment", *Physiology & Behavior*, Vol. 135, pp. 91–97.

Gaillet, L., (2012). "(Per)Forming Archival Research Methodologies", *College Composition and Communication*, Vol. 64, No. 1, pp. 35–58.

Groat, L., and Wang, D., (2013). *Architectural Research Methods*, Hoboken, NJ: John Wiley & Sons.

Hay, R., Samuel, F., Watson, K., and Bradbury, S., (2017). "Post-Occupancy Evaluation in Architecture: Experiences and Perspectives from UK Practice", *Building Research & Information*, Vol. 46, No. 6, pp. 698–710.

Hensen, J., and Lamberts, R., eds., (2011). *Building Performance Simulation for Design and Operation*, Abingdon, UK: Spon Press.

Hershberger, R., (2015). *Architectural Programming and Predesign Manager*, New York: Routledge.

Hochscheid, E., and Halin, G., (2018). "BIM Implementation in Architecture Firms: Interviews, Case Studies and Action Research Used to Build a Method that Facilitates Implementation of BIM Processes and Tools", *Proceedings of the 36th International Conference on Education and Research in Computer Aided Architectural Design in Europe (eCAADe)*, Lodz, Poland, September 19–21, pp. 231–240.

Hong, T., Chou, S., and Bong, T., (2000). "Building Simulation: An Overview of Developments and Information Sources", *Building and Environment*, Vol. 35, No. 5, pp. 347–361.

Li, P., Froese, T., and Brager, G., (2018). "Post-Occupancy Evaluation: State-of-the-Art Analysis and State-of-the-Practice Review", *Building and Environment*, Vol. 133, pp. 187–202.

Mack, N., Woodsong, C., Macqueen, K., Guest, G., and Namey, E., (2005). *Qualitative Research Methods: A Data Collector's Field Guide*, Research Triangle Park, NC: Family Health International.

Martin, D., Nettleton, S., and Buse, C., (2019). "Affecting Care: Maggie's Centres and The Orchestration of Architectural Atmospheres", *Social Science & Medicine*, Vol. 240, pp. 112563.

Merriam, S., and Tisdell, E., (2016). *Qualitative Research: A Guide to Design and Implementation*, 4th ed., San Francisco, CA: Jossey-Bass.

Mertler, C., (2019). *Introduction to Educational Research*, Thousand Oaks, CA: SAGE Publications.

Mulligan, K., Calder, A., and Mulligan, H., (2018). "Inclusive Design in Architectural Practice: Experiential Learning of Disability in Architectural Education", *Disability and Health Journal*, Vol. 11, No. 2, pp. 237–242.

Preiser, W., White, E., and Rabinowitz, H., (2015). *Post-Occupancy Evaluation*, New York: Routledge.

Ryan, E., and Sanquist, T., (2012). "Validation of Building Energy Modeling Tools Under Idealized and Realistic Conditions", *Energy and Buildings*, Vol. 47, pp. 375–382.

Sarvimaki, M., (2018). *Case Study Strategies for Architects and Designers: Integrative Data Research Methods*, New York: Routledge.

Siva, J., and London, K., (2011). "Investigating the Role of Client Learning for Successful Architect-Client Relationships on Private Single Dwelling Projects", *Architectural Engineering and Design Management*, Vol. 7, No. 3, pp. 177–189.

Srivastava, C., Yang, Z., and. Jain, R., (2019). "Understanding the Adoption and Usage of Data Analytics and Simulation Among Building Energy Management Professionals: A Nationwide Survey", *Building and Environment*, Vol. 157, pp. 139–164.

Stewart, D., Shamdasani, P., and Rook, D., (2009). "Group Depth Interviews: Focus Group Research", in *The SAGE Handbook of Applied Social Research Methods*, 2nd ed., Bickman, L., and Rog, D., eds., Thousand Oaks, CA: SAGE Publications, pp. 589-616.

Tong, S., Wong, N., Tan, E., and Jusuf, S., (2019). "Experimental Study on the Impact of Facade Design on Indoor Thermal Environment in Tropical Residential Buildings", *Building and Environment*, Vol. 166, pp. 106418.

Twombly, R., (2001). "Louis Sullivan's First National Bank Building (1919–1922), Manistique, Michigan", *Journal of the Society of Architectural Historians*, Vol. 60, No. 2, pp. 200–207.

Upadhyay, N., and Sharma, A., (2018). "Understanding and Recreating Historical Landscapes through Oral History, Architectural and Archival Research—A Methodology: The Case of the Royal Gardens of Rajnagar, Bundelkhand", *Journal of Heritage Management*, Vol. 2, No. 2, pp. 202–220.

Van Steenwinkel, I., de Casterle, B., and Heylighen, A., (2017). "How Architectural Design Affords Experiences of Freedom in Residential Care for Older People", *Journal of Aging Studies*, Vol. 41, pp. 84–92.

Wood, M., (1999). *From Craft to Profession: The Practice of Architecture in Nineteenth-Century America*, Berkeley, CA: University of California Press.

Zeisel, J., (2006). *Inquiry by Design: Environment/Behavior/Neuroscience in Architecture, Interiors, Landscape, and Planning*, New York: W.W. Norton.

PART 4

INTEGRATION OF RESEARCH IN ARCHITECTURAL PRACTICE

4 Integration of Research in Architectural Practice

4.1 THE ROLE OF RESEARCH IN INNOVATIVE PRACTICES

Research in architectural design is not a new phenomenon. Gradual technological changes, such as the development of new materials, construction techniques, and design representations, have accelerated the need for research over time (Groat and Wang, 2013). Today, however, research is more important than ever, and it is becoming an integral component in design practices (Aksamija, 2016; Aksamija and Green, 2013). A variety of factors have made designers' jobs more complex, including technological advancements, changing client expectations, and new design methods and processes.

Architectural and design research has evolved in fundamental ways during the last 100 years (Nigel, 1999). Prior to the 1950s, the major focus of research related to architectural history and theory. This focus shifted in the post-WWII era as research broadened to include mass-produced construction, alternative construction materials, engineering, and economics-related topics. During the 1970s, the oil crisis resulted in unprecedented energy concerns, and architectural research expanded to include environmental topics and methods for improving energy efficiency of buildings. More recently, during the 1980s and 1990s, research expanded to include behavioral research in architecture, focusing on occupants' responses to internal and external conditions (daylight, nature, indoor air quality, etc.), and continued to expand with advances in information technologies and digital design.

Contemporary architectural firms must continuously adapt to complex and changing conditions and can survive and thrive in changing market conditions only if they are able to respond to these changes. However, the motives and goals should be identified in such a way so that the changing market conditions do not impact the core values and strategies. The skills and services might change and adapt, as well as the design processes, project delivery methods, and design technologies.

The role of research in innovative practices is paramount. Research, within this context, is defined as systematic investigation and creation of new knowledge and applications, utilizing rigorous research methods. Figure 4.1 indicates relationships between design and research and illustrates how integrating research with the design process is essential for developing new knowledge, solving design and technical problems, overcoming different types of challenges present in the

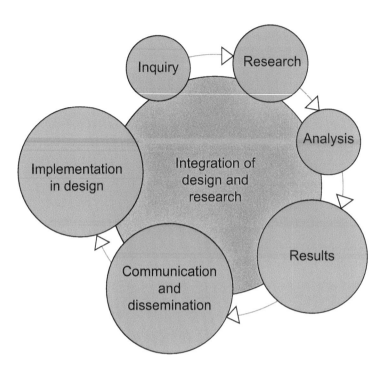

Figure 4.1:
Innovative archi-
tectural practices
integrate inquiry
and research into
the design process,
implement results,
and disseminate
new knowledge to
the wider design
community.

contemporary profession, and improving the design process and architectural work. Research results can be implemented on specific architectural projects but should also be disseminated to the wider design community in order to improve the knowledge base and architectural profession (Aksamija et al., 2015).

Over the past two decades, research in architecture has diversified and now often involves interdisciplinary approaches. Topics are wide-ranging, encompassing advanced materials, building technologies, environmental and energy concerns, design computation, automation in construction, management, and economics. The true value of research today lies in the evaluation and benchmarking of different types of design interventions, including operational efficiency, design effectiveness, building performance, and project delivery. The knowledge derived from these investigations helps to inform and propagate a culture of design innovation. The practical value of this knowledge is enhanced by the new direction in architectural research in which research originates in practice. Research questions, methods, and results must be closely tied to architectural projects, design processes, and services.

There are three stages that constitute the innovation process: research and development, commercialization or implementation, and dissemination, as seen in Figure 4.2. During each stage, there are activities that require inputs of knowledge and investments of time and resources. For example, the research and development stages require basic research, applied research, and development and testing. The outcomes include discoveries, new ideas, and development of new knowledge, as well as development of prototypes, testing, and experimental

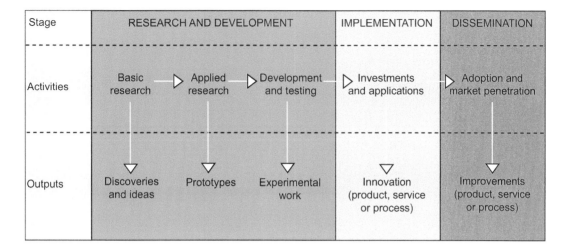

Stage	RESEARCH AND DEVELOPMENT			IMPLEMENTATION	DISSEMINATION
Activities	Basic research ▷	Applied research ▷	Development and testing	▷ Investments and applications	▷ Adoption and market penetration
Outputs	▽ Discoveries and ideas	▽ Prototypes	▽ Experimental work	▽ Innovation (product, service or process)	▽ Improvements (product, service or process)

Figure 4.2:
Three of stages
of the innovation
process, where
research and
development are
the essential steps
towards com-
mercialization or
implementation.
Dissemination and
knowledge sharing
are also impor-
tant, since these
steps are neces-
sary to improve or
transform products,
services, or the
design process.

work. The next stage constitutes implementation, and the last stage is the dissemination and wider adoption. It is important to note that innovation is rarely a linear progression through the indicated stages, but rather specific outputs influence activities of consequent stages.

Research and development can bring immense value to any organization for which innovation is important (Hult et al., 2004). However, considering the lack of universal models for integrating research with practice, the realities of client requirements, schedules, and budgets, as well as risks and liability—research in the architectural profession is challenging. Organizing and maintaining research departments within architectural design practices can be costly, time-consuming, and risky. Therefore, taking a careful and systematic approach to establishing research departments and defining operational models and relationships between research, design practice, and business performance are essential. It is necessary to balance and determine different priorities, including short-term goals and long-term strategic focus, alignment with firm's motives and values, developing internal capabilities, or outsourcing and partnering with external research partners. It is also essential to align research objectives and methods with the objectives of innovation. These following aspects should be considered in integrating research with design practice:

- How to establish the research arm of the firm and its structure and organization.
- What are the connections and relationships between the firm's core values, practice and research?
- What are the long-term strategies and objectives of research vs. short-term actions?
- How to fund research activities and how to mitigate risk and liability issues.
- How to translate results of research efforts into practice.

The next sections discuss and illustrate methods for integrating research with design practice.

4.2 ORGANIZATION, RESEARCH MANAGEMENT, AND MODELS FOR INTEGRATING RESEARCH IN PRACTICE

Innovative design practices support organizational change, incorporate integrated design methods, integrate research and development into their operations, embrace technological change, and improve employee performance, thus increasing business performance. The key aspect is that organization and management must support research, since traditional management of architectural firms often is driven by models whose priority is not research and innovation but the profitability of the firm. Innovative firms should set the context, create a strategy and goals, incorporate research and development, manage and guide the process of innovation, and welcome change (Hensel and Nilsson, 2016). The role of management then becomes essential in providing a work environment where research and innovation are welcome.

Creating an environment that fosters innovation, exchange of ideas, research and development, creative thinking, continuing education, and experimentation is essential for innovative architectural practices, regardless of the size of the firm. However, organizational structure impacts the culture of the firm, as well as its operation. There are three basic categories of firms, based on the operational models: strong delivery firms, strong service firms, and strong idea firms. These typologies are intensely influenced by the firm's values. The strong delivery firms are organized for efficiency and rely on standard solutions. They tend to have a strong formal structure and stable working environment and often specialize in specific building types. The design processes and production are standardized. The strong service firms are organized for service and have highly dynamic internal environments that allow changes to managerial structure. This allows the firms to respond to the different needs of their clients, and they typically cover a wider range of building types. Strong idea firms tend to primarily focus on conceptual processes and design thinking, but organizational structure is flexible. They provide unique results, and standard solutions are rarely considered since clients typically employ these types of firms for a unique project. Architectural firms fit within these categories and may operate within two or three categories simultaneously, as seen in Figure 4.3. It is necessary to find a balance between the firm's culture, underlining values, and organizational model. Cultural environment and organizational model are important in producing the best design work, but also for attracting and retaining new talents and clients. Innovative, research-based firms nurture success, openness and flexibility, internal communication and knowledge dissemination, professionalism, risk-taking, appreciation of employees, and collaboration. Therefore, the organizational structure and management should cultivate these qualities.

The roles in innovative, research-based firms should also be shifting. Traditionally, architectural firms have been organized according to the types of activities and project stages. Design, project management, and technical teams are the three basic pillars for any project. Design teams tend to be primarily involved during the conceptual and schematic design phases, project managers are involved from the beginning to the end stages, with varying levels of

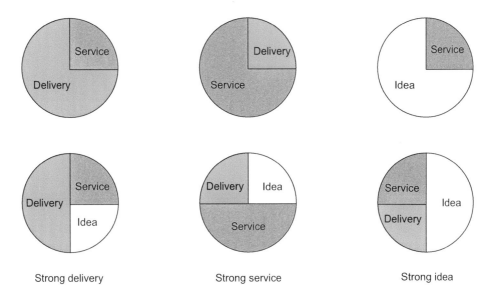

Strong delivery   Strong service   Strong idea

Figure 4.3:
Basic operational
models of architec-
tural firms.

responsibility during different design phases, and technical teams are primarily involved during design development, construction documentation, and construction administration. Changing design processes and technologies are influencing this paradigm, requiring more integration and collaboration during all design phases (Elvin, 2007). Moreover, research teams must also be part of the design team, or architectural practitioners should be trained to conduct basic research in order to integrate research into the design process. Traditional roles are blurred in research-based practices since improved collaboration between project team members is necessary. Besides internal collaboration, an integrated design process that involves architectural, engineering, fabrication, and construction disciplines from the beginning of the project is also a key aspect for innovative practices. Complexity of the projects, economic drivers, and technological changes are the primary factors for integrated project delivery. Outside of the design and engineering disciplines, innovative firms also involve team members or consultants from other disciplines, including computer scientists, material scientists, chemists, psychologists, etc. Interdisciplinary collaboration becomes especially crucial for research and development since research methods often require input from these specialized fields.

There are different models of operation for research activities within design practices—internal, external, and hybrid, as shown in Figure 4.4 (Aksamija, 2016). These models depend on several factors, including the size of the firm, its dedication to research and development, funding, types of research activities, etc. Internal research practices are internally funded by the firm or included as part of the firm's services (thus, client-driven and funded), where researchers are employees of the firm. Research activities are closely related to the firm's operation, research projects are driven by design projects, and results are directly implemented in practice. The external model constitutes involvement with external partners, where the design firms may fund activities of various research centers

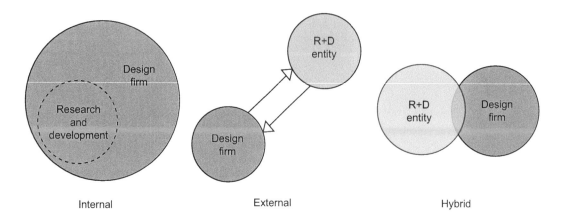

Internal   External   Hybrid

or universities. In this model, researchers are not employed by the firm, but rather act as consultants, or the firm has an opportunity to impact the research agenda of the external research center. Research projects may or may not be influenced by the firm's projects, and implementation of results highly depends on the way that the research projects are structured and executed. The hybrid model constitutes a mixture of the previous two types. For example, some design firms are establishing separate non-profit organizations that are dedicated to research, but are highly influenced by the firm's values, strategies, and projects. Part of the research work may be funded by the firm, while other activities may be funded by other sources.

Figure 4.4:
Models for integrating research into an architectural design practice.

CASE STUDY 4.1: INTERNAL MODEL FOR INTEGRATING RESEARCH INTO PRACTICE

Internal research departments in architectural firms require initial investments from the firms but also provide significant benefits to the firms that employ this model for integrating research into practice. Researchers are then employees of the firm and can be involved in a variety of projects and can be fully integrated into the design process. They can perform short-term and long-term studies, depending on the firm's objectives and strategic plans. The following case study illustrates one of these entities and demonstrates a specific research project as an example of how research results are integrated into practice.

The Building Technology Laboratory (Tech Lab) was formed in 2008 as an internal research entity within Perkins and Will, with the aim of enhancing project designs through dedicated research. Tech Lab's research agenda encompasses advanced building technologies, materials, sustainability, high-performance buildings, renewable energy sources, and computational design (Haymaker et al., 2016). Its work focuses on developments in building systems and materials and emerging technologies that can have a direct impact on the course of architectural design, and it investigates building systems and technologies that can significantly improve the value, quality, and performance of architectural projects. Examples of Tech Lab's research projects include performance and life cycle cost analysis for building integrated photovoltaic systems, the performance of double skin facades, renewable energy systems optimization, properties and performance of facade systems, emerging materials, etc. Tech Lab was set-up to work with project teams on specific design projects, with a large part of its research agenda relating to ongoing architectural projects. Other efforts were aimed at investigating emerging technologies and practices that can have a direct impact on the course of architectural design, as well as collaborations with universities and research laboratories.

Primary research methods include simulations and modeling, which are used to investigate different design scenarios and strategies but also include other qualitative and experimental methods. The typical research process encompasses: 1) determination of research objectives and questions based on the needs of specific architectural/design projects; 2) identification of appropriate research methods; 3) identification of the timeline, schedule, and research procedures; 4) execution of the study; and 5) dissemination and implementation of research results. Besides the implementation of research results on architectural and design projects, sharing and dissemination of findings with the larger architectural and design community has been a key aspect of Tech Lab's work. Publications of research data and methods, analysis processes, and results benefit the entire industry; therefore, research studies and results have been publicly shared and disseminated through comprehensive reports, as shown in Figure 4.5 (Aksamija, 2010a, 2011, 2012, 2013).

The primary challenges for Tech Lab's operation relate to the time and budget constraints of project-driven research efforts, which often influence the duration and depth of research projects. This indicates that project-driven research efforts must be focused, rapid, and within the financial constraints of the project. However, these types of research activities are essential since they directly influence the outcomes of specific projects. Since the formation of Tech Lab, Perkins and Will has formed other research laboratories that focus on more diverse research topics using the same model.

Figure 4.5:
Publicly shared Tech Lab Annual Reports, a research publication of Perkins and Will's Building Technology Laboratory.

CASE STUDY 4.2: COLLABORATIVE RESEARCH BETWEEN PRACTICE AND ACADEMIA AS AN EXTERNAL MODEL FOR INTEGRATING RESEARCH INTO PROFESSION

Collaborative research projects between architectural firms and academic institutions or research laboratories are the most common method for the external model. The benefits for the firms are that researchers do not have to be employees of the firm, and significant overhead costs are not needed for running research departments, as in the internal model. The drawbacks are that architectural firms have less control over research activities and projects, and it is typically complex and difficult to apply this model to short-term, individual architectural projects that require research. But the model is applicable to long-term studies that focus on design processes, methods, and services. The following case study illustrates one example of such collaboration.

Perkins and Will and the University of Cincinnati collaborated on a specific research project and initiated a unique design studio that was part of this collaboration. The studio investigated the relationships between performance-driven design, computational design techniques, integration of building performance analysis tools with the design process, and digital fabrication for a building facade retrofit. The project focused an existing cold storage facility, which was converted into a commercial office building, as seen in Figure 4.6. The purpose was to design a new building skin for this project, using digital design methods and performance analysis, and to construct physical prototypes using digital fabrication methods. The objective of this collaboration was to integrate building performance simulations and modeling to drive design decisions, to use parametric design tools to explore building skin design, and to investigate fabrication/prototyping methods for testing constructability and material choices, as seen in Figure 4.7.

Figure 4.6:
Adaptive reuse project, which was the focus of collaboration between Perkins and Will and the University of Cincinnati.

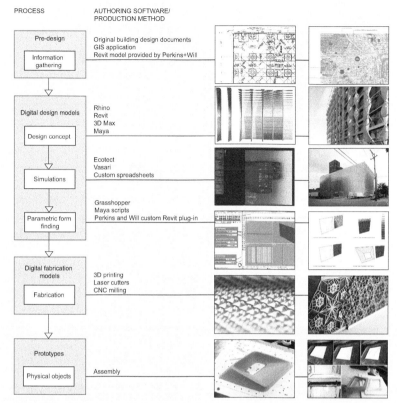

Figure 4.7:
Design and production process for research collaboration.

The central feature of this collaboration was examining new, emerging digital technologies and their applications for facade designs. The benefits for design practice are that emerging design approaches, technologies, and computational design methods were explored in relation to a real project. Several research questions were investigated during this process:

- Which tools are appropriate for the performance-based design approach? How do they relate to different design stages?
- What is the relationship between digital models and fabrication? What are the appropriate approaches for using design models to fabricate actual components?
- What are the best tools and practices for the translation of a digital design model to the physical prototype?

The practitioners provided all the background information about the project and presented and instructed students on the best methods for integration of building performance analysis tools into the design process. Remote video conferencing, podcasts, and online collaboration tools were used effectively to monitor the progress of the course and to provide guidance for further development of design solutions and fabrication of prototypes, as seen in Figure 4.8.

Figure 4.8:
Collaborative efforts, meetings, and reviews of research progress.

The collaboration offered the research team a route to investigate inno-vative design methods, observe the design and development, document results and applications, and share the outcomes and insights into the changing nature of design, affected by the emerging computational design methods. The collaboration resulted in a research article, which reviewed the research process, collaboration, and results and provided recommendations for best practices for collaborative research efforts between design practice and academic research institutions (Aksamija et al., 2012).

CASE STUDY 4.3: NON-PROFIT RESEARCH ENTITIES AS HYBRID MODELS FOR INTEGRATING RESEARCH INTO THE PROFESSION

Traditionally, there has been a divide between practice-based and academic research, but this gap needs to be restricted in the context of the contem-porary profession. The profession and academia, as well as other research entities, can greatly benefit from engaging in collaborative research efforts, especially for long-term studies. Research institutes and other organizations can benefit from teaming with practitioners, who could help identify problems relevant to practice and validate the practical application of research. At the same time, design professionals need better venues and academic partnerships to engage in non-project-specific, longer duration research efforts. The following case study illustrates one method to accomplish this, which requires architectural firms to establish non-profit research entities. These entities can be used as a channel to establish relationships with many other research organizations and partners.

AREA Research, established in 2011, is an independent 501(c)(3) non-profit organization operating parallel to Perkins and Will. Two primary conditions drove the formation of this company. First was the growing need for research institutes and other organizations to team with professional partners that represent the potential practical application of their research.

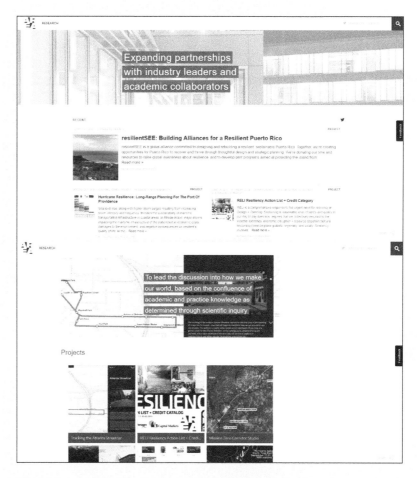

Figure 4.9:
Publicly shared results of collaborative research efforts between AREA Research and other research entities. Courtesy of Perkins and Will.

Second was the design professions' need for a venue to investigate issues that are not project-specific but longer duration efforts. Founded to address both demands, the true potential of AREA Research lies in its ability to bridge basic and applied research. AREA Research aims to bridge the divide of basic and applied research by providing a platform that connects the design professions, academia, and research institutions and supports innovative research that results in a higher-quality built environment.

The name AREA translates this mission as Advancing Research and Expanding Application. AREA is a conduit for partnerships, bringing information garnered in the research process to the broader design profession and providing knowledge from professional sources back to the research community. The organization's initial focus was on several different channels, including healthcare, workplace environments, education, building technologies, sustainability, and urban design. Projects can be structured within AREA Research in a number of ways, including externally funded projects in which AREA Research is a supporting member of a larger team, externally funded projects with AREA Research as the lead, and small, unfunded or internally funded projects. These partnership arrangements are meant to allow AREA Research to facilitate stronger relationships between basic research and applied research, combining the value of sustained research with project-specific data and expertise. Research results and reports are publicly shared, as seen in Figure 4.9.

4.3 FUNDING MECHANISMS

Architectural design practices function like many other business enterprises—they operate based on revenue received for services and overhead costs encumbered for operation. Profit is the difference between revenue and overhead costs and is influenced by many factors, including the billing rates for design services, costs of operation (salaries and benefits of employees, office space and equipment, consultant fees, and professional insurance), market demands, and economic conditions. Establishment of billing rates and costs of operation are within the direct control of the design firms, while market demands and the general state of the economy are outside factors. But where does funding for research come from, and how does it fit within the financial operations of design practices? There are three major mechanisms for funding research: internal funding (overhead costs), project-based research that is included in project budgets (client-driven), and obtaining external research funding, such as funding from federal agencies, foundations, professional organizations, etc. Each of these funding mechanisms requires different strategies and timelines for executing research projects. For example, internal funding can be used for short-term and long-term studies, focusing on different research projects (such as investigating new materials and their applications, building systems and building performance, design effectiveness, design process, new design and construction technologies, etc.). Project-based research is typically short-term and directly applicable to a single architectural project, but the results can be used for other similar projects. External funding is typically associated with long-term studies, and although they can focus on specific building typologies, systems, materials, and technologies, these types of studies must be applicable to a wide range of architectural projects.

Figure 4.10 summarizes these funding mechanisms and their relationships to operational models and timelines. For example, internal funding is typically used to fund internal research and development departments, which can be used to fund both short-term and long-term research studies. In this model, researchers are part of an architectural firm; they are employees of the firm and can be involved in a variety of projects. Internal funding can also be used to fund an external research entity, but these projects tend to be short-term, and they need to be related to the firm's research objectives and goals. Project-based funding can be used to fund internal short-term studies, but this type of research must be related to specific architectural projects. Similar mechanisms can be used to fund external research entities, but in this case, external researchers are acting as consultants on the project. External funding is typically used for long-term studies and is applicable to all three models of operation. In the case of internal research entities, researchers are expected to submit proposals and apply for external funding to execute research studies. For the external model, the collaborative research work is the primary mechanism to obtain external research funding. And in the

Figure 4.10: Funding mechanisms for research as they relate to different models for integrating research into practice.

MODELS FOR INTEGRATING RESEARCH INTO PRACTICE

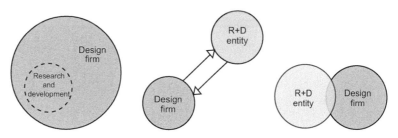

FUNDING MECHANISMS		INTERNAL		EXTERNAL		HYBRID	
		Short-term	Long-term	Short-term	Long-term	Short-term	Long-term
	Internal funding (overhead)	▲	▲	▲			
		Short-term	Long-term	Short-term	Long-term	Short-term	Long-term
	Project-based funding	▲		▲			
		Short-term	Long-term	Short-term	Long-term	Short-term	Long-term
	External funding (federal agencies, foundations, professional organizations)		▲		▲		

case of a hybrid model, the non-profit statue of the research arm might qualify for more funding opportunities than the for-profit part of the firm.

Nevertheless, architectural firms that are interested in integrating research into their work must invest in research. A typical question that the firms must address is how much of the internal funding to use towards research and development activities, since this funding needs to come from overhead costs. This is highly dependent on the firm's size, aspirational goals and mission, research objectives, and strategies. All design practices strive to increase profit while minimizing overhead costs. But innovative design practices should reinvest larger portions of their profit into activities that help them address innovation strategies, including development and establishment of research and development departments, employee incentives for innovative projects and results, infrastructure and equipment, and marketing. Strategies for increasing profit include:

- Balancing costs of design services, time, and rates
- Providing specific value, satisfying market demands, and offering unique perspectives for a variety of projects
- Leveraging capital and effort
- Controlling design processes through effective management

Therefore, architectural practices should try to reduce overhead costs for typical work activities so that the larger percentage can be used towards research and development. Methods for reducing overhead costs include streamlining work processes, effective management of schedules, controlling the scope of services, employing control quality programs, and financial accountability.

Innovative design practices often also categorize investments based on the type of research projects (building, service, or process). Service and process innovations should be based on internal funding, where part of the firm's profit is used to advance design services and processes. On the other hand, research projects that are project or building-specific should be funded accordingly, where contracts are drafted in such a way as to allow integrated design services, including research and development, to be considered as part of the firm's services. For example, if a certain project requires extensive simulations and modeling to investigate building performance, those activities should be included in the contract since they are project-specific tasks.

Determining reasons for investments in research and associated value is essential for any design organization. Competitive advantage, market expansion, and extension of firm's services may have financial benefits for the firm to invest in research, but there are also other intangible benefits, including improvement in design services and processes. In determining the value of research, design firms should establish a value proposition that reflects the core services, market niche, and benefits. For example, improving technical expertise and embracing new building and design technologies are benefits for investing in research and directly influence value. Figure 4.11 shows the impacts of research and innovation on revenue (as a direct measure) and value (as a measure of all indirect benefits).

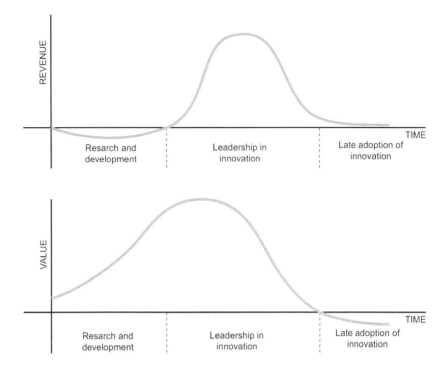

Figure 4.11:
Impacts of invest-
ments in research
on revenue and
value over time.

Investments in research and development require initial capital, but results impact
the activities and practices of the firm, influencing design services and methods. Cutting-edge firms and leaders in innovation create a niche market, thus
increasing the revenue for their services due to increased market demand. On
the other hand, late adopters of innovation do not possess value differentiation.
Continuous investment in and implementation of innovative strategies maintains
higher revenues for firms whose core values focus on research and development
and improvement of design services and methods, as seen in Figure 4.12.

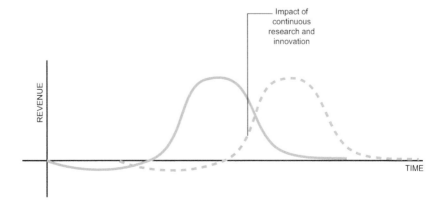

Figure 4.12:
Impact of continu-
ous research and
innovation on rev-
enue over time.

4.4 IMPLEMENTATION OF RESEARCH AND INTEGRATION WITH THE DESIGN PROCESS

Implementation of research and integration with the design process are essential for any firm interested in establishing research and development departments. But what are the appropriate strategies for successfully integrating research into the design? Research projects must relate to the firm's core values, projects, and strategic plan, while research activities must align with the firm's operations and timelines for executing projects. For example, short-term studies that are focusing on specific architectural projects and are funded by the clients must align with the overall project timeline and budget. This means that, typically, available time to conduct the research is very limited, and it must be conducted much faster than academic research. At the same time, the quality of research work cannot be compromised, which is the major challenge for integrating research into the architectural profession—maintaining high-quality research work while adhering to timelines and project budgets. This is the core difference between academic and practice-based research, since the timeframes for executing research projects are quite different. For long-term studies, practice-based research is similar to academic research but should relate to the funding mechanisms and operation of the firm.

In order to address this challenge, firms must develop strategic plans for research, establish procedures for organizing and structuring research activities, and determine the right research methods for different types of research projects. The previous two chapters provided in-depth explanations of the research process and its steps, types of studies in architectural research, different research methods, and procedures for executing research projects. Therefore, firms can follow these steps and procedures in executing specific research studies.

CASE STUDY 4.4: RESEARCH CONDUCTED DURING THE DESIGN OF RUSH UNIVERSITY MEDICAL CENTER

Rush University Medical Center (RUMC) is located in Chicago, Illinois. In 2004, RUMC revealed plans to initiate the most comprehensive construction and facilities improvement project in its history, known as the Campus Transformation Project. This plan called for investments in new technologies and facility design that would modernize operations for the 21st century and reorient the campus around the comfort of patients and their families. RUMC enlisted Perkins and Will to plan and design parts of the medical campus, which included a new 840,000 ft^2 (78,039 m^2) state-of-the-art hospital building (Tower), a new medical office building and orthopedics care facility, and a centralized power plant/parking garage, as shown in Figure 4.13. The design of this major healthcare facility started in 2006, and the building was completed in early 2012. The existing hospital building is connected to the new Tower with the Edward A. Brennan Entry Pavilion.

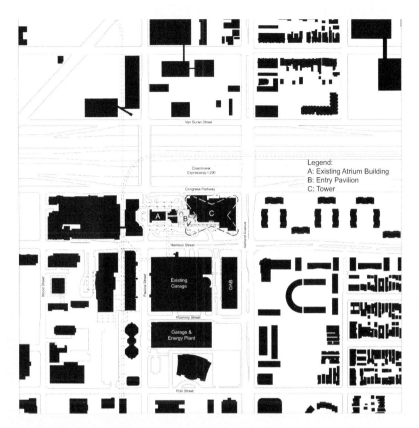

Figure 4.13:
Rush University Medical Center Transformation Plan and its components (Tower, Entry Pavilion, Orthopedics Ambulatory Care Building, Garage, and Centralized Energy Plant). Courtesy of Perkins and Will.

The building program for the RUMC Tower included an emergency department, a center for advanced emergency response, a non-invasive diagnostics department, an interventional platform, women's services and neo-natal critical care units, a critical care unit, and patient rooms. The distinctive butterfly shape of the bed tower was directed by the operational and pragmatic requirements, with the intention to minimize travel distances between medical staff and patients. The findings of previous research indicated that design layouts and locations of nurses' stations that minimize staff walking increase patient care time and support staff activities, such as communication and collaboration among medical staff (Hendrich et al., 2009; Rechel et al., 2009). This concept directly correlates to the guiding principles of the project and was a driving factor for the design and layout of the Tower.

Figure 4.14 shows the Tower, Entry Pavilion and the existing Atrium Building on the west side. The Entry Pavilion connects the existing Atrium Building and the Tower and provides an inviting lobby and entry space for the patients, families, and medical staff. A series of bridge connections that

Figure 4.14:
Rush University Medical Center Tower and Entry Pavilion. Courtesy of James Steinkamp.

link the existing Atrium Building to the Tower were also designed and constructed. Figure 4.15 shows an exploded axonometric view of the Tower.

The Entry Pavilion is a grand public entry space connecting the Tower with the Atrium Building. It was designed to address the arrival experience for those coming to the large, medical, urban campus. Figure 4.16 shows an exploded axonometric of the Entry Pavilion in relation to the overall building footprint of the RUMC Tower. On the ground level, an open-to-above "terrarium" greets incoming guests with trees and a forest floor garden. A publicly accessible roof garden on the fourth level provides an outdoor space, specifically designed to allow building occupants access to nature. Also, two large circular skylights provide daylight to the interior space.

Previous research studies have produced evidence that hospital gardens can lower stress levels for medical staff and improve their productivity, improve patients' outcomes, and improve patient and family satisfaction with the overall quality of care (Ulrich, 1999). For example, based on post-occupancy evaluations of four hospital gardens, it was concluded that many nurses and other healthcare workers used the gardens for achieving escape and recuperation from stress (Cooper-Marcus and Barnes, 1995). Other post-occupancy studies indicated that patients and family members who use hospital gardens report positive mood changes and reduced stress (Whitehouse et al., 2001). Therefore, access to nature, roof gardens, and terrariums were important design elements. A "staff only" roof garden was specifically designed at the ninth level as a respite area for caregivers.

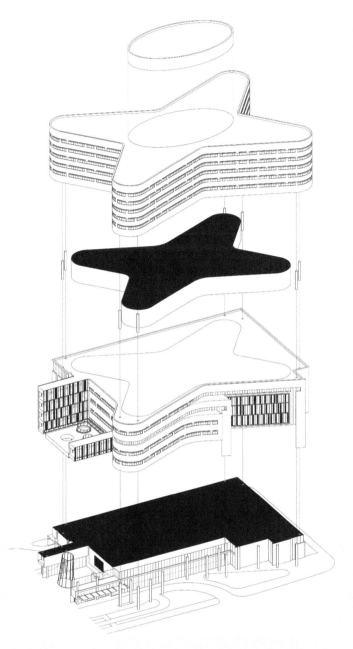

Figure 4.15:
Exploded axonometric view of the RUMC Tower. Courtesy of Perkins and Will.

The design of the RUMC Entry Pavilion was started with the goal of achieving the Living Building Challenge, which required significant research during the design process (Abdullah and Aksamija, 2012). The Living Building Challenge is a certification program that promotes one of the most advanced measurements of sustainability in the built environment. The Living Building Challenge comprises seven performance areas: site, water, energy, health,

Figure 4.16:
Exploded axonometric view of the RUMC Entry Pavilion. Courtesy of Perkins and Will.

materials, equity, and beauty. These can be applied to buildings (new construction and renovation of existing structures), landscape, urban design, community development, and infrastructure. This certification program is based on
actual performance, which must be measured and verified after the building or
development project is completed and occupied. Among other requirements,
it specifies that the building or development be designed and operated as
net-zero energy, where all the project's energy needs are supplied by on-site
renewable energy. It also requires that all water usage needs come from captured precipitation or closed loop water systems that are appropriately purified
without the use of chemicals, and that all occupied spaces have direct access
to operable windows and daylight. The design process of the Entry Pavilion
considered multiple sustainability strategies for meeting the Living Building
Challenge, as seen in Table 4.1 and Figure 4.17.

TABLE 4.1: Considered design strategies for RUMC Entry Pavilion in response to the Living Building Challenge.

Performance area	Requirements	Design strategies
Site design	Responsible site selection Limits to growth Habitat exchange	Habitat preservation on the campus
Energy	Net-zero energy	Building-integrated PVs on skylights, south facades of bridges PV panels on Atrium roof Daylighting Stored solar energy for nighttime Displacement ventilation Heat recovery systems Double skin facade along the south facade of the bridge Radiant heating system in the floor Solar hot water system
Materials	Materials red list Carbon footprint Responsible industry Appropriate materials radius Construction waste	Alternatives to thin-set epoxy-based terrazo Calculations for carbon footprint Recycled wood Local stone and wood
Water	Net-zero water Sustainable water discharge	Rainwater use for green roof irrigation Rainwater use for toilets Rainwater diversion from roofs into cisterns
Health	Civilized work Ventilation	Operable windows Daylighting Double skin facade along the south facade of the bridge Exhaust hot air from the atrium via double skin wall cavity
Beauty	Design for spirit Inspiration and education	Plant Terrarium Art mural Energy performance LED screen Exposed rainwater retention system Permanent displays explaing building's features

Building performance analysis was used to investigate several key aspects during the design, such as solar exposure and shadows for the roof garden, performance of a double skin facade along the bridge corridor, solar access analysis for several facades, performance of a photovoltaic system, and daylight analysis. The use of simulations and building performance analysis during the design process improves design decision-making (Aksamija, 2010b). The following sections demonstrate the results of various studies and performance analyses conducted for the RUMC Entry Pavilion.

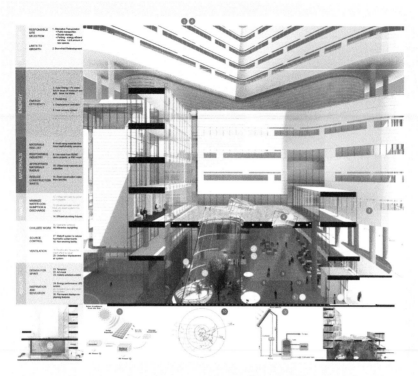

Figure 4.17:
Entry Pavilion section and the considered sustainable design strategies. Courtesy of
Perkins and Will.

The objective of the solar exposure study was to investigate the amount
of solar radiation available for the Entry Pavilion roof area. The primary driver
was to investigate whether this area would have access to enough solar radiation, since this portion of the building is used as a roof garden. Figure 4.18
indicates solar exposure and shading hours for the Entry Pavilion roof area
on June 21 and December 20. There are approximately thirteen hours of
sunlight available on June 21 and only seven on December 20. Diffuse solar
radiation was found to be comparable for both dates.

The next step considered hourly shadow ranges for two specific dates
during the summer and winter seasons. Since this study showed that the
Tower and the Existing Atrium Building partially shade the roof garden, hourly
solar position and shadows were studied to determine how much time the
roof garden spends in shade on two specific dates (June 21 and December
21). The diagrams in Figure 4.19 show the hourly sun position and projected
shadows on June 21 from 7 AM to 6 PM. The roof garden is in total shadow
from 7 to 9 AM, as well as from 5 PM to sunset. Partial shadows are present
from 10 to 11 AM and from 2 to 5 PM. From noon to 1 PM, roof garden is
fully exposed to the sun. The diagrams shown in Figure 4.20 show the hourly
sun position and projected shadows on December 21 from 7 AM to 6 PM.
The roof garden is in total shadow from 8 to 10 AM. Partial shadows are

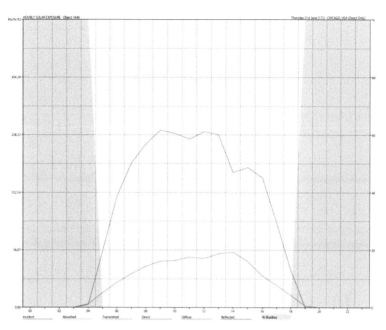

June 21
Hourly solar exposure for roof area

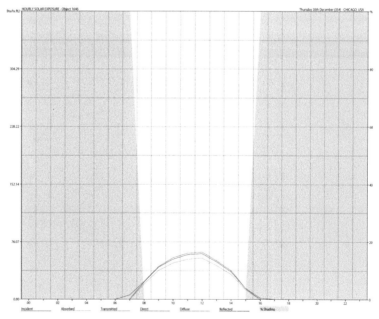

December 20
Hourly solar exposure for roof area

Figure 4.18:
Solar exposure and shading hours study for the Entry Pavilion roof area.

June 21 shadows

7 AM to 6 PM (1 hour increments)

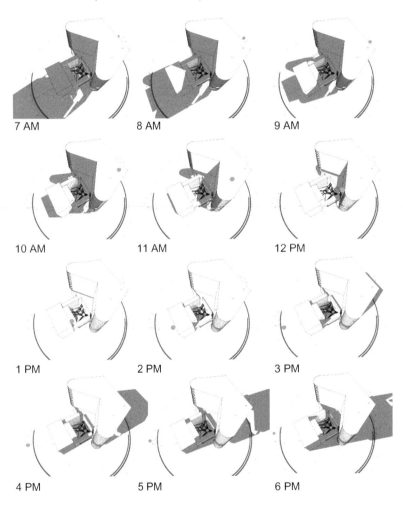

Figure 4.19:
Hourly sun position in relation to the roof garden and projected shadows on June 21 from
7 AM to 6 PM.

December 21 shadows
7 AM to 6 PM (1 hour increments)

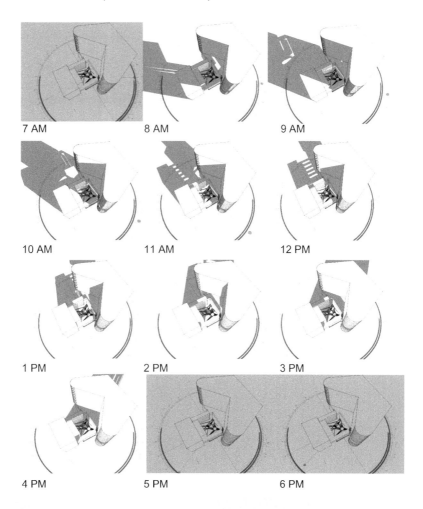

Figure 4.20:
Hourly sun position in relation to the roof garden and projected shadows on December 21 from 7 AM to 6 PM.

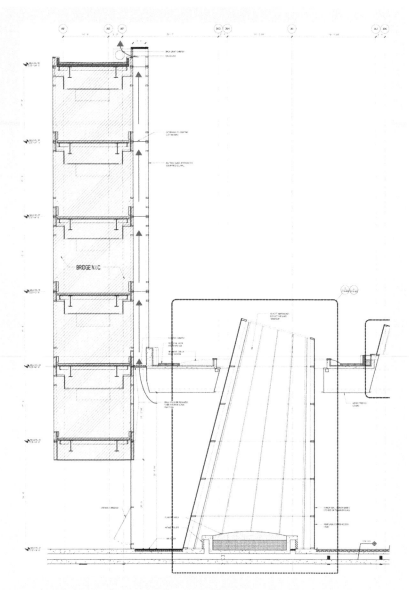

Figure 4.21:
Double skin wall section. Courtesy of Perkins and Will.

present most of the day, from 10 AM to 4 PM. However, the roof garden would not be widely used by building occupants during the winter months, but some solar exposure is necessary for plants. Therefore, it was concluded that there is enough solar exposure for plant life and landscaping, as well as occupants' comfort.

A double skin glazed facade along the south side of the bridge (connecting the RUMC Tower to the existing building) was considered during the schematic design as one of the energy-efficient design methods, shown in Figure 4.21. Double skin facades improve the thermal performance of

TABLE 4.2: Dynamic variables for different double skin design options.

Scenarios	Location of double glazing	Air flow type	Air cavity depth
Base model	-	-	-
Scenario 1	In	Exhaust air (interior vent supply, exterior vent exhaust)	1.5 ft (0.5 m)
Scenario 2	In	Exhaust air (interior vent supply, exterior vent exhaust)	2 ft (0.6 m)
Scenario 3	In	Exhaust air (interior vent supply, exterior vent exhaust)	3 ft (0.9 m)
Scenario 4	In	Exhaust air (interior vent supply, exterior vent exhaust)	4 ft (1.2 m)
Scenario 2.1	Out	Combination (exhaust air summer, air curtain winter)	2 ft (0.6 m)
Scenario 3.1	Out	Combination (exhaust air summer, air curtain winter)	3 ft (1.2 m)
Scenario 2.1.1	Out	Combination (exhaust air summer, air curtain winter)	2 ft (0.6 m)
Scenario 3.1.1	Out	Combination (exhaust air summer, air curtain winter)	3 ft (1.2 m)

exterior walls and subsequently the energy performance (Aksamija, 2018). Several design parameters and their effects on energy consumption, such as air cavity dimensions between the two skins, location of double air-insulated glazing, and the differences in operation during winter and summer months were studied using energy modeling (Aksamija, A., 2009). In order to study the effects of changing air cavity geometry, location of double skin, and different air flow types, different design scenarios were investigated, shown in Table 4.2. The base model included a single skin facade with low-e glazing, consisting of a curtain wall with double air-insulated low-e glazing unit. For double skin facade options, the location of the double glazing was varied from the internal to external side, as was cavity depth. Two different types of air flow were investigated—exhaust air all year round, as well as the combination of exhaust air during the summer months and air curtain during the winter months. This combined air flow type would allow use of warm air during winter to preheat the air cavity. All double skin scenarios included blinds within the air cavity for shading.

Results are shown in Figure 4.22. The base model (double glazed single skin facade) has the highest overall energy demand; however, comparing the annual energy demand reveals that some cases of double skin wall have higher heating loads during the winter months. Air flow type has a major effect since the exhaust air type increases heating demand. Results indicate

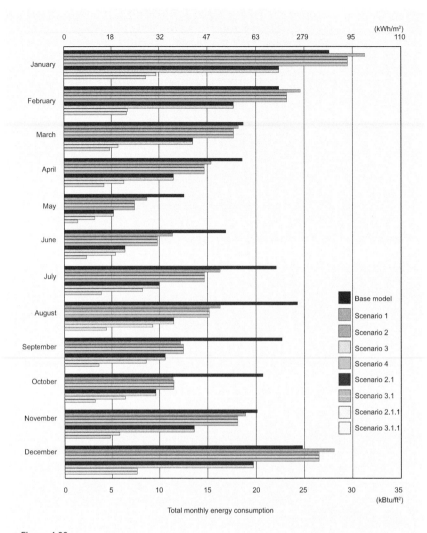

Figure 4.22:
Annual energy demand for the investigated double skin facade design options, compared against the baseline model (single skin facade).

that trapping air within the air cavity during the winter months insulates the double wall, thus significantly lowering the heating loads. Air cavity size influences energy consumption; however, results indicated that the location of the double glazing is more important and has a greater effect on energy consumption. Results show that exterior placement of double glazing would significantly reduce energy consumption, compared to placement on the interior side. The size of the air cavity also has an effect; a cavity with a small opening can negatively influence natural buoyancy and stack effect. Also, air cavities that are too large increase the cost of the facade systems.

Based on the performed energy analysis for several possible design scenarios, it was concluded that the best possible candidate would contain double glazing on the exterior and single glazing on the interior side, with an air

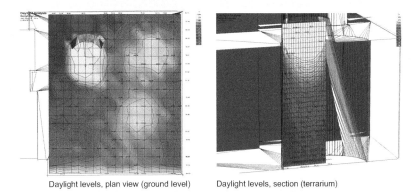

Daylight levels, plan view (ground level)   Daylight levels, section (terrarium)

Figure 4.23:
Daylight analysis on the horizontal plane of the first floor and along the vertical plane of
the terrarium.

cavity depth of 3 ft (1.2 m), and a hybrid airflow mode (exhausted air during
summer months assisted with mechanical fans and an air curtain during
the winter months to decrease heating loads). However, the double skin
wall was eliminated in the design development stage due to the high initial
costs and relatively low return on investment. The final design incorporated
a curtain wall facade with fritted glass to limit the solar heat gain and reduce
cooling demand.

Daylight analysis was performed for two areas of the Entry Pavilion.
The first study analyzed available daylight levels in the terrarium, as seen in
Figure 4.23. The research question was whether enough daylighting would
be present in the terrarium on the ground level for plants and landscaping. Results of the daylight analysis indicated that natural lighting levels in
the terrarium would be approximately 120 foot-candles (1,333 lux) for the
horizontal plane (ground level). Analysis of the vertical distribution indicated
that the terrarium would receive between 110 and 330 foot-candles (1,222
and 3,667 lux) of natural light. The middle section would receive between
120 and 150 foot-candles (1,333 and 1,667 lux). Therefore, the results of the
analysis indicated that enough lighting levels would be present for the plants
and landscaping in the terrarium. The results also indicated that areas of the
Entry Pavilion directly below the skylights would have high daylight levels;
therefore, subsequent analysis focused on two design options for distribut-
ing daylight evenly within the interior space. Results are shown in Figure 4.24
for the two design scenarios. The model on the left side shows daylight levels where ceramic frit is incorporated in both facades (40%). The daylight
levels range from 60 to 90 foot-candles (667 to 1,000 lux). The model on the
right side shows daylight levels for a scenario that incorporates ceramic frit
coverage in the skylight glass as well as the building facades. This would
reduce daylight levels directly underneath the skylights and would create a
more uniform distribution of natural light. The daylight levels would be in the
range of 60 to 80 foot-candles (667 to 889 lux). Figure 4.25 shows the final

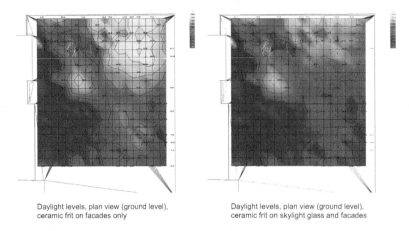

Daylight levels, plan view (ground level),
ceramic frit on facades only

Daylight levels, plan view (ground level),
ceramic frit on skylight glass and facades

Figure 4.24:
Comparison of daylighting levels for different types of glass incorporated into skylights
and building facades (40% frit coverage for south and north building facades vs. 50% frit
coverage for skylight and 40% frit coverage for building facades).

Figure 4.25:
Final design outcome, showing the interior of the RUMC Entry Pavilion and the terrarium.
Courtesy of Steve Hall © Hall + Merrick.

design outcome and built terrarium, while Figure 4.26 shows the roof garden
and upper portion of the terrarium and skylights.

A photovoltaic system was also considered during the design process,
and an analysis was performed to understand solar access for the roof area

Figure 4.26:
Roof garden on the fourth floor, showing the top of the terrarium and skylights. Courtesy of Steve Hall © Hall + Merrick.

of the Atrium building. Two different photovoltaic arrays were studied—one being placed on the rooftop of the Atrium Building, covering 2238 ft² (208 m²) and with a 35 kW rating, and the second on the roof of the Tower, covering 9873 ft² (917 m²) and with a 143 kW rating. The results showed that the surrounding buildings would not overshadow the photovoltaic array on the Atrium Building; however, the payback time for both arrays was found to be too high to justify investments into this renewable energy source.

Although building performance analyses that were performed during the design process were useful for the assessment of different sustainable design strategies and to investigate different design options, the RUMC Entry Pavilion was not able to meet the Living Building Challenge. Primary obstacles that were encountered during the design were:

- Multiple energy-efficiency design strategies were employed to minimize energy consumption; however, it was not possible to design a net-zero energy facility without using renewable energy sources. The initial high costs of renewable energy systems, such as photovoltaics, were prohibitive for including them in the design. Therefore, one of the major requirements of the Living Building Challenge was not met.

- Use of natural ventilation for healthcare facilities (even the lobby areas such as the Entry Pavilion) is not acceptable for most North American hospitals due to infection control strategies. Therefore, inclusion of operable windows, which is one of the requirements of the Living Building Challenge, could not be met.

Nevertheless, the employed design strategies resulted in significant energy savings. The modelled Energy Usage Intensity (EUI) for the Entry Pavilion was 62 kBtu/ft^2 (196 kWh/m^2), compared to the 155 kBtu/ft^2 (489 kWh/m^2) for a baseline building, resulting in 60% energy reduction. The research conducted during the design process was essential for many design decisions as described in this case study. Significant reductions in energy consumption would not have been achieved for this project if extensive building performance simulations and modeling were not used to investigate the effects of different design decisions.

4.5 RISK AND LIABILITY

Uncertainty is one of the major inherent characteristics of research and innovation, and as such, it poses risks to firms and organizations that are engaged in innovative design practices and research. It is important to manage risks and develop management techniques that align with the organization's strategy and performance measurement system (Emmitt et al., 2009). Major sources of risk in architectural design practices include poor project management; loss of control over costs, changes, and time on projects; poor contracts with open-ended commitments; poor budgeting and financial control; and lack of quality control protocols and lack of accountability. But design practices that integrate research and innovative design methods face additional risks and must be prepared to manage them effectively.

Risk management is a structured approach to managing uncertainty and includes several steps: risk identification, risk assessment, risk response planning, and risk monitoring and control. The purpose of risk identification is to distinguish risks that may influence the outcomes of various projects and design practices. Risk assessment evaluates the probability of an identified risk, as well as its effect on a project or design practice. Risk response planning identifies appropriate actions that can be taken to reduce potential threats to projects and practices. The risk management strategies should be developed based on these considerations:

- What are the significant risks that are acceptable to the design practice?
- What are significant risks that are not acceptable?
- Is there a clear understanding of the magnitude and nature of risks that the design practice is willing to accept to achieve its goals and mission?
- What are the appropriate steps to reduce and manage risks?

Risk management strategy should not be a rigid set of rules, but rather it should provide guidance for assessing the magnitude of potential threats, as well as methods for reducing, monitoring, and controlling those threats, while still engaging in research and innovative design practices. It is important to communicate risk management strategy to all employees, develop tools and training materials, and implement monitoring and control techniques but also develop a culture that balances risks and innovation. Risks associated with research and innovation should not be regarded as negative, rather—they should be understood, assessed, and effectively managed.

One of the important steps of any research project is dissemination of results and implementation. Firms should establish procedures for publishing and sharing the results of their research efforts—transparency and dissemination of research results benefits the entire design industry. It is pertinent that firms that conduct research share the results in peer-reviewed research publications and articles, reports, and technical guidelines. However, this last step of any research project may seem to increase risks and liability for the firms that are conducting research and sharing obtained knowledge. Firms should establish mechanisms and procedures for sharing and disseminating knowledge that aligns with their risk management strategies.

4.6 CHAPTER SUMMARY

We are entering an era of unprecedented changes in the architectural and building industry. The paradigm shifts that have been initiated in the last two decades are all having an impact on the way that architectural and design firms are operating, designing, and delivering buildings, collaborating with industry-wide stakeholders, and creating the built environment. On the other hand, economic, social, and environmental factors are also influencing the building industry and posing challenges to create better performing, environmentally sensitive buildings, which are designed and constructed faster, cost less, and have a positive impact on the environment, health, and productivity of the buildings' occupants. These challenges require the architectural profession to engage in research and to find novel solutions for these issues, since only through systematic investigations is it possible to find optimal answers for often conflicting objectives.

This chapter discussed the role of research in architectural practice, different methods for integrating research into the profession, models for establishing research mechanisms, institutional organization, and management of research projects. It also presented various funding models for research, as well as risk and liability issues. Case studies were used to illustrate the concepts, especially different models for integrating research into the profession.

We have discussed the fact that integrating research into the architectural profession is challenging, but research is essential for innovative practices. Therefore, the following recommendations are provided as guidelines for establishing and maintaining research activities in the profession:

- Firms and organizations interested in research, regardless of their size, should first determine their objectives for engaging in research activities and determine what is the value for their own organization.
- Then, firms should develop strategic goals, set priorities, and determine a plan for integrating research, considering the short-term and long-term objectives.
- Based on these goals and objectives, firms should determine what is the best model and funding mechanism for their own practice (internal, external, hybrid) and what is the organizational structure of the research arm. If engaging in collaborative research activities with other entities (external and hybrid models), firms should determine what are the objectives of these activities, how they relate to the firm's core values and goals, what types of research projects to focus on, and how to fund these activities.
- Finally, firms should determine best practices for integrating research into their own design practices, considering research objectives, goals, and appropriate research methods that align with the research objectives and activities. Also, firms should determine best practices for implementation of research results and dissemination of obtained knowledge. The first step is implementation of research results within specific design projects, but firms should also determine how to share results with the wider design community. Transparency and sharing research results benefits the entire industry and creates a culture of innovation within the architectural profession.

REFERENCES

Abdullah, A., and Aksamija, A., (2012). "Sustainable Design Strategies and Technical Design Development: Rush University Medical Center Entry Pavilion", *Perkins and Will Research Journal*, Vol. 4, No. 1, pp. 51–81.

Aksamija, A., (2009). "Context-Based Design of Double Skin Facades: Climatic Considerations during the Design Process", *Perkins and Will Research Journal*, Vol. 1, No. 1, pp. 54–69.

Aksamija, A., (2010a). *Tech Lab Annual Report 2009*, Chicago, IL: Perkins and Will.

Aksamija, A., (2010b). "Analysis and Computation: Sustainable Design in Practice", *Design Principles and Practices: An International Journal*, Vol. 4, No. 4, pp. 291–314.

Aksamija, A., (2011). *Tech Lab Annual Report 2010*, Chicago, IL: Perkins and Will.

Aksamija, A., (2012). *Tech Lab Annual Report 2011*, Chicago, IL: Perkins and Will.

Aksamija, A., (2013). *Tech Lab Annual Report 2012*, Chicago, IL: Perkins and Will.

Aksamija, A., (2016). *Integrating Innovation in Architecture: Design, Methods and Technology for Progressive Practice and Research*, Chichester, UK: John Wiley & Sons.

Aksamija, A., (2018). "Thermal, Energy and Daylight Analysis of Different Types of Double Skin Facades in Various Climates", *Journal of Facade Design and Engineering*, Vol. 6, No. 1, pp. 1–39.

Aksamija, A., and Green, D., (2013). "Visibility of Research in Design Practice: Current and Emerging Trends", *Proceedings of the Architectural Research Centers Consortium (ARCC) 2013 Conference*, Charlotte, March 27–30, pp. 661–668.

Aksamija, A., Haymaker, J., and Aminmansour, A., eds., (2015). *Future of Architectural Research: Proceedings of the Architectural Research Centers Consortium Conference*, Chicago, IL: Perkins and Will.

Aksamija, A., Snapp, T., Hodge, M., and Tang, M., (2012). "Re-Skinning: Performance-Based Design and Fabrication of Building Facade Components: Design Computing,

Analytics and Prototyping", *Perkins and Will Research Journal*, Vol. 4, No. 1, pp. 15–28.

Cooper-Marcus, C., and Barnes, M., (1995). *Gardens in Healthcare Facilities: Uses, Therapeutic Benefits, and Design Recommendations*, Martinez, CA: Center for Health Design.

Elvin, G., (2007). *Integrated Practice in Architecture: Mastering Design-Build, Fast-Track, and Building Information Modeling*, Hoboken, NJ: John Wiley & Sons.

Emmitt, S., Prins, M., and Den Otter, A., eds., (2009). *Architectural Management: International Research and Practice*, Chichester, UK: John Wiley & Sons.

Groat, L., and Wang, D., (2013). *Architectural Research Methods*, Hoboken, NJ: John Wiley & Sons.

Haymaker, J., Aksamija, A., and Green, D., (2016). "Research Mechanisms and Projects at Perkins and Will", in *The Changing Shape of Practice - Integrating Research and Design in Architectural Practice*, Hensen, M., and Nillson, F., eds., New York: Routledge, pp. 14–24.

Hendrich, A., Chow, M., Bafna, S., Choudhary, R., Heo, Y., and Skierczynski, B., (2009). "Unit-Related Factors that Affect Nursing Time with Patients: Spatial Analysis of the Time and Motion Study", *Health Environments Research & Design Journal*, Vol. 2, No. 2, pp. 5–20.

Hensel, M., and Nilsson, F., eds., (2016). *The Changing Shape of Practice, Integrating Research and Design in Architecture*, New York: Routledge.

Hult, T., Hurley, R., and Knight, G., (2004). "Innovativeness: Its Antecedents and Impact on Business Performance", *Industrial Marketing Management*, Vol. 33, No. 5, pp. 429–438.

Nigel, C., (1999). "Design Research: A Disciplined Conversation", *Design Issues*, Vol. 15, No. 2, pp. 5–10.

Rechel, B., Buchan, J., and McKeea, M., (2009). "The Impact of Health Facilities on Healthcare Workers' Well-Being and Performance", *International Journal of Nursing Studies*, Vol. 46, No. 7, pp. 1025–1034.

Ulrich, R., (1999). "Effects of Gardens on Health Outcomes: Theory and Research", in *Healing Gardens*, Cooper-Marcus, C. and Barnes, M., eds., New York: John Wiley & Sons, pp. 27-86.

Whitehouse, S., Varni, J., Seid, M., Cooper-Marcus, C., Ensberg, M., and Jacobs, J. R., and Mehlenbeck, R., (2001). "Evaluating a Children's Hospital Garden Environment: Utilization and Consumer Satisfaction", *Journal of Environmental Psychology*, Vol. 21, No. 3, pp. 301–314.

PART 5

CASE STUDIES

5 Case Studies

5.1 QUALITATIVE AND QUANTITATIVE RESEARCH FOR A HISTORICALLY SIGNIFICANT BUILDING: BUILDING PERFORMANCE ANALYSIS OF A BRUTALIST BUILDING

Historically significant buildings can be defined as buildings with distinctive physical and spatial qualities that manifest architectural and historic value, improve our understanding of the past, and typically demonstrate exemplary design techniques associated with a certain architectural style or historic period. To be classified as a historically significant building, a structure needs to be of sufficient age, a relatively high degree of physical integrity, and demonstrate historical significance. In terms of sufficient age, structures that are more than 50 years old are generally considered historic. Physical integrity refers to the state of the building—to be classified as historically significant, a building must be relatively unchanged, maintaining its characteristics and exemplary features. Historic preservation, in the context of architecture, is the process of preserving and protecting historically significant buildings. The primary goal of preserving historically significant buildings is to maintain the original character, architectural features, materials, and overall design intent. If historically significant buildings need to be renovated, the procedures are quite specific and different from other buildings—all the interventions need to be planned and executed in such a way as to maintain the original architectural design intent.

This case study reviews research that was conducted for a historically significant building to determine and analyze original design features, assess the building's current state and performance, evaluate how its current performance relates to the original design, and propose renovation strategies that would improve the building's performance while maintaining the original design intent, particularly focusing on the building skin. The building, Spomen Dom (literal translation "Remembrance Home"), is an exemplary building of the Brutalist architectural style built between 1971 and 1975, located in Kolašin, Montenegro (formerly Yugoslavia) and shown in Figure 5.1. Designed by the Slovenian architect Marko Mušič, the building abstractly expresses vernacular forms present in this region, specifically traditional sloped residential roofs shaped in response to harsh winters, but in a different material—concrete. Figure 5.2 shows a sketch of Spomen Dom's form and relation to the surrounding context. It was originally designed as a memorial and cultural center, but parts of it have been repurposed.

Figure 5.1:
Spomen Dom,
current state.
Courtesy of Sunčica
Milosević.

Figure 5.2:
Spomen Dom and
sketch of its sur-
rounding context.

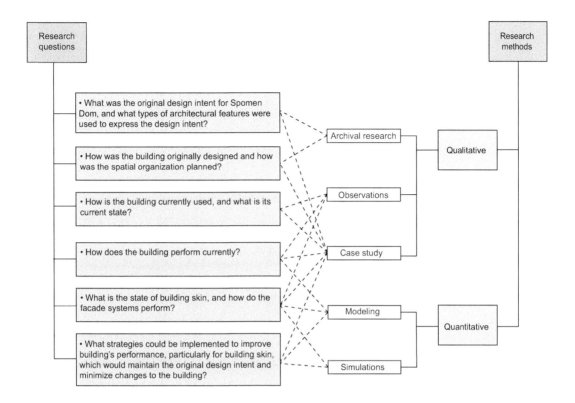

Figure 5.3:
Overview of
research ques-
tions and research
methods.

The historical significance of this building lies in its expressive architecture, relationship to the context and history of this region, and exemplary design features that reflect the Brutalist architectural style. After the initial literature review relating to this building and the research goals, it was found that current studies that focus on analysis of its performance do not exist. Some literature sources were identified that captured design features, historical context, and significance of this building. However, existing studies that focus on its current state and performance do not exist.

The research questions that were addressed include:

• What was the original design intent for Spomen Dom, and what types of architectural features were used to express the design intent?

• How was the building originally designed, and how was the spatial organization planned?

• How is the building currently used, and what is its current state?

• How does the building perform currently?

• What is the state of the building skin, and how do the facade systems perform?

• What strategies could be implemented to improve the building's performance, particularly for the building skin, which would maintain the original design intent and minimize changes to the building?

In order to address these questions, qualitative and quantitative research methods were chosen, as shown in Figure 5.3. Particularly, archival research was used to address the first two questions, which included collection of the original architectural records, drawings, diagrams, documents, and photographs. The original documents had to be translated, since they were written in the Serbo-Croatian or Slovenian language. Observations were used to address the third research question, which included visits to the building, observations of the exterior and interior spaces, documentation, and photographing. The results of archival research and observations were used in the subsequent research process. Simulations and modeling were used to address the remainders of the research questions, where a BIM model of the building was developed to represent the original and current spatial organization and to analyze its performance in relation to passive design techniques (solar radiation and window-to-wall ratio). Combined heat and moisture transport analysis was conducted to analyze building skin performance. Lastly, the entire study is a case study because it focuses on detailed analysis of a single building. However, it demonstrates research procedures that can be applied to other types of research studies that focus on building performance analysis of historically significant buildings.

The results of the archival research showed that the conceptualization of this unusual building with multiple civic and administrative programs was a result of the political movement and economic prosperity of its time. The reviewed archives included the original architect's documentation, city hall archives, and local university's archives. The primary purpose of Spomen Dom was to symbolically commemorate Yugoslavia's victory over fascism during World War II, to inspire, celebrate, and strengthen its ideology, and to promote collective participation in cultural events. Spomen Dom was designed as a cultural center, memorial museum, and an administrative municipal building. The building is a prime example of Brutalism, an architectural style based on expressive geometric forms and concrete construction. In the context of Yugoslavian architecture, Brutalism was used from the 1950s to the 1980s as the dominant style to demonstrate the country's progressive ideology (Stierli and Kulic, 2018). Civic buildings like Spomen Dom were especially designed as futuristic, progressive structures with extremely high budgets that reflected cultural identity in a modern way (Niebyl, 2018). The main goal was to democratize architecture and to make it widely available for people to enjoy, use, and inhabit. Buildings like this were meant to create innovative forms of public spaces, where education, cultural events, entertainment, and political activities were intertwined. However, with the collapse of Yugoslavia in 1991, these ambitious and stylistically explorative projects abruptly ended. Currently, many of the buildings are systematically neglected, abandoned, in ruin, demolished, or repurposed. Some of the buildings faced targeted destruction as the political context changed, and socialist ideology was no longer widely accepted. The observations that were conducted showed that Spomen Dom is currently in partial ruin, while a portion of the building is used as office spaces for the municipal services. Public gathering and cultural spaces have ceased to function. In the late 2000s, demolition and redevelopment of the project were planned, but these plans were abandoned. Little effort has been made to preserve the building's existence, regardless of its historical significance and architectural qualities.

Figure 5.4:
Floorplans of
Spomen Dom,
according to origi-
nal design intent,
and spatial organi-
zation. Courtesy of
Sunčica Milosević.

The building was initially composed of three types of spaces, which were differentiated through size, volume, and materials. These included public halls, office spaces, and support spaces. The core compromised a "citizen's vestibule", which was surrounded by public halls. Two administrative wings—one longer on the west and one shorter on the east—extended from the public part of the building. The support spaces were placed on the lower level. Figure 5.4 illustrates the building program and spatial organization according to the design intent, while

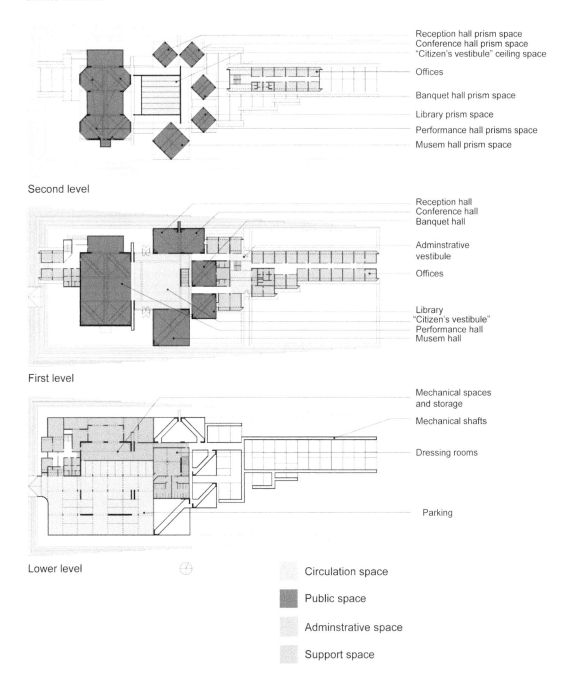

Reception hall prism space
Conference hall prism space
"Citizen's vestibule" ceiling space

Offices

Banquet hall prism space

Library prism space

Performance hall prisms space

Musem hall prism space

Second level

Reception hall
Conference hall
Banquet hall

Adminstrative
vestibule

Offices

Library
"Citizen's vestibule"
Performance hall
Musem hall

First level

Mechanical spaces
and storage

Mechanical shafts

Dressing rooms

Parking

Lower level

Circulation space

Public space

Adminstrative space

Support space

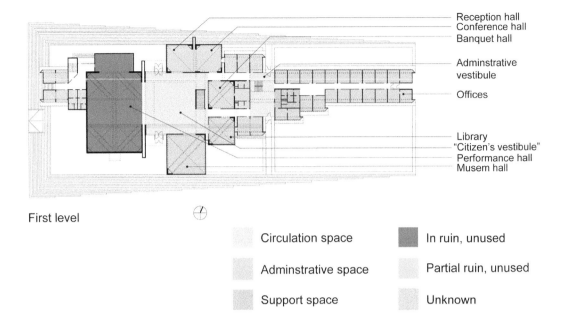

Reception hall
Conference hall
Banquet hall

Adminstrative
vestibule

Offices

Library
"Citizen's vestibule"
Performance hall
Musem hall

First level

Circulation space	In ruin, unused
Adminstrative space	Partial ruin, unused
Support space	Unknown

Figure 5.5 shows the current state and indicates parts of the building that are in ruin. Figure 5.6 shows photographs of the current state of the interior of the building.

The results of archival research and observations were used to develop a detailed BIM model of Spomen Dom, using the Revit software program, shown in Figure 5.7. This model was used to evaluate building performance (passive design strategies), response to solar radiation, shading, window-to-wall ratio, and building skin performance. Spomen Dom's north and south facades are elongated, while those of the east and west are minimized. The building's shape responds to solar orientation, but there are very few differences in facade treatment for different orientations. Moreover, the relatively equal window-to-wall ratio between south and north facades is present. The solid mass prisms with triangular windows have a similar exterior treatment and size of glazing, regardless of the orientation.

A BIM model was used to study shadows during different times of the year, as seen in Figure 5.8. Insight 360 Solar Analysis software was used as a simulation tool to evaluate solar radiation, as shown in Figure 5.9. Results indicate that the north elevation is exposed to direct daylight, and there is potential for solar heat gain in the early morning of the summer season—at all the other times, it is in complete shade. Since the building is located in a heating dominated climate where approximately eight months of the year require heating, the glazing along this elevation does not utilize passive solar heating. The results for the south elevation indicated that the administrative wings are facing direct sun at almost all times, and the only time that the offices are in shade is early morning in the summer. The solar radiation along this orientation is high.

A double skin glazed facade is utilized along the south orientation, shown in Figure 5.10, which was quite an advanced building technology for the time when

Figure 5.5:
Floorplan of
Spomen Dom's first
level, as currently
used. Courtesy of
Sunčica Milosević.

Figure 5.6:
Spomen Dom,
current state of the
interior spaces.
Courtesy of Sunčica
Milosević.

SPOMEN DOM CURRENT STATE

Banquet hall

Banquet hall prism skylight

Performance space

Performance stage

Performance space view from the stage

Figure 5.7:
BIM model of
Spomen Dom.
Courtesy of Sunčica
Milosević.

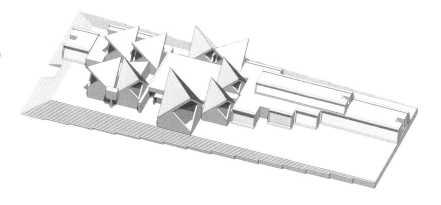

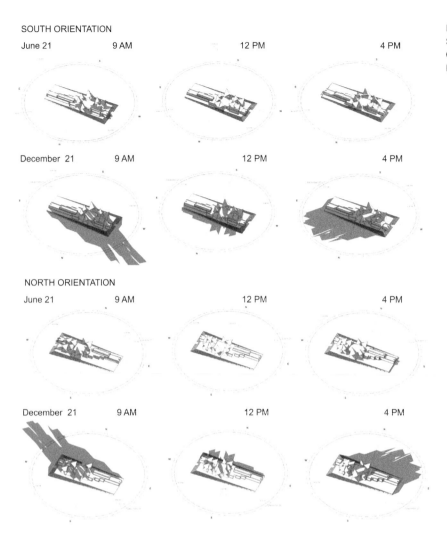

SOUTH ORIENTATION

June 21   9 AM   12 PM   4 PM

December 21   9 AM   12 PM   4 PM

NORTH ORIENTATION

June 21   9 AM   12 PM   4 PM

December 21   9 AM   12 PM   4 PM

Figure 5.8:
Shadow analysis.
Courtesy of Sunčica
Milosević.

Spomen Dom was built. The main advantage of double skin facades is improved thermal performance. This double skin facade is vertically compartmentalized, spans from the ground level to the roof, and includes windows on the exterior side for ventilation, consisting of single glazing units. The adjoining offices have operable windows at the base and at the head of each level, which improve air circulation within the double skin cavity. Since air conditioning systems were not common at the time when the building was designed, the operable windows were intended to provide natural ventilation and cooling in the summer. There are some discrepancies between the original drawings and the constructed double skin facade. The operable windows were drawn as 180-degree rotational panels, but the actual installed windows only partially open at about 45 degrees. Also, horizontal blinds are shown in the air cavity as shading mechanisms, but these are not present in the current building (only vertical shades that are located further away on the interior side). Therefore, deviance from the construction documents may have negatively impacted the performance of this system. Installing

Figure 5.9:
Solar radiation anal-
ysis. Courtesy of
Sunčica Milosević.

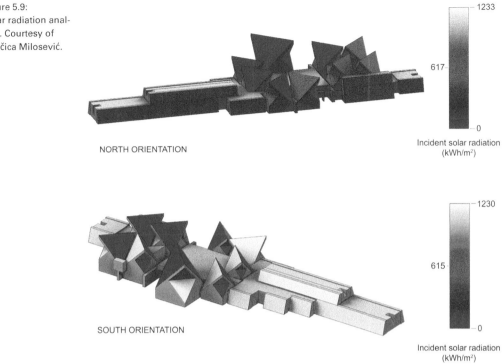

NORTH ORIENTATION

1233

617

0

Incident solar radiation
(kWh/m²)

1230

615

0

Incident solar radiation
(kWh/m²)

SOUTH ORIENTATION

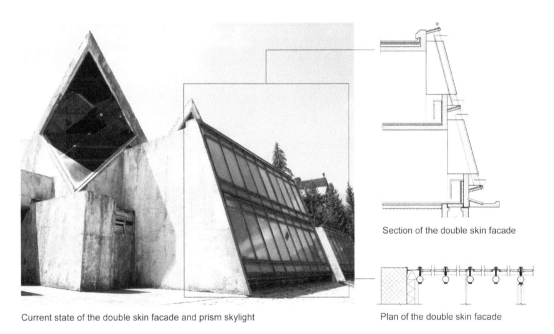

Current state of the double skin facade and prism skylight

Section of the double skin facade

Plan of the double skin facade

Figure 5.10:
Double skin glazed facade, and its current state. Courtesy of Sunčica Milosević.

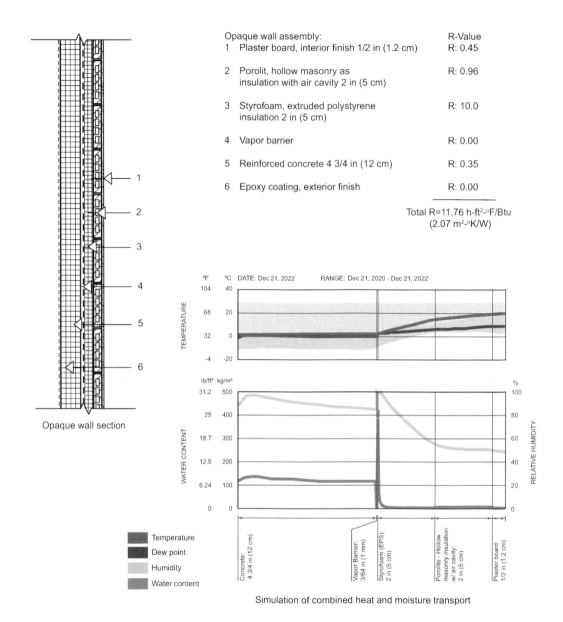

Opaque wall section

Opaque wall assembly:
1 Plaster board, interior finish 1/2 in (1.2 cm)
2 Porolit, hollow masonry as insulation with air cavity 2 in (5 cm)
3 Styrofoam, extruded polystyrene insulation 2 in (5 cm)
4 Vapor barrier
5 Reinforced concrete 4 3/4 in (12 cm)
6 Epoxy coating, exterior finish

R-Value
R: 0.45
R: 0.96
R: 10.0
R: 0.00
R: 0.35
R: 0.00

Total R=11.76 h-ft²-°F/Btu (2.07 m²-°K/W)

Temperature
Dew point
Humidity
Water content

Simulation of combined heat and moisture transport

a mechanical fan on the roof may help with air circulation and ventilation of the double skin cavity, as well as adding shading devices in the cavity.

Solid wall assemblies were also analyzed. The typical concrete exterior wall was investigated, as seen in Figure 5.11. Material components and their properties were identified, and the overall thermal resistance of the assembly was calculated, which slightly exceeds the minimum recommended values for this climate. Simulations were performed to investigate combined heat and moisture transport using the WUFI software tool. The results have shown that significant moisture is retained on the building interior, likely due to the lack of an air cavity, insufficient insulation, two material layers that are trapping vapor within the assembly (epoxy coating on the exterior surface of the concrete and a vapor

Figure 5.11: Typical concrete exterior wall assembly, thermal resistance, and simulations of combined heat and moisture transport. Courtesy of Sunčica Milosević.

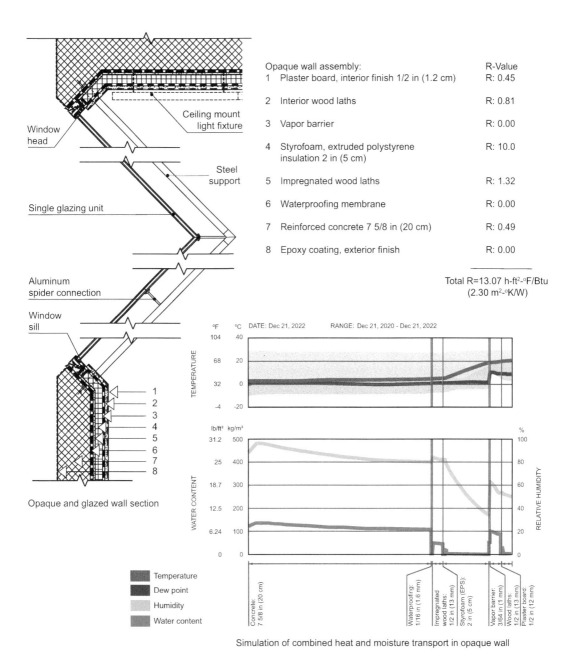

Opaque wall assembly:	R-Value
1 Plaster board, interior finish 1/2 in (1.2 cm)	R: 0.45
2 Interior wood laths	R: 0.81
3 Vapor barrier	R: 0.00
4 Styrofoam, extruded polystyrene insulation 2 in (5 cm)	R: 10.0
5 Impregnated wood laths	R: 1.32
6 Waterproofing membrane	R: 0.00
7 Reinforced concrete 7 5/8 in (20 cm)	R: 0.49
8 Epoxy coating, exterior finish	R: 0.00

Total R=13.07 h-ft²-°F/Btu
(2.30 m²-°K/W)

Window head

Ceiling mount light fixture

Steel support

Single glazing unit

Aluminum spider connection

Window sill

Opaque and glazed wall section

°F °C   DATE: Dec 21, 2022   RANGE: Dec 21, 2020 - Dec 21, 2022

Temperature
Dew point
Humidity
Water content

Simulation of combined heat and moisture transport in opaque wall

Figure 5.12:
Typical prism exterior wall assembly, thermal resistance, and simulations of combined heat and moisture transport. Courtesy of Sunčica Milosević.

barrier between concrete and insulation), and the porous nature of the hollow masonry that is the support plasterboard interior finish. The solid wall and the triangular skylight for the typical prism component were also investigated, as seen in Figure 5.12. Thermal resistance of this assembly was calculated and exceeds minimum recommendations. This assembly includes a punched pyramidal opening with thick single layer glazing units—two per volume. Simulations were also performed for this assembly, and the results indicated that moisture is retained in this assembly as well.

The final research results showed that the building skin of Spomen Dom is not well-performing and is adding to the deterioration of this architecturally important building. In order to preserve its state, careful renovations of the building skin would be required. These should include adding insulation on the building interior for the solid walls, incorporating continuous waterproofing, and adding air cavities. The skylights would also benefit from double insulated glazing units, to improve thermal performance. The double skin glazed facades would need to incorporate double insulated glazing units on the exterior skins, add shading elements within the cavity, and integrate small mechanical fans on the roof to help with the ventilation of the cavity. These changes would maintain the original design intent but would improve the building performance of Spomen Dom. Buildings like this deserve to be cherished and celebrated.

5.2 QUALITATIVE AND QUANTITATIVE RESEARCH FOR ADAPTIVE REUSE: DESIGNING FOR NET-ZERO ENERGY

Adaptive reuse of existing buildings is a growing area of architectural design, engineering, and construction. Adaptive reuse is the process of renovating an existing building, applying retrofit strategies, and transforming the building's function to a new purpose. Adaptive reuse often focuses on buildings that do not have historic significance; therefore, the design and retrofit approaches are different from historic preservation projects. The architectural expression, choice of materials, and design interventions do not necessarily have to reflect the building's original design intent.

Adaptive reuse is an important aspect in sustainable and resilient design because it reduces our reliance on new construction, as well as the embodied energy and carbon emissions associated with new construction. Energy-efficient retrofitting of existing buildings can significantly lower our dependency on fossil fuels and improve building performance across the board. Through reusing and upgrading existing buildings, performance of the existing building stock can be improved, thus bringing more opportunities to reinvigorate and benefit local economies in the long run. Moreover, integrating Net-Zero Energy Building (NZEB) concepts into building retrofits can improve the energy efficiency levels in existing buildings and apply renewable energy sources to reduce their dependence on external energy infrastructure. Since the life of existing buildings is extended and possible demolition waste is avoided, net-zero energy retrofits also contribute to the development of sustainable and resilient urban environments.

Typically, achieving net-zero energy goals can be realized through implementing passive design strategies, improving building enclosures, installing high performance HVAC systems to reduce heating and cooling loads, and reducing lighting and other electric loads, thus making it possible to offset the required energy balance with renewable means, such as photovoltaics or wind turbines. Figure 5.13 shows appropriate steps that should be implemented in achieving net-zero energy buildings, as well as the economic impacts, risks, and benefits associated with advanced building technologies. Passive design strategies should be implemented to reduce energy consumption as much as possible, since their

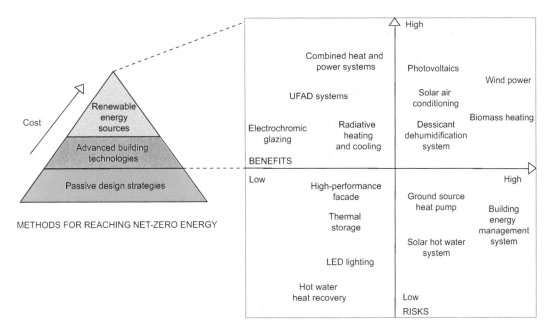

METHODS FOR REACHING NET-ZERO ENERGY

ASSOCIATED RISKS AND BENEFITS

Figure 5.13:
Design methods for achieving net-zero energy in buildings, and associated benefits and risks.

costs are relatively low. Advanced building technologies, such as energy-efficient lighting and HVAC systems, as well as high-performance building envelopes, should then be employed, since their costs are higher, but they can significantly reduce a building's energy consumption. Lastly, renewable energy sources must be used, but only after passive design strategies and advanced building technologies are exhausted since their costs are high. Figure 5.13 shows appropriate steps that should be implemented in achieving net-zero energy buildings, as well as economic impacts, risks, and benefits associated with advanced building technologies. Achieving net-zero energy goals is a challenging objective, especially when it comes to retrofit projects, because more constraints are typically imposed on existing buildings than new construction.

This research study explored applicable passive and active design approaches that can be integrated to achieve energy savings by investigating feasible retrofitting techniques for building performance upgrading. The research focused on a specific case study, a commercial building located in Holyoke, Massachusetts (Aksamija, 2016; Aksamija and Wang, 2017). Also, the study investigated the ways to combine renewable energy generation installations to provide on-site renewable energy to meet net-zero energy goals. These following research questions were addressed:

- How was the building originally designed?
- What is the current state of the building?
- What are the adaptive reuse design strategies that can be implemented to improve the building's performance and reach net-zero energy goals?
- What types of passive design strategies can be implemented by manipulating building massing, volume, and building envelope design to reduce energy

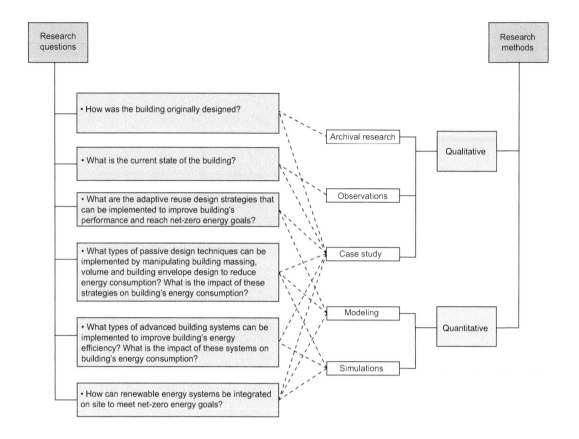

consumption? What is the impact of these strategies on the building's energy consumption?

- What types of advanced building systems can be implemented to improve the building's energy efficiency? What is the impact of these systems on the building's energy consumption?

- How can renewable energy systems be integrated on site to meet net-zero energy goals?

The research methods that were used to address these questions included qualitative and quantitative methods, as seen in Figure 5.14. Archival research was used to collect information about the existing building and its history, while observations were used to assess the current state of the building. Information about the original building was obtained and analyzed to develop redesign strategies that would facilitate the achievement of net-zero energy goals. Case study research was used throughout the research process since the study focused on a specific building. Simulations and modeling were used to assess the impacts of adaptive reuse design strategies on energy consumption and to quantify the performance of renewable energy systems. Energy modeling was used to drive design decisions, where the initial energy model that was built assessed the impact of retrofitting design strategies, such as change in building massing, impacts of daylight, improvement in building envelope, and retrofitting of lighting and HVAC systems.

Figure 5.14:
Overview of research questions and research methods.

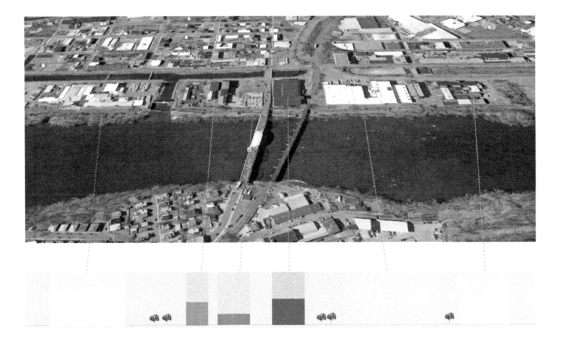

Then, an alternative energy model was developed which investigated the maximum energy savings that could be achieved by the combined design strategies. Different parameters within energy models were varied to perform a comparison of the base case and alternative design scenarios. Based on the calculation of annual energy balance and consideration of local climate and available resources, specific types of renewable energy generation installations were selected and integrated in the retrofit design program to ensure that sufficient energy could be generated on-site to offset the annual energy balance of the building to zero. Although the results of simulations and modeling are applicable only to the discussed case study building, the methods are applicable to any retrofit design project.

The building that was chosen as a case study for this research is a 200,000 ft² (18,587 m²) commercial building located in Holyoke, Massachusetts. The building was originally designed as a paper mill and built in 1895, but it has been renovated several times in its history. Currently, the majority of the building is abandoned, while a small part is used as a commercial office space. As part of the revitalization plan for this area, retrofits of commercial buildings would contribute to the development of a stable, healthy, and desirable neighborhood. Figure 5.14 shows the building's context and the surrounding area, while Figure 5.15 presents the building site and the current conditions.

The first step in adaptive redesign was to analyze the massing of the existing building, structure, and spatial organization and to determine how exactly the building form could be changed and improved. Building shape, orientation, and volume can significantly affect energy consumption (Aksamija, 2017). This is much easier to accommodate in new construction since the building form and massing can be determined from the early stages of the design process. In existing buildings,

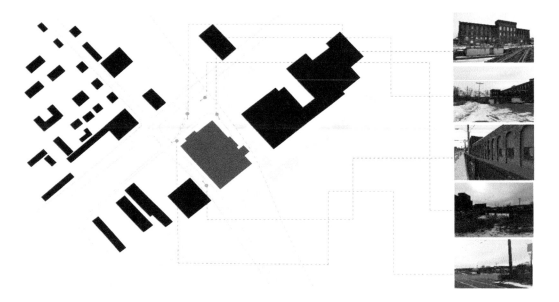

this is more complicated since the building form is already predetermined. For the case study building, building massing and form were modified to allow for daylighting and natural ventilation. Extensive BIM modeling was implemented to investigate changes to the building's form and shape. It was determined that parts of the building should be demolished (mainly, parts of the second and third floor) and that two additional floors would be added to accommodate the new building program, as seen in Figure 5.17. The new program includes offices, classrooms, gallery space, retail space, and public space (community center). The program for the first level is shown in Figure 5.18. The middle part of the building was redesigned into a courtyard, which allowed the building to get back to its original appearance (the initial interior courtyard was closed off in the 1960s). With this retrieved courtyard, daylighting and natural ventilation were integrated as passive design techniques to reduce electricity consumption. Extraction of the existing building mass and addition of a new building mass created several roof gardens, which would offer public space for occupants and provide an area for placement of photovoltaic panels. Figure 5.19 depicts vertical transportation, circulation diagrams, shading system, and green roofs.

Building envelope upgrade strategies included improving the exterior wall insulation to control the heat, air, and moisture transfer between the wall assemblies and the exterior environment. Newly added thermal insulation, an air barrier, and a vapor retarder would help the building acquire improved insulating and air sealing performance. For the top two floors, a new facade system was designed to provide an appropriate visual environment for the office areas and make full use of daylight to reduce energy consumption for lighting. A curtain wall system and an exterior horizontal sunshades system were combined to achieve environmental optimization and energy efficiency. The shading system would control the direct solar exposure and glare, making the interior daylighting environment ambient and comfortable. An energy-efficient HVAC system was integrated into the

Figure 5.16: Site plan and current state of the building.

ORIGINAL BUILDING

1 Added office levels

2 Added vertical circulation

3 Removed building elements
  to open up the original
  courtyard

4 Removed entrances

5 Removed ramp

Figure 5.17:
Comparison of the
original building
and its adaptive
reuse design, outlin-
ing major changes
to the building.

ADAPTIVE REUSE DESIGN

design, consisting of a radiant heating and cooling system and biomass heating. Since wood, agriculture residues, and crops are the most common fuels for biomass energy systems, easy accessibility to these organic matters in the western Massachusetts area would lead to reduced delivery and storage costs.

Simulations of energy performance were conducted using the eQuest energy modeling software program. Two different models were simulated and analyzed to explore the energy savings potential of different design strategies—the initial baseline design and an alternative design. Renewable energy sources are necessary to achieve net-zero energy goals, and the energy modeling results also indicated how much energy would be required to meet those goals. Comprehensive thinking towards energy conversion ratio, feasibility, accessibility, and cost contributed to the decision of selecting four types of renewable energy systems that

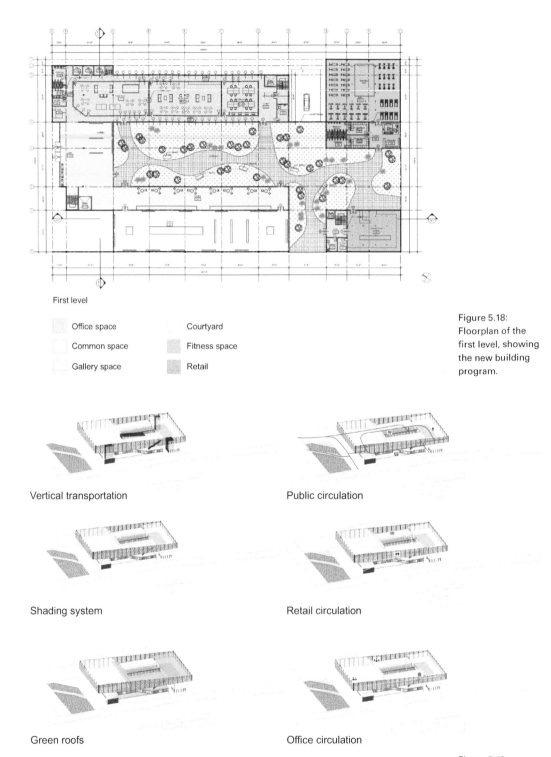

First level

Office space   Courtyard

Common space   Fitness space

Gallery space   Retail

Figure 5.18:
Floorplan of the
first level, showing
the new building
program.

Vertical transportation   Public circulation

Shading system   Retail circulation

Green roofs   Office circulation

Figure 5.19:
Adaptive reuse
building diagrams.
Courtesy of Yi Wang
Vizard.

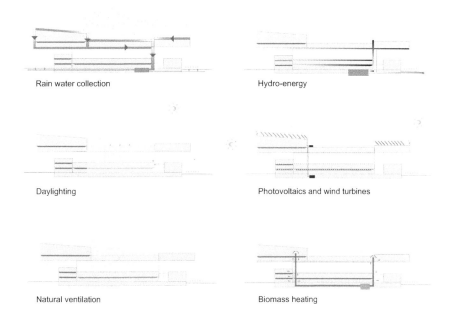

Rain water collection

Hydro-energy

Daylighting

Photovoltaics and wind turbines

Figure 5.20:
Sustainable adap-
tive reuse design
strategies and
renewable energy
sources. Courtesy
of Yi Wang Vizard.

Natural ventilation

Biomass heating

generated enough energy to support the operation of the building. Figure 5.20 shows sustainable design strategies that were considered in this adaptive reuse project, as well as renewable energy sources. Table 5.1 shows basic inputs for the energy models, and Table 5.2 shows occupancy schedules.

The baseline simulation results showed relatively high annual energy consumption, with an Energy Use Intensity (EUI) of 120 kBtu/ft^2 (378 kWh/m^2). Deep retrofit measures designed to address this problem incorporated control of internal loads and operating schedules, lighting, and improvement in the building envelope. For museums, classrooms, retail spaces, and offices, different demands for the interior lighting environment and occupancy schedules were taken into consideration in the energy modeling improvement process. Lighting power density (LPD), which is an important value associated with energy efficient lighting design, was reduced for all spaces in the building. In addition, planning and rescheduling work time for every functional room made it possible that significant lighting energy could be saved according to occupancy levels, and integrated occupancy sensors would ensure that lighting electricity is minimized. Other energy efficiency approaches included using materials that have high thermal mass and durability, as well as applying glazing with lower U-values. Since windows account for most of the energy loss, improving glazing is an effective way to reduce energy transfer through the windows. Double glazing with a low-e coating and argon gas fill was selected to substitute glazing for windows, thus significantly reducing heat transfer through the building envelope. After applying all the possible energy saving strategies, an alternative simulation run in eQuest was conducted to acquire a comparison analysis, lowering the EUI value to 52 kBtu/ft^2 (163 kWh/m^2). By comparing the baseline run and the alternative run, it was evident that energy performance improvement can be achieved. Figure 5.21 shows

■ Case Studies

TABLE 5.1: Inputs used for energy modeling.

Building program	Office	Retail	Museum	Community center
Area	75,000 ft² (6,970 m²)	11,200 ft² (1,041 m²)	10,700 ft² (994 m²)	47,600 ft² (4,424 m²)
Energy code	ASHRAE 90.1	ASHRAE 90.1	ASHRAE 90.1	ASHRAE 90.1
Heating and cooling system	Cooling: DX coils Heating: hot water coils	Cooling: DX coils Heating: hot water coils	Cooling: DX coils Heating: hot water coils	Cooling: DX coils Heating: hot water coils
Daylighting	As designed, light controls considered (photosensors)	As designed, light controls considered (photosensors)	As designed, light controls considered (photosensors)	As designed, light controls considered (photosensors)
Lighting power density	Office spaces: 1.10 W/ft² (0.10 W/m²) Conference rooms: 1.30 W/ft² (0.12 W/m²) Lounge 0.80 W/ft² (0.07 W/m²) Corridor 0.90 W/ft² (0.08 W/m²)	Retail: 1.25 W/ft² (0.12 W/m²) Storage: 0.60 W/ft² (0.08 W/m²) Corridor 0.90 W/ft² (0.08 W/m²)	Museum: 1.06 W/ft² (0.10 W/m²) Storage: 0.90 W/ft² (0.08 W/m²)	Workshop: 1.20 W/ft² (0.11 W/m²) Library: 1.18 W/ft² (0.11 W/m²) Common space: 0.80 W/ft² (0.07 W/m²) Dining: 1.30 W/ft² (0.12 W/m²) Fitness: 1.00 W/ft² (0.09 W/m²)
Glass types	Double low-e air insulated glazing unit	Double low-e air insulated glazing unit	Double low-e air insulated glazing unit	Double low-e air insulated glazing unit

the energy model, as well as the results associated with the baseline model and the alternative run.

In order to meet the net-zero energy goals, several renewable energy systems had to be implemented. High efficiency commercial photovoltaics (PVs) were considered to be placed on the roofs. Considering the limited site around the existing building, high efficiency PV panels can be used to provide a significant portion of the building's energy demand. In addition, the working schedule for most spaces in the building are during daytime, so PV system can deliver power during the peak time when utility rates are relatively high. The design of PV arrays involved a series of 240 PV panels, covering 50,000 ft² (4,646 m²) of roof area to provide 45% of the building's energy demand. The monthly energy output for PV system is shown in Figure 5.22. In addition, installing wind turbines on top of the building to capture wind energy on site was considered. Medium vertical axis wind turbines with 2 KW generators were selected to be installed on the roof to generate 20% of the building's energy demand. The reasons for choosing this type of wind turbines included their high efficiency, ability to catch wind from all directions, and simplicity of mechanical configuration. Since vertical axis wind turbines are without downwind coning, rudders, and yaw mechanisms, and their electrical generators are positioned close to

TABLE 5.2: Occupancy schedules used for energy modeling, according to building program.

Building program	Office	Retail	Museum	Community center
Occupancy schedule	M, T, W, Th, F (9 am to 5 pm, occupancy at 90%, lights at 90%, equipment at 90% load)	M, T, W, Th, F (9 am to 7 pm, occupancy at 90%, lights at 90%, equipment at 90% load)	M, T, W, Th, F (9 am to 5 pm, occupancy at 90%, lights at 90%, equipment at 90% load)	M, T, W, Th, F (11 am to 7 pm, occupancy at 90%, lights at 90%, equipment at 90% load)
	Sat (10 am to 4 pm, occupancy at 10%, lights at 10%, equipment at 10% load)	Sat, Sun (9 am to 10 pm, occupancy at 90%, lights at 90%, equipment at 90% load)	Sat (10 am to 4 pm, occupancy at 10%, lights at 10%, equipment at 10% load)	Sat (10 am to 8 pm, occupancy at 90%, lights at 90%, equipment at 10% load)
	Sun (unoccupied)		Sun (unoccupied)	Sun (10 am to 10 pm, occupancy at 90%, lights at 90%, equipment at 10% load)

the base, they are easy to install and maintain. Biomass and hydropower were also considered, based on the availability of resources and site-specific factors. Holyoke is located in western Massachusetts, which has significant agricultural resources, and it is cost-efficient to collect and deliver biomass materials. The biomass system was sized based on the heating demand and the capacity of the heating system and furnace. The last renewable energy source that was considered for the retrofit design of the building's energy system was hydro-power. The location of this building was the primary reason for including hydro-power. Right beside an important canal of Holyoke, this building can integrate the hydro-power system with ease. Although site-based hydro-power is not widely used in commercial buildings due to specific site requirements and access to water, this particular building has great potential because of its proximity to the canal and existing hydro-power turbines in the City of Holyoke. Different from solar power, which only works during the daytime with enough solar radiation, hydro-power's availability is very flexible, so it is possible to get a long-term, stable, and dependable payback with a one-time investment. For this building scale, a

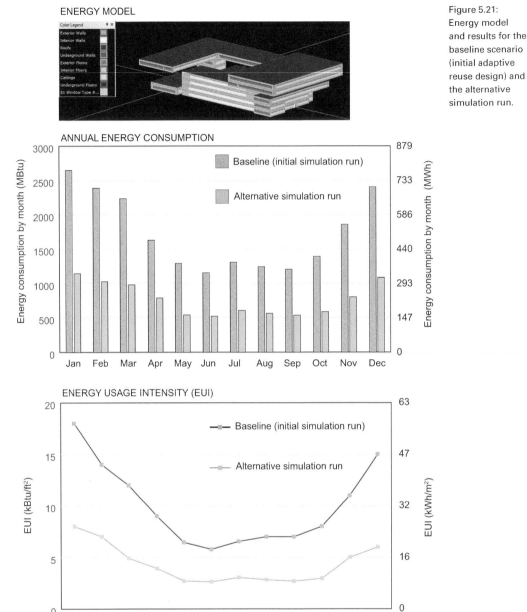

Figure 5.21:
Energy model
and results for the
baseline scenario
(initial adaptive
reuse design) and
the alternative
simulation run.

micro hydro system is suitable for placement, and a turbine can be applied to transform potential energy from the water flow into mechanical energy first, and this mechanical energy can be transformed into electric power later for building usage. The renewable energy systems that incorporate solar energy, wind energy, biomass, and hydro-energy made it possible to achieve net-zero energy goals, thus meeting the energy demand of the building with renewable energy sources on site. The breakdown of the supplied energy by renewable sources is shown in Figure 5.22.

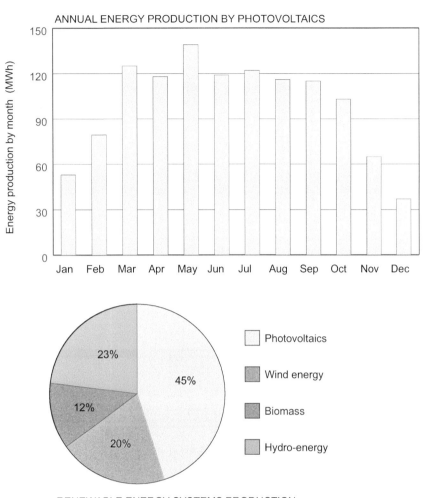

ANNUAL ENERGY PRODUCTION BY PHOTOVOLTAICS

RENEWABLE ENERGY SYSTEMS PRODUCTION
FOR MEETING NET-ZERO ENERGY

5.3 QUANTITATIVE RESEARCH FOR BUILDING SYSTEMS: COMPARATIVE ANALYSIS OF FACADE SYSTEMS AND IMPACTS OF CLIMATE CHANGE

The facade is one of the most significant contributors to the energy budget and the comfort parameters of any building, and control of environmental factors must be considered during the design process. High-performance facades need to block adverse external environmental effects and maintain internal comfort conditions with minimum energy consumption (Aksamija, 2013). The purpose of this research was to analyze the thermal and energy performance of different facade types, as well as the impacts of climate change on facade performance. Improving thermal performance and minimizing thermal bridging are extremely important design strategies for high-performance facades. Thermal bridging within a wall occurs when a highly conductive material such as a metal support penetrates the facade's insulation layer. This can significantly affect the thermal performance of

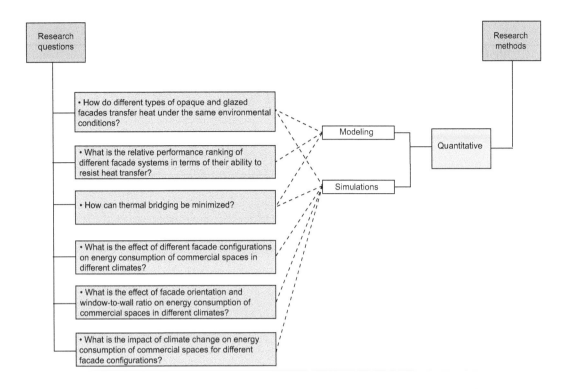

the wall and decrease its effective thermal resistance. Thermal bridging can occur in all types of facades and significantly impacts thermal performance, energy consumption, and the thermal comfort of building occupants. Thermally improved facades limit thermal bridging and can improve thermal performance by using materials that reduce heat transfer between different components.

Figure 5.23: Overview of research questions and research methods.

The purpose of this research was to investigate heat transfer in several exterior wall types, methods for minimizing thermal bridging and improving thermal performance, and the effects of climate change on energy consumption (Aksamija and Peters, 2016a, 2016b). The following research questions were addressed:

* How do different types of opaque and glazed facades transfer heat under the same environmental conditions?
* What is the relative performance ranking of different facade systems in terms of their ability to resist heat transfer?
* How can thermal bridging be minimized?
* What is the effect of different facade configurations on the energy consumption of commercial spaces in different climates?
* What is the effect of facade orientation and window-to-wall ratio on the energy consumption of commercial spaces in different climates?
* What is the impact of climate change on the energy consumption of commercial spaces for different facade configurations?

Quantitative research methods were used to answer these questions, as seen in Figure 5.23. Modeling and simulations were used to execute the research study, in which seven different facade systems were studied. Thermal modeling was performed to address the first three questions. The individual material layers of each facade system and their properties were modeled in detail, as well as the boundary conditions for exterior and interior temperatures. Four exterior temperatures were used as boundary conditions (variables) to represent different climate types, while interior temperature was constant. Heat transfer coefficients (U-values) were also calculated for each facade system. The energy performance of the seven facade types was studied using whole year energy simulations for a typical office space. The total yearly energy values included heating, cooling, lighting, and fans. Simulations were conducted for 15 cities in the U.S., representing different climate zones for three time periods: present day, the year 2050, and the year 2080. Weather files for 2050 and 2080 were created using a weather file generator that considers the impacts of climate change on weather patterns (Jentsch et al., 2013).

Seven different facade systems were investigated, and their components are shown in Figures 5.24 to 5.30:

- Type 1: Brick cavity wall with metal framing
- Type 2: Rainscreen facade with terracotta cladding and metal framing
- Type 3: Rainscreen facade with glass-fiber reinforced concrete (GFRC) cladding and metal framing
- Type 4: Curtain wall with aluminum framing
- Type 5: Curtain wall with thermally broken aluminum framing
- Type 6: Rainscreen facade with terracotta cladding and thermal spacers
- Type 7: Rainscreen facade with terracotta cladding and thermal isolators

Thermal modeling was conducted for each facade system in the THERM software program, where four different models were developed to represent different exterior environmental conditions, representative of different climate types and seasons. These included exterior temperatures of 90°F, 60°F, 30°F, and 0°F (32°C, 16°C, -1°C and -18°C), while the interior temperature was set at 72°F (22°C). This modeling was conducted to understand the behavior of these different exterior wall types under various conditions and to determine thermal gradients since this information is useful for the design decision-making process. Figures 5.31 to 5.34 illustrate the results for thermal gradients through all facade types. U-values were also calculated for all the analyzed facade systems using THERM software. Heat transfer through exterior walls depends on the following factors: 1) the difference in temperature between the exterior and interior environment, 2) the materials of the wall and their thicknesses, and 3) the thermal conductivity of material layers. The total rate of heat transfer through an opaque wall assembly is calculated by an area-weighted approach, where separate heat transfer contributions of different material layers are taken into account, based on the relative area that they occupy within the wall system. For glazed facades, the area-weighted approach is also used to calculate heat transfer, where the center-of-glass, edge-of-glass, and frame U-values are taken into account. Therefore, a total of 35 thermal models were developed and simulated. Figure 5.35 shows

TYPE 1

Simulated section

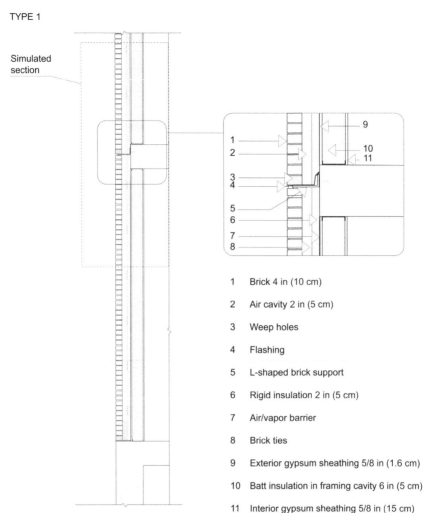

Figure 5.24: Overall section, material components, and simulated section for Type 1 facade system (brick cavity wall with metal framing).

1   Brick 4 in (10 cm)

2   Air cavity 2 in (5 cm)

3   Weep holes

4   Flashing

5   L-shaped brick support

6   Rigid insulation 2 in (5 cm)

7   Air/vapor barrier

8   Brick ties

9   Exterior gypsum sheathing 5/8 in (1.6 cm)

10 Batt insulation in framing cavity 6 in (5 cm)

11 Interior gypsum sheathing 5/8 in (15 cm)

the results for U-value calculations and compares the thermal performance of the investigated facade types. The results show that Type 4 (conventional curtain wall) is the worst thermally performing facade system, while Types 6 and 7 are the best since their U-value is the lowest. These thermally improved systems would minimize thermal bridging in the building envelope, which would reduce energy consumption.

The energy modeling was performed using the EnergyPlus simulation software program, simulating whole year total energy use for an office space enclosed by the seven different exterior wall types. The five opaque walls were modeled with window-to-wall ratios of both 20% and 40% for occupant views and daylighting, while the curtain walls were modeled with an 80% window-to-wall ratio. A single zone office space was chosen to highlight the thermal properties of the different wall types at different orientations. The dimensions of the office space were modeled at 13 ft (4 m) high by 12 ft (3.7 m) wide and 16 ft (4.9 m) deep. The facade was 13 ft (4 m) high by 12 ft (3.7 m) wide. The floor, ceiling, and

TYPE 2

Figure 5.25:
Overall section,
material com-
ponents, and
simulated section
for Type 2 facade
system (rainscreen
facade with terra-
cotta cladding and
metal framing).

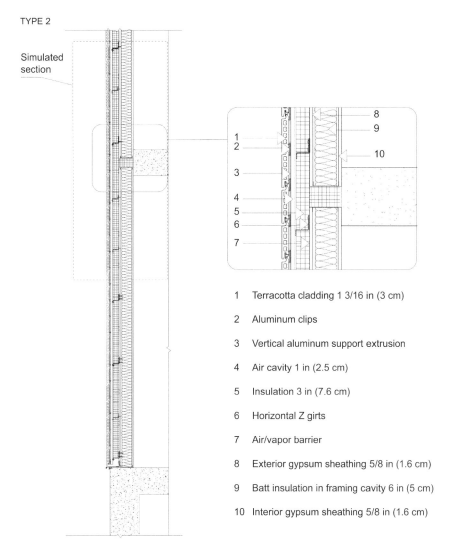

TYPE 2

Simulated
section

1   Terracotta cladding 1 3/16 in (3 cm)

2   Aluminum clips

3   Vertical aluminum support extrusion

4   Air cavity 1 in (2.5 cm)

5   Insulation 3 in (7.6 cm)

6   Horizontal Z girts

7   Air/vapor barrier

8   Exterior gypsum sheathing 5/8 in (1.6 cm)

9   Batt insulation in framing cavity 6 in (5 cm)

10 Interior gypsum sheathing 5/8 in (1.6 cm)

three interior walls were modeled as adjacent to other interior spaces with the same thermal conditions without heat transfer occurring, but they would retain and release heat due to their thermal mass. The interior walls were modeled as gypsum board over steel studs, the floor was carpet over a concrete slab, and the ceiling was a drop ceiling of standard acoustical tiles. The Ideal Loads Air System component was used in EnergyPlus to study the performance of the office space without modeling a full HVAC system. Lighting was designed with a 0.5 W/ft^2 (0.05 W/m^2) load density and continuous daylighting control. The equipment load for the office was modeled at 0.7 W/ft^2 (0.07 W/m^2), and the occupancy load was one person.

The single office space with each type of exterior wall was modeled and rotated in 12 different orientations at 30° increments, using climate data for three time periods (present day, the year 2050, and the year 2080), for 15 different cities, representing all climate zones in the United States, as shown in Table 5.3.

TABLE 5.3: Climate zones and representative cities used for energy modeling.

	Climate zone	City	Zone	Subzone
1	1A	Miami, FL	very hot	moist
2	2A	Houston, TX	hot	moist
3	2B	Phoenix, AZ	hot	dry
4	3A	Memphis, TN	warm	moist
5	3B	El Paso, TX	warm	dry
6	3C	San Francisco, CA	warm	marine
7	4A	Baltimore, MD	mixed	moist
8	4B	Albuquerque, NM	mixed	dry
9	4C	Salem, OR	mixed	marine
10	5A	Chicago, IL	cool	moist
11	5B	Boise, ID	cool	dry
12	6A	Burlington, VT	cold	moist
13	6B	Helena, MT	cold	dry
14	7	Duluth, MN	very cold	
15	8	Fairbanks, AK	subarctic	

TYPE 3

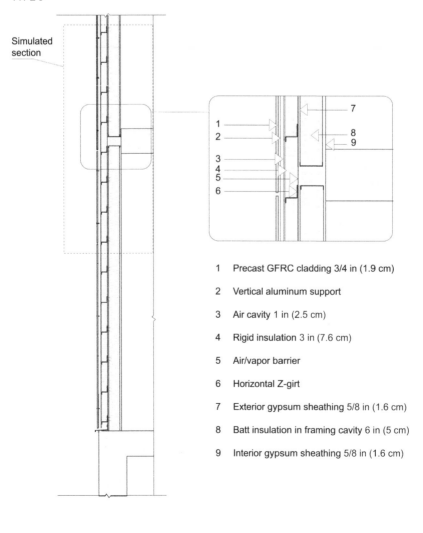

Simulated section

1 Precast GFRC cladding 3/4 in (1.9 cm)

2 Vertical aluminum support

3 Air cavity 1 in (2.5 cm)

4 Rigid insulation 3 in (7.6 cm)

5 Air/vapor barrier

6 Horizontal Z-girt

7 Exterior gypsum sheathing 5/8 in (1.6 cm)

8 Batt insulation in framing cavity 6 in (5 cm)

9 Interior gypsum sheathing 5/8 in (1.6 cm)

Figure 5.26: Overall section, material components, and simulated section for Type 3 facade system (rainscreen facade with glass-fiber reinforced concrete cladding and metal framing).

Figure 5.27:
Overall section,
material com-
ponents, and
simulated section
for Type 4 facade
system (curtain
wall with aluminum
framing).

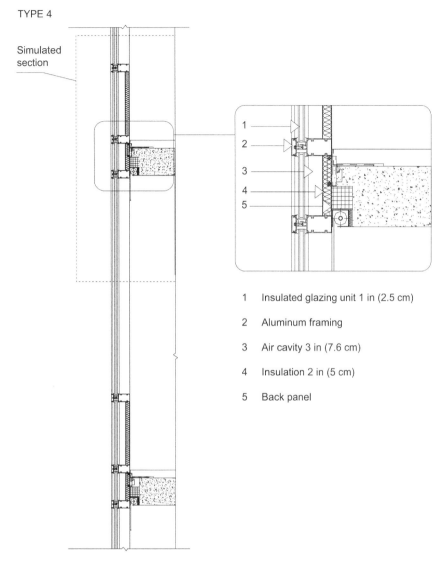

TYPE 4

Simulated
section

1   Insulated glazing unit 1 in (2.5 cm)

2   Aluminum framing

3   Air cavity 3 in (7.6 cm)

4   Insulation 2 in (5 cm)

5   Back panel

Future predicted climate change weather files were created for the 15 climate zones for the years 2050 and 2080 using the climate change world weather file generator tool CCWorldWeather. These files were used to simulate and compare present day energy use with future energy use for each of the facade types. A total of 3,780 simulations were run.

The plotted results, shown in Figure 5.36, indicate general patterns for each of the different wall types in the 15 climate zones, considering current climate data. The results of the simulations show that the facades with a lower U-value have better energy performance for the whole year in all climates and orientations. In general, the opaque facades all performed better than the transparent curtain walls, despite the energy reducing possibility of heat gain in winter and daylight harvesting. The opaque walls also performed similarly for all orientations,

TYPE 5

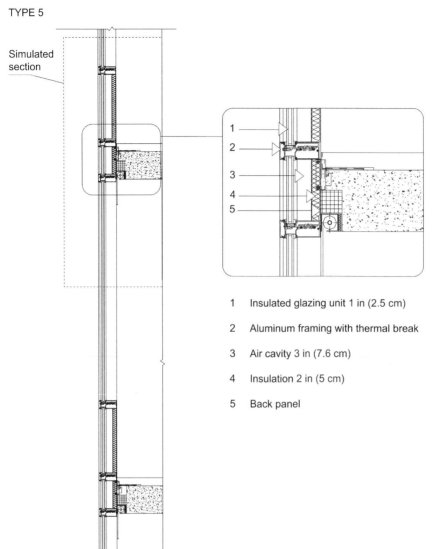

Figure 5.28:
Overall section,
material com-
ponents, and
simulated section
for Type 5 facade
system (curtain
wall with thermally
broken aluminum
framing).

Simulated
section

1 Insulated glazing unit 1 in (2.5 cm)

2 Aluminum framing with thermal break

3 Air cavity 3 in (7.6 cm)

4 Insulation 2 in (5 cm)

5 Back panel

with slightly better performance towards the north in warm climates and towards the south in cold climates. Orientation had a greater effect for the glazed walls, with the east and west orientations performing the worst. The south orientation performed the best in the coldest climates, but north facing walls performed the best for most of the other climate zones. In climate zones 1A through 3C, the north facing glazed facades performed nearly as well as the opaque facades.

Simulation runs that considered impacts of climate change, which utilized weather files for the year 2050 and the year 2080, increased the total energy use for all climates and facade types. The north facing facades performed the best for most of the climate zones due to lower cooling loads. All facade types

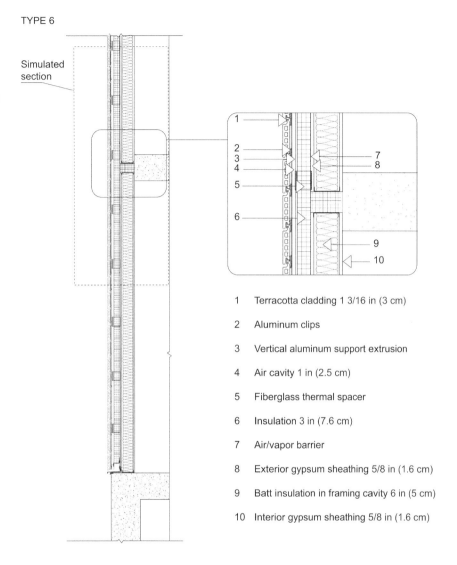

Figure 5.29: Overall section, material components, and simulated section for Type 6 facade system (rainscreen facade with terracotta cladding and thermal spacers).

TYPE 6

Simulated section

1   Terracotta cladding 1 3/16 in (3 cm)

2   Aluminum clips

3   Vertical aluminum support extrusion

4   Air cavity 1 in (2.5 cm)

5   Fiberglass thermal spacer

6   Insulation 3 in (7.6 cm)

7   Air/vapor barrier

8   Exterior gypsum sheathing 5/8 in (1.6 cm)

9   Batt insulation in framing cavity 6 in (5 cm)

10 Interior gypsum sheathing 5/8 in (1.6 cm)

showed the highest total energy use in the year 2080. The next highest was the year 2050, and the lowest total energy use was for present day weather files. The results for a rainscreen facade with terracotta cladding and thermal isolators (Type 7) and a curtain wall with thermally broken aluminum framing (Type 5) were plotted and compared to represent typical results of all the wall types. Type 7 had the lowest conductance in this study for the opaque assembly, and Type 5 had the lowest conductance for a glazed facade. Figures 5.37 and 5.38 show impacts of climate change on energy performance, considering current climate data, year 2050 simulations, and year 2080 simulations for the best performing opaque and glazed exterior wall assemblies (Type 7 and Type 5). Figure 5.37 shows the total energy consumption, while 5.38 shows heating and cooling loads only. Type

TYPE 7

Simulated section

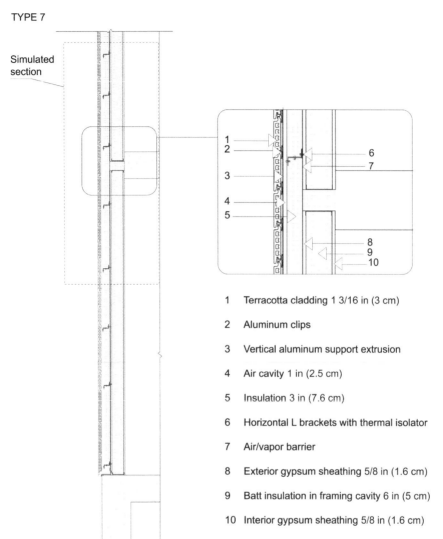

Figure 5.30: Overall section, material components, and simulated section for Type 7 facade system (rainscreen facade with terracotta cladding and thermal isolators).

1   Terracotta cladding 1 3/16 in (3 cm)

2   Aluminum clips

3   Vertical aluminum support extrusion

4   Air cavity 1 in (2.5 cm)

5   Insulation 3 in (7.6 cm)

6   Horizontal L brackets with thermal isolator

7   Air/vapor barrier

8   Exterior gypsum sheathing 5/8 in (1.6 cm)

9   Batt insulation in framing cavity 6 in (5 cm)

10 Interior gypsum sheathing 5/8 in (1.6 cm)

7 with a 20% window-to-wall ratio had lower total energy use than Type 7 with a 40% window-to-wall ratio. Heating and cooling loads were compared for Type 7 with a 20% window-to-wall ratio, which shows that cooling loads dominate the energy use for the office space, except in climate zones 7 and 8. Cooling loads increase by a greater amount than the decrease in heating loads; therefore, net energy use is increased with climate change. Similar results are evident for the curtain wall.

Figure 5.31:
Results of thermal
modeling, indi-
cating thermal
gradients within
all facade systems,
under exterior
temperature of 90°F
(32°C).

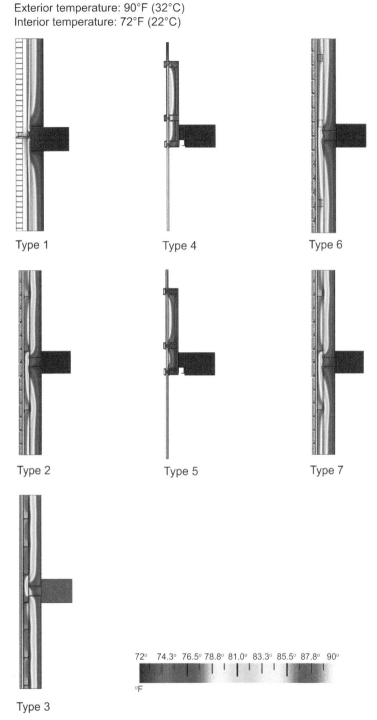

Exterior temperature: 90°F (32°C)
Interior temperature: 72°F (22°C)

Type 1   Type 4   Type 6

Type 2   Type 5   Type 7

Type 3

72° 74.3° 76.5° 78.8° 81.0° 83.3° 85.5° 87.8° 90°

°F

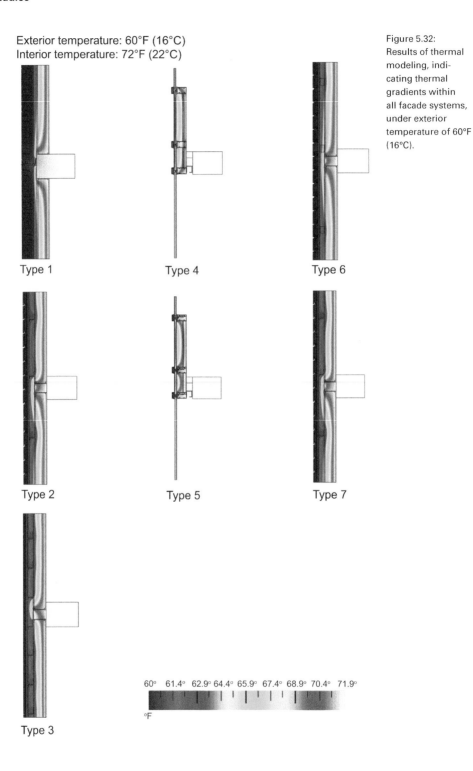

Exterior temperature: 60°F (16°C)
Interior temperature: 72°F (22°C)

Type 1

Type 4

Type 6

Type 2

Type 5

Type 7

Type 3

60° 61.4° 62.9° 64.4° 65.9° 67.4° 68.9° 70.4° 71.9°
°F

Figure 5.32:
Results of thermal modeling, indicating thermal gradients within all facade systems, under exterior temperature of 60°F (16°C).

Figure 5.33:
Results of thermal
modeling, indi-
cating thermal
gradients within
all facade systems,
under exterior
temperature of 30°F
(-1°C).

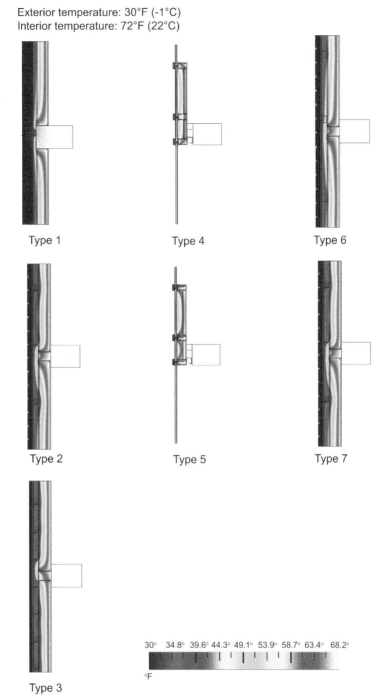

Exterior temperature: 30°F (-1°C)
Interior temperature: 72°F (22°C)

Type 1

Type 4

Type 6

Type 2

Type 5

Type 7

Type 3

30° 34.8° 39.6° 44.3° 49.1° 53.9° 58.7° 63.4° 68.2°

°F

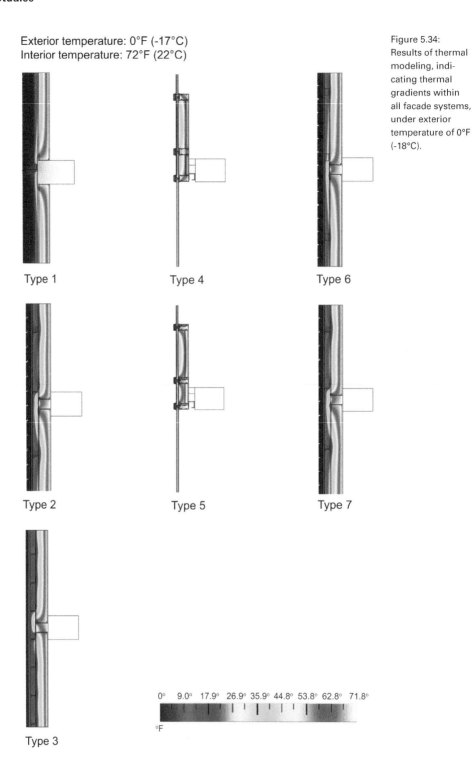

Exterior temperature: 0°F (-17°C)
Interior temperature: 72°F (22°C)

Type 1

Type 2

Type 3

Type 4

Type 5

Type 6

Type 7

0° 9.0° 17.9° 26.9° 35.9° 44.8° 53.8° 62.8° 71.8°

°F

Figure 5.34:
Results of thermal
modeling, indi-
cating thermal
gradients within
all facade systems,
under exterior
temperature of 0°F
(-18°C).

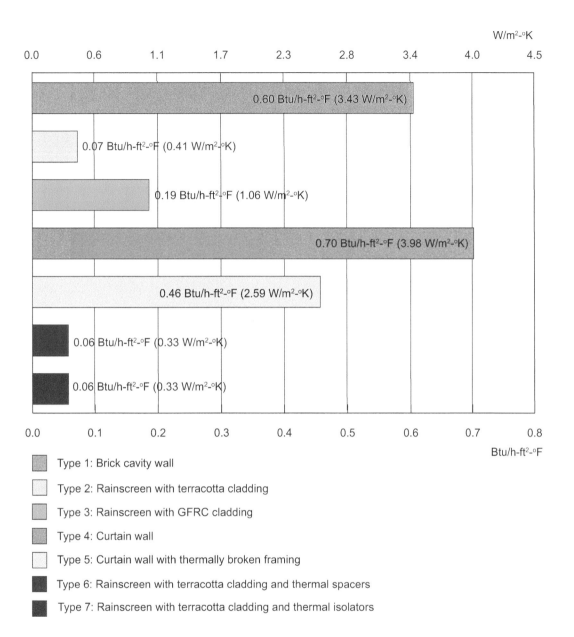

W/m²-°K

| 0.0 | 0.6 | 1.1 | 1.7 | 2.3 | 2.8 | 3.4 | 4.0 | 4.5 |

0.60 Btu/h-ft²-°F (3.43 W/m²-°K)

0.07 Btu/h-ft²-°F (0.41 W/m²-°K)

0.19 Btu/h-ft²-°F (1.06 W/m²-°K)

0.70 Btu/h-ft²-°F (3.98 W/m²-°K)

0.46 Btu/h-ft²-°F (2.59 W/m²-°K)

0.06 Btu/h-ft²-°F (0.33 W/m²-°K)

0.06 Btu/h-ft²-°F (0.33 W/m²-°K)

| 0.0 | 0.1 | 0.2 | 0.3 | 0.4 | 0.5 | 0.6 | 0.7 | 0.8 |

Btu/h-ft²-°F

Type 1: Brick cavity wall

Type 2: Rainscreen with terracotta cladding

Type 3: Rainscreen with GFRC cladding

Type 4: Curtain wall

Type 5: Curtain wall with thermally broken framing

Type 6: Rainscreen with terracotta cladding and thermal spacers

Type 7: Rainscreen with terracotta cladding and thermal isolators

Figure 5.35:
Comparison of cal-
culated U-values for
all facade systems.

EFFECT OF ORIENTATION ON TOTAL ENERGY USE-CURRENT CLIMATE

Energy consumption (GJ)

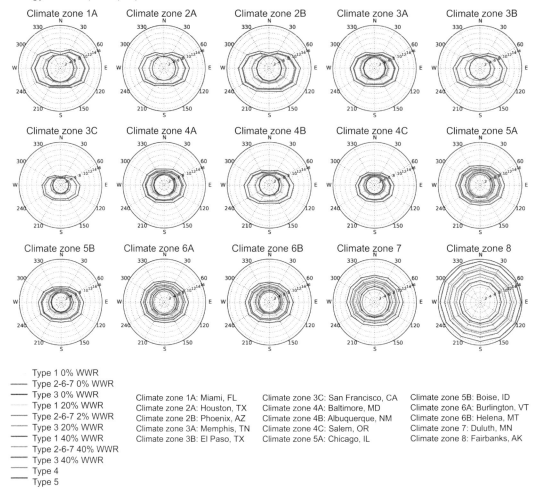

Type 1 0% WWR
Type 2-6-7 0% WWR
Type 3 0% WWR
Type 1 20% WWR
Type 2-6-7 2% WWR
Type 3 20% WWR
Type 1 40% WWR
Type 2-6-7 40% WWR
Type 3 40% WWR
Type 4
Type 5

Climate zone 1A: Miami, FL
Climate zone 2A: Houston, TX
Climate zone 2B: Phoenix, AZ
Climate zone 3A: Memphis, TN
Climate zone 3B: El Paso, TX

Climate zone 3C: San Francisco, CA
Climate zone 4A: Baltimore, MD
Climate zone 4B: Albuquerque, NM
Climate zone 4C: Salem, OR
Climate zone 5A: Chicago, IL

Climate zone 5B: Boise, ID
Climate zone 6A: Burlington, VT
Climate zone 6B: Helena, MT
Climate zone 7: Duluth, MN
Climate zone 8: Fairbanks, AK

Figure 5.36:
Effects of orientation and different window-to-wall ratios on energy consumption for investigated facade types in different climates.

ENERGY USE-CURRENT CLIMATE, 2050 AND 2080

Total energy consumption (GJ)
Type 7 (best performing opaque facade system)

Total energy consumption (GJ)
Types 7 and 5 (best opaque and glazed systems)

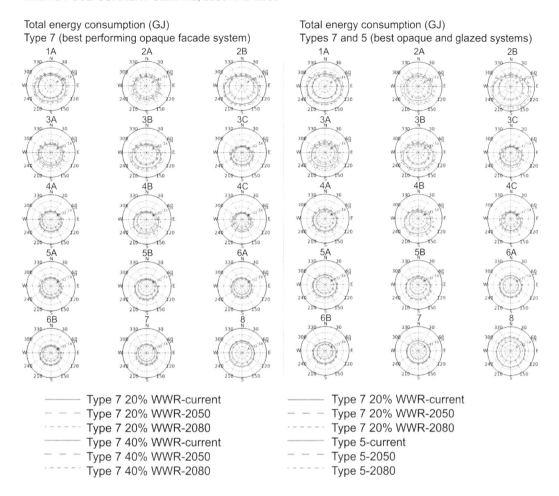

——————	Type 7 20% WWR-current	
– – –	Type 7 20% WWR-2050	
··········	Type 7 20% WWR-2080	
——————	Type 7 40% WWR-current	
– – –	Type 7 40% WWR-2050	
··········	Type 7 40% WWR-2080	

——————	Type 7 20% WWR-current	
– – –	Type 7 20% WWR-2050	
··········	Type 7 20% WWR-2080	
——————	Type 5-current	
– – –	Type 5-2050	
··········	Type 5-2080	

Climate zone 1A: Miami, FL
Climate zone 2A: Houston, TX
Climate zone 2B: Phoenix, AZ
Climate zone 3A: Memphis, TN
Climate zone 3B: El Paso, TX

Climate zone 3C: San Francisco, CA
Climate zone 4A: Baltimore, MD
Climate zone 4B: Albuquerque, NM
Climate zone 4C: Salem, OR
Climate zone 5A: Chicago, IL

Climate zone 5B: Boise, ID
Climate zone 6A: Burlington, VT
Climate zone 6B: Helena, MT
Climate zone 7: Duluth, MN
Climate zone 8: Fairbanks, AK

Figure 5.37:
Impacts of climate
change on total
energy consump-
tion for best ther-
mally performing
opaque and glazed
facade systems.

ENERGY USE-CURRENT CLIMATE, 2050 AND 2080

Heating and cooling loads (GJ)
Type 7 (best performing opaque facade system)

Heating and cooling loads (GJ)
Type 5 (best performing glazed facade system)

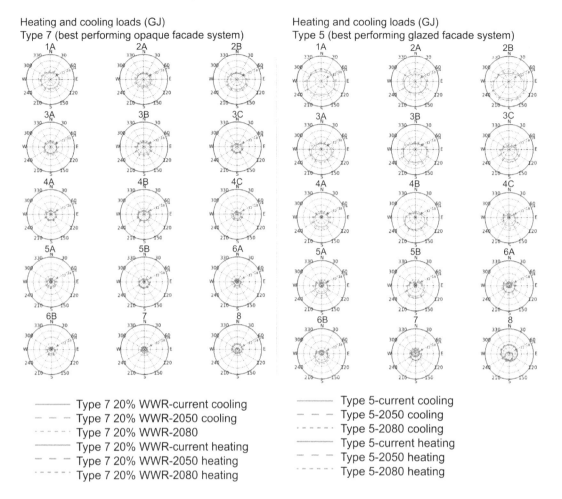

Type 7 20% WWR-current cooling
— — — Type 7 20% WWR-2050 cooling
- - - - - Type 7 20% WWR-2080
Type 7 20% WWR-current heating
— — — Type 7 20% WWR-2050 heating
- - - - - Type 7 20% WWR-2080 heating

Type 5-current cooling
— — — Type 5-2050 cooling
- - - - - Type 5-2080 cooling
Type 5-current heating
— — — Type 5-2050 heating
- - - - - Type 5-2080 heating

Climate zone 1A: Miami, FL
Climate zone 2A: Houston, TX
Climate zone 2B: Phoenix, AZ
Climate zone 3A: Memphis, TN
Climate zone 3B: El Paso, TX

Climate zone 3C: San Francisco, CA
Climate zone 4A: Baltimore, MD
Climate zone 4B: Albuquerque, NM
Climate zone 4C: Salem, OR
Climate zone 5A: Chicago, IL

Climate zone 5B: Boise, ID
Climate zone 6A: Burlington, VT
Climate zone 6B: Helena, MT
Climate zone 7: Duluth, MN
Climate zone 8: Fairbanks, AK

Figure 5.38:
Impacts of climate
change on heating
and cooling loads
for best thermally
performing opaque
and glazed facade
systems.

5.4 QUALITATIVE, QUANTITATIVE, AND EXPERIMENTAL RESEARCH FOR THE DESIGN PROCESS: INTEGRATION OF AUGMENTED AND VIRTUAL REALITY WITH DESIGN

Augmented reality (AR) and virtual reality (VR) are computer-generated, simulated representations of real or imagined environments, where users can interact with simulated representations using various digital technologies. The similarities between AR and VR technologies are that they rely on digital representations of real or imagined scenes, objects, and environments and utilize advanced 3D modeling and visualization strategies. However, the major differences relate to the level of interaction— AR can only be "viewed", while VR can be "experienced". AR superimposes computer-generated visuals into a real-world environment and utilizes mobile devices, tablets, and computer displays to augment the physical environment with digital projections. On the other hand, VR offers a fully immersive digital environment and uses 3D computer-generated visuals to produce representations of the real world or imagined environments.

AR and VR applications are a promising new direction for architectural design. A literature review was conducted to identify the current state-of-knowledge. Improved understanding of architectural design and communication procedures are the primary benefits of these novel technologies (de Freitas and Ruschel, 2013). These tools offer exploration of designed environments that is not possible with the traditional forms of representation, since they allow users to immerse themselves, visualize, and explore spaces during different design stages and before they are built. Besides advanced visualization, AR and VR tools enhance collaboration and communication among design teams (Fernando et al., 2013; Heydarian et al., 2015). However, studies focusing on the integration of these advanced digital technologies in the architectural curriculum are limited (Wang et al., 2013). Therefore, the primary research objectives of this study were to investigate implementation of AR/VR tools in architectural education and to determine whether these novel digital technologies are beneficial for the educational experience of students.

Specific research questions that were addressed, shown in Figure 5.39, are:

Figure 5.39: Overview of research questions and research methods.

- How can AR/VR tools be utilized during the different stages of the design process?
- What is the appropriate workflow for integrating such tools into architectural design?

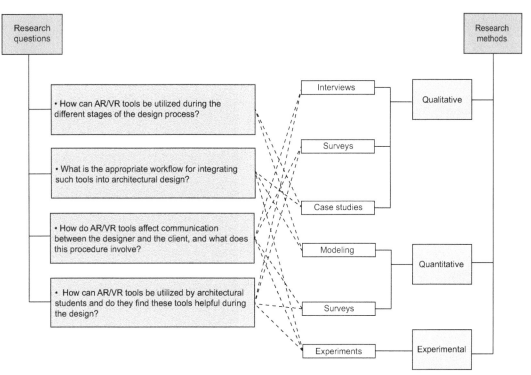

- How do AR/VR tools affect communication between the designer and the client, and what does this procedure involve?
- How can AR/VR tools be utilized by architectural students, and do they find these tools helpful during the design?

A combination of qualitative, quantitative, and experimental research methods was used to address these questions, as seen in Figure 5.39. The research methods included interviews, qualitative and quantitative surveys, case studies, modeling, and experiments. The experiments were conducted during the different stages of the design process and involved three different groups of users. The first experiment analyzed the effectiveness of AR/VR tools on the design process (personal assessment) during the conceptual design, schematic design, and design development. The second experiment investigated the effectiveness of these tools in collaboration and communication between the designer and the "client" during the conceptual design, schematic design, and design development (communication procedures), considering that in the context of architectural education, faculty members are acting as clients. The third experiment involved graduate architecture students, and evaluations were conducted in a group setting (student effectiveness), during the design development phase. These evaluations only included VR applications, since results of earlier studies indicated that AR tools are most suitable for the early stages of the design process. Table 5.4 summarizes the research procedures, survey methods, and design phases investigated in this study.

Identical workflow for data exchange, design models, and AR/VR models were utilized for all evaluations. In terms of design elements that were included in the digital model during different design phases, the models increased in complexity and amount of information in later stages. The design development model included more detailed information than the schematic and conceptual design models, as seen in Table 5.5. The workflow involved preparation of AR/VR models (exported from design software programs and visualized through AR and VR applications), based on specific design phases and the level of detail. A BIM tool was used to create a design model (Autodesk Revit). Then, the model was exported as an FBX file type, which can be used for both AR and VR viewing/immersive purposes. SketchFab was utilized to view the models in AR. An Apple iPhone device was used to visualize this model, and the evaluations were performed in a typical office setting. Figure 5.40 shows AR models superimposed within physical space. To view and explore the models using VR, the Unity software program was used for a full immersive experience. Unity is a game development platform with the capabilities to build high-quality 3D virtual environments for immersive experiences. FBX files were exported for each evaluation, imported to Unity, and visualized with a VR headset and controllers. Figure 5.41 shows VR model visualized through a headset. In this research, a controlled setting was used for VR evaluations—a green room, equipped with a computer workstation (which included the Unity software program), headset, and controllers (HTC Vive headset and controllers). Figure 5.42 shows the experimental setting.

TABLE 5.4: Summary of research procedures.

	Evaluations		
	Personal Assessment	Communication Procedures	Student Effectiveness
Investigated methods	AR and VR	AR and VR	VR
Investigated design phases	Conceptual design, schematic design, and design development	Conceptual design, schematic design, and design development	Design development
Research procedure	Experimental evaluation of impacts of AR/VR tools on architectural design, followed by a survey (quantitative)	Experimental evaluation of architectural design, visualized and experienced through AR/VR tools, followed by a survey (qualitative and quantitative) and interviews	Initial survey about familiarity with VR tools (qualitative and quantitative), followed by an experimental evaluation of architectural design visualized and experienced through VR tools, a second survey and interviews
Survey method	Self-administered questionnaire	Questionnaire	Questionnaires (for both surveys)

TABLE 5.5: Summary of design elements and features included in the digital models according to different design phases.

Design phase	AR	VR
Conceptual design	Basic building site and surrounding buildings Building massing and geometry Building volume Individual levels of the building	Basic building site and surrounding buildings Building massing and geometry Building volume Individual levels of the building
Schematic design	Not investigated	Schematic site design Surrounding buildings Building geometry Building volume Interior spatial arrangement Schematic facade design Schematic building structure
Design development	Not investigated	Developed building site and surrounding buildings Infrastructure and transportation Building geometry Interior spatial arrangement and circulation Detailed facade design Detailed building structure Materials Furniture

AR model viewed on a mobile device

Figure 5.40:
AR model.

VR headset

VR model viewed through a headset

Figure 5.41:
VR headset, and VR
model visualization.

In this study, ten different evaluations were conducted to investigate the difference between AR and VR tools, their effects on design and communication protocols during different stages of the design process, and the perspectives of various
participants, as shown in Figure 5.43. Each step involved evaluation of the AR or
VR building model, which lasted approximately 30 minutes for every participant,
followed by a survey (qualitative and quantitative), and interviews (for open-ended
questions). For investigating student effectiveness, a survey was also administered
before the evaluations to assess students' familiarity with AR/VR tools.

In the case of AR, the digital model was visualized within the physical environment by superimposing a 3D digital model in the real environment, and the
walk-throughs were conducted by simply rotating the smartphone to visualize different aspects of the model. In the case of VR, each study participant was fully
immersed within the VR environment, where they had an opportunity to "experience" the VR model. This immersive experience included visualization of the

Figure 5.42:
Experimental
setting for VR
experiments.

Experimental setting for VR experiments

VR experiments

VR model (the scale, building geometry, surrounding buildings, building structure, etc.), as well as a walk-through within the site and the building.

Surveys included different questions for different participants, but all used a 10-point rating scale to investigate these following aspects:

- Workflow: complexity of the overall process and data exchange
- Design: effects on the design process
- Navigation: ease of navigation through the design
- Visualization: effects on the visualization techniques of the design
- Success: how important was it to use AR/VR tools (for design process or design communication) or interest (for student effectiveness)

Figure 5.44 shows specific survey questions that were used to evaluate the impacts of VR during the different design stages (for the designer and the client), while Figure 5.45 shows questions for students.

	Conceptual design	Schematic design	Design development
AR Evaluations	*Step 1: Personal assessment* • Evaluation of the AR model by the Designer, followed by responding to self-administered survey • Participants: 1 (Designer) *Step 2:* *Communication procedure* • Evaluation of the AR model by Designer and Client, followed by a survey and interviews • Participants: 2 (Designer and Client)		
VR Evaluations	*Step 3: Personal assessment* • Immersive walk-through and evaluation of the VR model by the Designer, followed by responding to self-administered survey • Participants: 1 (Designer) *Step 4:* *Communication procedure* • Immersive walk-through and evaluation of the VR model by the Designer and Client, followed by a survey and interviews • Participants: 2 (Designer and Client)	*Step 6: Personal assessment* • Immersive walk-through and evaluation of the VR model by the Designer, followed by responding to self-administered survey • Participants: 1 (Designer) *Step 7:* *Communication procedure* • Immersive walk-through and evaluation of the VR model by the Designer and Client, followed by a survey and interviews • Participants: 2 (Designer and Client)	*Steps 8 and 9:* *Student effectiveness* • Initial survey administered to students to assess familiarity with VR • Participants: 16 (Graduate architecture students) • Immersive walk-through and evaluation of the VR model by students, followed by a survey and interviews • Participants: 6 (Graduate architecture students)

Figure 5.43: Evaluations and research procedures.

Figure 5.46 shows the results of AR evaluations conducted during the conceptual design, where the top part of the figure shows the results of a personal assessment (designer), and the bottom part of the figure shows the results for communication procedures (designer and client). The results of the personal assessment indicated that the use of AR at this stage was not very important for the designer. Although the workflow was simple and effective in terms of exporting model geometry from BIM and importing into AR software, the use of AR did not have a major impact on the design decisions. It was useful for visualizing the overall design concept and presenting it to others. The results of the interactive evaluation focusing on design communication showed that AR was beneficial for visualizing the overall site and scale of the building and its relationships to the surrounding context. However, it had limited use for resolving design problems. The results indicated that the AR is useful for understanding the overall building massing and relaying large-scale ideas to the client. The application of this technology in the early stages of the design process is similar to physical models, which are very typical in architectural education. The main benefit of AR is that digital models can be created automatically from BIM software and displayed in AR environments, thus saving time and resources compared to building physical

		Conceptual design	Schematic design	Design development

Figure 5.44:
Example of surveys
questions for
VR evaluations
(designer and
client).

VR Evaluations

Steps 3 and 6: Personal assessment
1. Workflow: How easy was the VR workflow process?
2. Design: How much did VR help you to solve design problems?
3. Navigation: How easy or difficult was it to navigate through the design model in VR environment?
4. Visualization: How much did the VR immersion affect the way you visualize the design?
5. Success: How important was it to use VR tools at this phase of the design process?

Steps 4 and 7:
Communication procedure
Questions for the Designer
1. Workflow: How easy was it to present the design model to the client?
2. Design: How much did VR help you to communicate and solve design problems with client?
3. Navigation: How easy or difficult was it for you and your client to navigate through the design model?
4. Visualization: How much did the VR immersion affect the way you and your client visualize the design?
5. Success: How important was it for you and your client to use VR tools at this phase of the design process?

Questions for the Client
1. Workflow: How easy or difficult was it to adapt to the V workflow that the designer was presenting?
2. Design: How much did VR help you and the designer to solve design problems?
3. Navigation: How easy or difficult was it for you and the designer to navigate through the design model in the VR environment?
4. Visualization: How much did the VR immersion affect the way you and the designer visualize the design?
5. Success: How important was it for you and the designer to use VR tools at this phase of the design process?

				Design development

Figure 5.45:
Example of surveys
questions for
VR evaluation
(students).

VR Evaluations

Steps 8 and 9:
Student effectiveness
Questions before evaluations
1. Workflow: How familiar are you with VR tools?
2. Design: How much do you think that VR would help you to understand and solve design problems?
3. Navigation: How easy or difficult would it be for you to navigate through a design model using VR technology?
4. Visualization: How much do you think VR will affect the way you visualize and understand a design model?
5. Interest: How likely are you to use VR tools in your architecture studio?

Questions after evaulations
1. Workflow: How easy was the VR workflow process?
2. Design: How much did VR help you to find potential problems in the design model?
3. Navigation: How easy or difficult was it to navigate through the design model in the VR environement?
4. Visualization: How much did the VR immersion affect the way you visualize the design model?
5. Interest: How likely are you to use VR tools in architecture studio for your own projects now that you have used the technology?

Conceptual design

**AR
Evaluations
Survey Results**

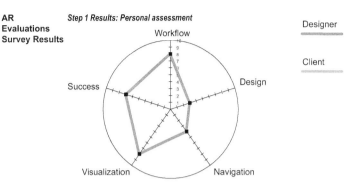

Step 1 Results: Personal assessment

Designer

Client

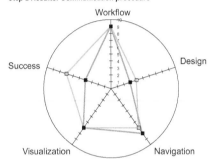

Step 2 Results: Communication procedure

models. The results of the interview indicated that AR would have been more useful for investigating different building forms, early design studies, and the overall building shape.

Figure 5.47 shows the results of VR evaluations conducted during the different stages of the design process, considering the designer's and client's perspectives. The immersive nature of the VR and the ability to experience the building helped to provide an insight as to what would it be like to explore this architectural design in person. From the designer's perspective, the primary benefit of using VR at this stage was the ability to explore and visualize the design, but it was not greatly helpful for making design decisions. The results of the interactive evaluation and communication procedures between the designer and client indicated that the primary benefits of using VR in the conceptual design stage are the ability to explore and visualize the scale of the building, its relationship to the site, the overall form, and movement through the building. The last aspect—the ability to experience the building from the perspective of a building occupant and circulate through the digital model as if moving through the real building—is the most important one, because no other visualization technique offers this capability. The client was more satisfied with the design, workflow,

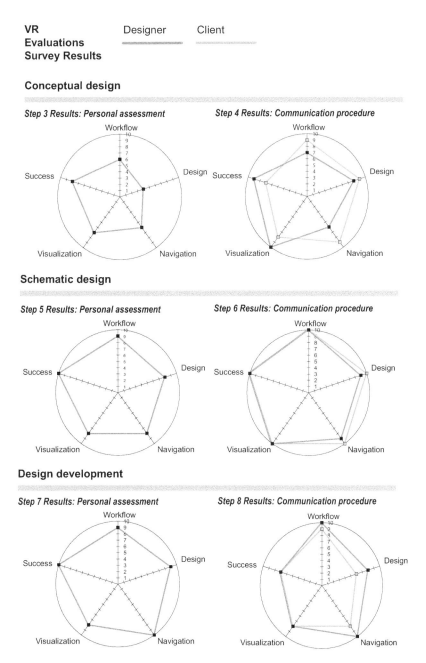

VR Evaluations Survey Results   Designer   Client

Figure 5.47:
Results of the VR evaluations.

and navigation than the designer, while the designer gave higher scores for visualization and success. The results of the interviews indicated that VR would be more effective if it included materials, interior partitions, and many other details to represent the real design, which relates to schematic design and information that would typically be included in this design phase. The results for schematic design evaluations were much better and indicated that the designer was more satisfied with the VR model and its effect on design decisions than with the VR model for the conceptual design. The VR model was more developed and included the overall structure, interior partitions, building envelope treatment, and circulation elements (stairs and elevators). Therefore, the immersive experience was more beneficial since it was easier to notice design problems that would be difficult to notice in typical architectural drawings. The designer also indicated that understanding the building scale and relationships between different spaces was extremely helpful. The results of the interactive evaluation and communication procedures between the client and the designer indicated that the use of VR at this design stage was extremely helpful. The client provided the highest scores for all aspects of the evaluation, and the designer gave higher scores than in the personal assessment. The more complete model was beneficial for the client to fully understand the scale of the building, spatial organization, interior partitions, stairs, and circulation cores, etc. The client also indicated some design deficiencies, which were modified in the later stages of the design process. The final evaluations conducted during the design development implemented the most detailed VR model. The design issues raised during earlier stages were resolved, and the model was updated to reflect these changes. The immersive experience was the most convincing at this stage, because it was possible to fully explore all aspects of the VR model (integration of the building with the site and surrounding context, structural systems, building envelope design, circulation, etc.). The results of the personal assessment indicated that the designer was most satisfied with the use of VR during this stage of the design process, compared to earlier stages. From the client's perspective, use of VR was slightly less effective than for the previous design stages. The results of the open-ended evaluations and interview indicated that this was caused by the lack of materials in the VR model and that the immersive experience would be more effective if all materials were properly displayed.

The last part of the study investigated the effects of VR on students' perception and design effectiveness. Two different surveys were distributed—the first before the immersive VR experience to investigate students' familiarity with VR tools, their previous experiences, and their perspectives regarding the workflow and impacts on design, interest in these tools, and their perspectives regarding navigation and visualization. Then, students participated in the evaluations of the identical VR model, used for the previous step in the study (design development model). The second survey was administered to evaluate this immersive experience, followed by interviews and open-ended questions. Figure 5.48 shows the results of both surveys, where the data indicates average results for all participants. The top part of the figure shows "before" results, indicating students' familiarity with the VR tools and perspectives on the effects of this technology on the design process. It was found that students were not greatly familiar with the VR tools and workflows, and they did not fully understand how VR tools can be used or navigated. Their initial thoughts were that these tools can benefit the design process, and that VR offers better visualization techniques compared to

Figure 5.48:
Results of the VR
evaluations (stu-
dents' perspective),
conducted before
and after immersive
VR experience.

Design development

**VR
Evaluations
Survey Results**

Step 9 Results: Student effectiveness (familarity with VR tools)

Students

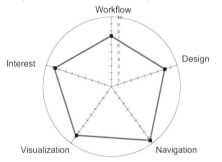

Average results
Number of participants: 16

Step 10 Results: Student effectiveness (evaluation of VR model)

Average results
Number of participants: 6

standard 2D or 3D architectural documents. Students also expressed great interest in learning these tools and applying them for their own design projects. The
participants were fully immersed within the VR model used in this study (an identical VR model to that used for the design development explorations between the
designer and the client), and then responded to a survey. Students' responses
indicated that they had a much better understanding of the workflow and data
exchange between the design and VR software applications after the immersive
experience, as well as navigation within the VR environment. Their perspective
on the impacts of VR on design were identical to the "before" survey, where they
indicated that the VR tools would be beneficial for the design process. Evaluations
"after" the immersive experience confirmed this aspect. Moreover, students'
interest in VR tools increased after the immersive VR experience because they
could visualize the model, explore, and understand the capabilities of VR software applications and implementation in architectural design. Figure 5.49 shows
individual students' responses as scatter plots. It is evident that many students
were not familiar with the workflows associated with VR technologies but were
aware of the benefits associated with the design process. Another aspect that
received the lowest scores before the immersive evaluation was the navigation—
students were generally not familiar with VR environments nor how to navigate

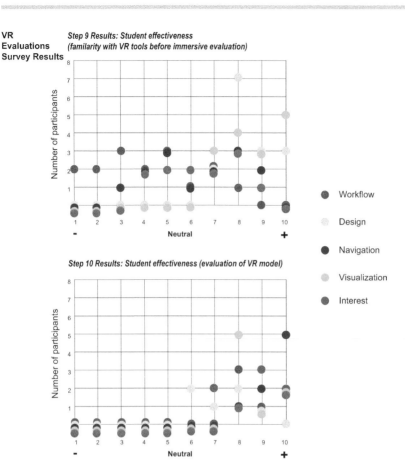

Design development

VR
Evaluations
Survey Results

Step 9 Results: Student effectiveness
(familarity with VR tools before immersive evaluation)

Step 10 Results: Student effectiveness (evaluation of VR model)

- ● Workflow
- ○ Design
- ● Navigation
- ○ Visualization
- ● Interest

Figure 5.49:
Individual students'
surveys responses,
before and after
immersive VR
experience.

VR models. Students were aware of the visualization potentials of VR technologies and were generally interested in these emerging digital technologies. After the immersive VR experience, students' interest in VR technologies drastically increased. Also, their understanding of the workflow and navigation significantly improved. Students' perspectives regarding the impacts of VR on the design process remained the same as before the immersive experience. Lastly, their understanding of the visualization capabilities of VR technologies slightly improved. The results of interviews and open-ended questions indicated that students very much appreciated being exposed to VR tools and expressed that they would start using these emerging technologies in their design projects, even if not required by studio instructors.

The results of this study indicate that AR and VR tools are beneficial for the architectural design process and can advance architectural education. These benefits include improved team collaboration, improved communication, investigation of design mock-ups, and visual, immersive reviews. Specific results of various evaluations indicated that VR and AR tools are useful for visualizing building form, scale, and design elements, as well as understanding movement and circulation through the building. No other design representation method offers such an immersive experience and visualization of design elements nor an ability to move through a digital representation of a building. Therefore, these technologies can greatly benefit spatial cognition, design communication, and visualization of architectural projects.

5.5 QUANTITATIVE AND EXPERIMENTAL RESEARCH: INTELLIGENT FACADE SYSTEMS

Intelligent facade systems can be defined as building enclosures that react to the exterior environment, adapt to environmental changes, regulate their performance and functioning (by self-regulation or by users), integrate smart materials and components, and, in some instances, provide renewable energy for building's operation. Intelligent facade systems are an important aspect of advanced building technologies that can revolutionize our buildings and significantly improve their performance.

This research focused on the development, design, evaluations, and applications of new, intelligent facade systems, which integrate thermoelectric materials (Aksamija et al., 2020, 2019). Thermoelectric materials are smart materials that can produce a temperature gradient when electricity is applied, exploiting the Peltier effect, or generate a voltage when exposed to a temperature gradient, utilizing the Seebeck effect. These types of materials can be used for heating, cooling, or power generation. Research and development has largely focused on thermoelectric modules (TEMs) that convert heat energy into electrical energy (Montecucco et al., 2012; Yilmazoglu, 2016) and novel TE materials that offer higher energy efficiency through nanoscale engineering (Snyder and Toberer, 2008). Heating and cooling modes can be switched by reversing the current direction. TEMs can offer low cost electricity without the use of mechanical parts or production of toxic wastes. Thermoelectric heating and cooling have several advantages over their conventional counterparts. The compact size of commercial TEMs, their light weight, reliability, lack of mechanical parts, and elimination of the need for chlorofluorocarbons (CFCs) make them environmentally friendly and appealing. But, applying thermoelectric systems for space heating and cooling remains much more challenging (Zhao and Tan, 2014). Few applications of TEMs in facade assemblies have been researched, proposed, or constructed. This has created a significant gap in knowledge of the potential architectural applications of TEMs. The research objective of this study was to investigate the potential integration of TEMs into building skin to create intelligent facade systems that utilize the temperature difference between the exterior environment to provide heating, cooling, and energy generation, as seen in Figure 5.50.

The research questions that were addressed, as seen in Figure 5.51, are:

- How can TE materials be integrated into architectural facade assemblies to provide localized heating and cooling?
- How do TE materials behave in typical thermal conditions for various climates?

Case Studies

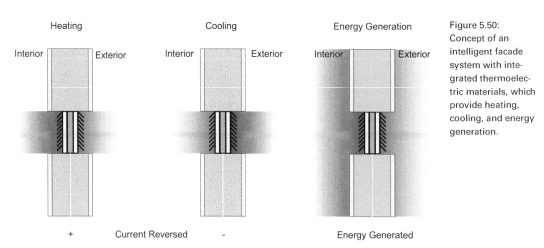

Figure 5.50: Concept of an intelligent facade system with integrated thermoelectric materials, which provide heating, cooling, and energy generation.

Heating — Interior / Exterior
Cooling — Interior / Exterior
Energy Generation — Interior / Exterior

+ Current Reversed -
Energy Generated

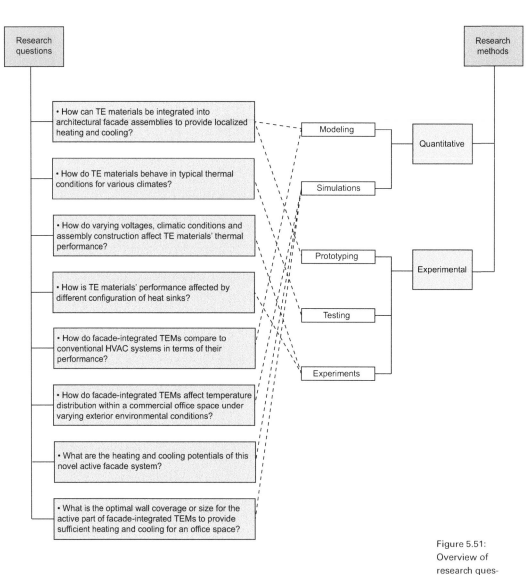

Research questions:

• How can TE materials be integrated into architectural facade assemblies to provide localized heating and cooling?

• How do TE materials behave in typical thermal conditions for various climates?

• How do varying voltages, climatic conditions and assembly construction affect TE materials' thermal performance?

• How is TE materials' performance affected by different configuration of heat sinks?

• How do facade-integrated TEMs compare to conventional HVAC systems in terms of their performance?

• How do facade-integrated TEMs affect temperature distribution within a commercial office space under varying exterior environmental conditions?

• What are the heating and cooling potentials of this novel active facade system?

• What is the optimal wall coverage or size for the active part of facade-integrated TEMs to provide sufficient heating and cooling for an office space?

Research methods: Modeling, Simulations — Quantitative; Prototyping, Testing, Experiments — Experimental

Figure 5.51: Overview of research questions and research methods.

- How do varying voltages, climatic conditions, and types of assembly construction affect TE materials' thermal performance?
- How is TE materials' performance affected by different configurations of heat sinks?
- How do facade-integrated TEMs compare to conventional HVAC systems in terms of their performance?
- How do facade-integrated TEMs affect temperature distribution within a commercial office space under varying exterior environmental conditions?
- What are the heating and cooling potentials of this novel active facade system?
- What is the optimal wall coverage or size for the active part of facade-integrated TEMs to provide sufficient heating and cooling for an office space?

Quantitative and experimental research methods, including modeling, simulations, prototyping, testing, and experiments were employed to address these questions as shown in Figure 5.51. Initially, two prototypes were designed and constructed, shown in Figure 5.52, with different configurations. These prototypes were first tested in ambient room conditions to measure the heating and cooling outputs of TEMs. Then, an experimental study was utilized to physically evaluate heating and cooling outputs, where a controlled thermal chamber was

Figure 5.52:
Initial prototypes
and testing in ambient conditions.

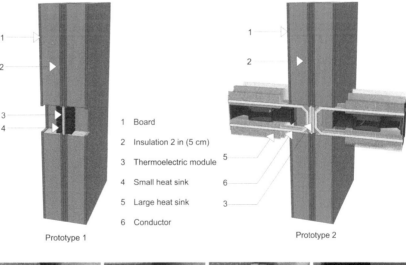

1   Board

2   Insulation 2 in (5 cm)

3   Thermoelectric module

4   Small heat sink

5   Large heat sink

6   Conductor

Prototype 1   Prototype 2

  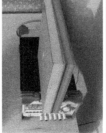 

Initial testing in ambient conditions

used to represent different exterior temperatures, and interior temperature was kept constant. Thermal imaging was used to measure the heating and cooling outputs under varying voltage and power supply. The results were promising and indicated that facade-integrated TEMs would provide sufficient heating and cooling. The coefficient of performance (COP) was numerically calculated based on the experimental results and compared to conventional HVAC systems. The next stage of the research focused on the integration of TEMs into various facade types, as well as implementation of these intelligent facade systems for commercial office spaces. Digital models were developed, and scaled physical prototypes of these systems were digitally fabricated. The last step of the research included simulations, where Computational Fluid Dynamic (CFD) analysis was performed to investigate optimal exterior wall coverage for maximizing heating and cooling output, as well as temperature distribution within the interior office space under different climatic conditions.

The dimensions of the TEM were 0.16 in x 0.16 in (40 mm x 40 mm), drawing up to 12 V, and operating conditions ranged from -22°F (-30°C) to 181°F (83°C). The small heat sink in the first prototype included aluminum fins, measuring 0.16 in x 0.16 in x 0.04 in (40 mm x 40 mm x 11 mm), which were bonded on to both sides of the TEM with silicone based thermal pads. The second prototype included two larger heat sinks, measuring 4.7 in (120 mm), with four direct copper pipes for heat dissipation, connected with thermal paste to both sides of the TEM. The first testing was conducted in ambient conditions. An independent module without a heat sink, a module with a small heat sink, and both prototypes were tested with applied voltage of 1V increments. Results were measured using a thermal imaging camera, as well as a power supply. Thermal images were taken at one volt increments up to 8V, and temperatures were recorded using a thermal camera. The temperatures that were measured during ambient testing ranged from 49°F (9°C) to 258°F (126°C) in both cooling and heating modes. The results also indicated that the small heat sinks in the first prototype were not as effective for heat dissipation; therefore, the second prototype was selected for further testing as a better performing system.

Further testing involved the use of a temperature controlled thermal chamber. The thermal chamber's opening was sealed using insulating foam with tape applied to provide a relatively air-tight seal for the testing. The prototype was inserted into the chamber and sealed again, as seen in Figure 5.53. The chamber was set to 90°F, 60°F, 30°F, and 0°F (32°C, 16°C, -1°C, and -18°C) to represent different exterior temperatures (winter, summer, and intermediate seasons). This method of testing represented typical exterior temperatures found in most climates while allowing for temperature data to be collected in a controlled setting. The heating mode was tested under 60°F, 30°F, and 0°F (16°C, -1°C, and -18°C) conditions, while the cooling mode was tested under 90°F and 60°F (32°C and 16°C). The thermal chamber was allowed time to stabilize (1 hr) before each testing session, and 20-minute breaks were taken in between each measurement. The ambient temperature of the room was kept relatively stable at 73°F. Voltage was applied in 1 V increments in both heating and cooling modes. Temperature measurements on the exterior surface of the prototype were recorded using a

Figure 5.53:
Thermal chamber
experimental set-
up, and examples of
measurements.

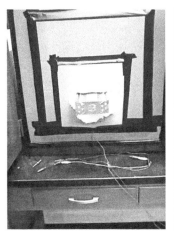

Thermal chamber testing and thermal imagining used for measurements

60°F (16°C) 30°F (-1°C) 0°F (-18°C)

Measurements (heating mode) at 3V, captured with a thermal camera

thermal camera. Table 5.6 shows results for the heating mode and Table 5.7 for the cooling mode. The results show that TEMs operate at effective heating and cooling temperatures even when exposed to variable exterior temperatures, represented by the thermal chamber.

The next step of the research focused on the design, modeling, and physical prototyping of real facade systems that would integrate thermoelectric materials. Figure 5.54 shows digital models of various facade systems. In all cases, the exterior heat sinks are seamlessly integrated into the exterior cladding since aesthetic considerations are important for any facade design. For example, aluminum fins can be used as exterior shading devices, but also as an external heat sink, connected to the TEMs with a copper conducting system and an interior heat sink (a radiant panel). Aluminum cladding in a rainscreen application can be used as an exterior heat sink. Lastly, in a curtain wall application, an aluminum panel, acting as exterior heat sink, can be integrated into the spandrel area. In all three cases, a radiant panel is placed on the interior side and would provide heating and cooling. Also, the facade-integrated TE system would be installed as a modular piece and would be insulated from the rest of the exterior wall. The modular nature of this system would be suitable for all building types, as well as retrofits of existing buildings. Figure 5.55 shows scaled physical prototypes of these systems, which

TABLE 5.6: Results of thermal chamber testing (heating mode).

Chamber Temperature°F (°C)	Voltage(Volts)	Current(Amps)	Power(Watts)	Temperature Output°F (°C)
0 (-18)	0	0	0	68 (20)
	1	0.17	0.17	67 (19)
	2	0.45	0.9	70 (21)
	3	0.74	2.22	73 (23)
	4	1.02	4.08	72 (22)
	5	1.12	5.6	76 (24)
	6	1.42	8.52	80 (27)
30 (-1)	0	0	0	52 (12)
	1	0.16	0.16	56 (14)
	2	0.45	0.9	70 (21)
	3	0.62	1.86	72 (22)
	4	0.87	3.48	69 (21)
	5	1.23	6.15	82 (28)
	6	1.4	8.4	76 (24)
60 (16)	0	0	0	73 (23)
	1	0.08	0.08	74 (23)
	2	0.73	1.46	74 (23)
	3	0.64	1.92	79 (26)
	4	0.9	3.6	81 (27)
	5	1.12	5.6	88 (31)
	6	1.41	8.46	97 (36)

TABLE 5.7: Results of thermal chamber testing (cooling mode).

Chamber Temperature°F (°C)	Voltage(Volts)	Current(Amps)	Power(Watts)	Temperature Output°F (°C)
60 (16)	0	0	0	76 (24)
	1	0.36	0.36	72 (22)
	2	0.65	1.3	70 (21)
	3	0.77	2.31	63 (17)
	4	1.08	4.32	46 (8)
	5	1.41	7.05	54 (12)
	6	1.82	10.92	50 (10)
90 (32)	0	0	0	73 (23)
	1	0.19	0.19	63 (17)
	2	0.43	0.86	67 (19)
	3	0.65	1.95	57 (14)
	4	0.92	3.68	67 (19)
	5	1.27	6.35	67 (19)
	6	1.6	9.6	61 (16)

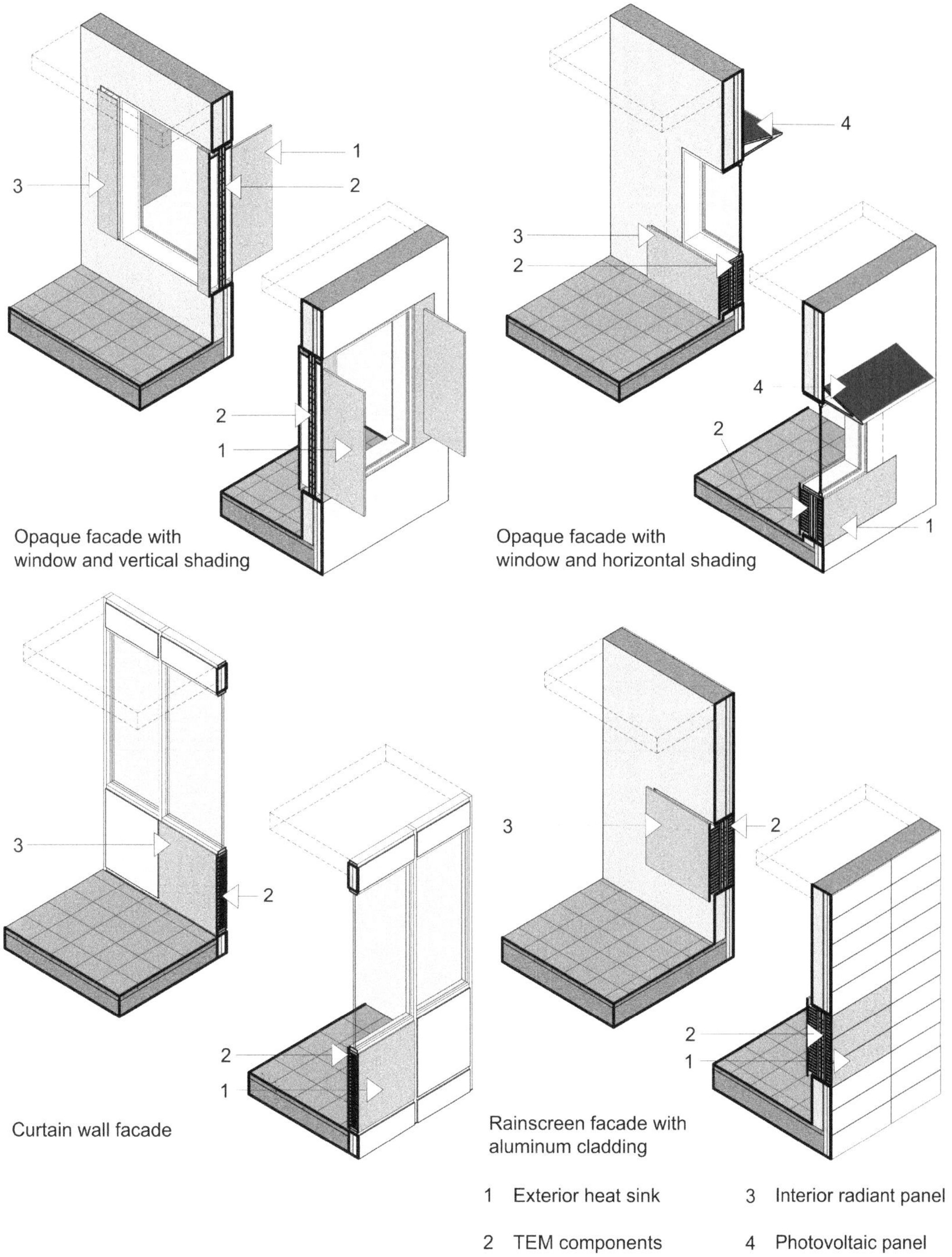

Opaque facade with
window and vertical shading

Opaque facade with
window and horizontal shading

Curtain wall facade

Rainscreen facade with
aluminum cladding

1	Exterior heat sink	3	Interior radiant panel
2	TEM components	4	Photovoltaic panel

Figure 5.54:
Digital models of
different facade
types with inte-
grated thermoelec-
tric components.

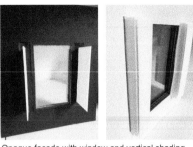 

Figure 5.55:
Physical scaled
prototypes of dif-
ferent facade types
with integrated
thermoelectric com-
ponents, digitally
fabricated.

Opaque facade with window and vertical shading   Opaque facade with window and horizontal shading

Curtain wall facade   Rainscreen facade with aluminum cladding

were digitally fabricated using 3D printers and laser cutting. These prototypes were used for visual evaluations. Figure 5.56 shows full scale working physical prototypes.

The last part of the study investigated the heating and cooling potentials of these novel systems for conditioning commercial office spaces. A typical commercial office space was used in the simulation study to investigate heating and cooling capabilities. In the simulation model, a single office space was modeled with an exterior wall consisting of a thermoelectric facade and interior walls as adiabatic partition walls. CFD simulations were conducted for different scenarios, using the SOLIDWORKS software program, varying the exterior environmental conditions and the percentage of wall coverage with thermoelectric components (5%, 10%, 15%, and 20%). The exterior temperature was identical to the experimental study, considering temperatures of 90°F, 60°F, 30°F, and 0°F (32°C, 16°C, -1°C, and -18°C). Simulations were conducted to calculate temperature distribution within the interior space for these different scenarios, and to determine heating and cooling outputs. Results of the 20 simulated scenarios indicated that 15% TE wall coverage was the most efficient option both for heating and cooling purposes within the simulated space. Examples of results are shown in Figure 5.57.

The results of this research indicated that TE materials are promising intelligent components that can be used in facade assemblies for heating and cooling purposes, controlling buildings' interior environments. This is an independent system that does not require moving parts or harmful substances and solely relies

Figure 5.56:
Physical full scale,
working prototypes
of facade systems
with integrated
thermoelectric
components.

PROTOTYPE 1: SOLID FACADE ASSEMBLY

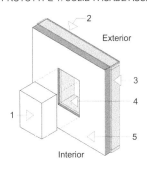

Exterior side

Interior side

PROTOTYPE 2: FACADE ASSEMBLY WITH A WINDOW

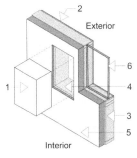

Exterior side

Interior side

1   TEM components and heat sinks

2   Exterior metal cladding

3   Wall framing and insulation

4   Insulation around TEM components

5   Interior gypsum sheathing

6   Window

on the temperature difference between the interior and exterior environments to operate. It relies on the capabilities of TEs to warm up in heating mode and cool down in cooling mode, when exposed to temperature differences between the inside and outside. However, a separate ventilation system would still be needed for the interior space, which cannot be provided by the stand-alone facade-integrated TEs. Maintenance of TE systems is easier than the conventional HVAC systems because they can be treated as individual components, with no need to shut down the whole system. Furthermore, they can be used as a personalized system which occupants of each room within the same building can use based on personal preferences.

Figure 5.57:
CFD models and
examples of simula-
tion results.

5%   10%   15%   20%

CFD simulation models with different exterior wall coverage with TEM components

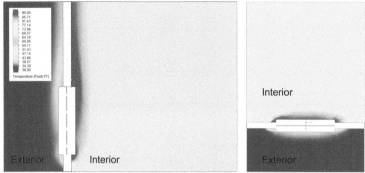

Results for 20% wall coverage, 30°F (-1°C) exterior temperature, heating mode

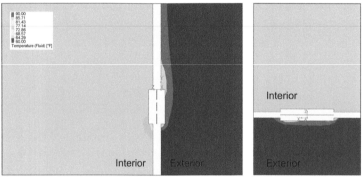

Results for 10% wall coverage, 60°F (16°C) exterior temperature, cooling mode

REFERENCES

Aksamija, A., (2013). *Sustainable Facades: Design Methods for High-Performance Building Envelopes*, Hoboken, NJ: John Wiley & Sons.

Aksamija, A., (2016). "Regenerative Design and Adaptive Reuse of Existing Commercial Buildings for Net-Zero Energy Use", *Journal of Sustainable Cities and Society*, Vol. 27, pp. 185–195.

Aksamija, A., (2017). "Impact of Retrofitting Energy-Efficient Design Strategies on Energy Use of Existing Commercial Buildings: Comparative Study of Low-Impact and Deep Retrofit Strategies", *Journal of Green Building*, Vol. 12, No. 4, pp. 70–88.

Aksamija, A., Aksamija, Z., Counihan, C., Brown, D., Upadhyaya, M., (2019). "Experimental Study of Operating Conditions and Integration of Thermoelectric Materials in Facade Systems", *Frontiers in Energy Research, Special Issue on New Materials and Design of the Building Enclosure*, Vol. 7, Article 6, pp. 1–10.

Aksamija, A., Aksamija, Z., Vignaeu, G., Upadhyaya, M., and Farid Mohajer, M., (2020). "Thermoelectric Facades: Simulation of Heating, Cooling and Energy Generation Potential for Novel Intelligent Facade Systems", *Proceedings of the Facade World*

Congress 2020, Virtual, August 5-27. https://www.facadetectonics.org/papers/t hermoelectric-facades.

Aksamija, A., and Peters, T., (2016a). "Climate Change and Performance of Facade Systems: Analysis of Thermal Behavior and Energy Consumption in Different Climate Types", *Perkins and Will Research Journal*, Vol. 8, No. 2, pp. 52–79.

Aksamija, A., and Peters, T., (2016b). "Heat Transfer in Facade Systems and Energy Use: Comparative Study of Different Exterior Wall Types", *Journal of Architectural Engineering*, Vol. 23, No. 1, pp. C5016002.

Aksamija, A., and Wang, Y., (2017). "Regenerative Design for Achieving Net-Zero Energy Commercial Buildings in Different Climate Types", in *Architectural Research Addressing Societal Challenges*, Couceiro da Costa, M., Roseta, F., Pestana Lages, P., and Couceiro da Costa, S., eds., Leiden, The Netherlands: CRC Press/Taylor & Francis Group, pp. 527–534.

de Freitas, M., and Ruschel, R., (2013). "What is Happening to Virtual and Augmented Reality Applied to Architecture?", *Proceedings of the 18th International Conference on Computer-Aided Architectural Design Research in Asia (CAADRIA 2013)*, Hong Kong, pp. 407–416.

Fernando, T., Wu, K., and Bassanino, M., (2013). "Designing a Novel Virtual Collaborative Environment to Support Collaboration in Design Review Meetings", *Journal of Information Technology in Construction*, Vol. 18, pp. 372–396.

Heydarian, A., Carneiro, J., Gerber, D., Becerik-Gerber, B., Hayes, T., and Wood, W., (2015). "Immersive Virtual Environments versus Physical Built Environments: A Benchmarking Study for Building Design and User-Built Environment Explorations", *Automation in Construction*, Vol. 52, pp. 116–126.

Jentsch, M., James, P., Bourikas, L., and Bahaj, A., (2013). "Transforming Existing Weather Data for Worldwide Locations to Enable Energy and Building Performance Simulation under Future Climates", *Renewable Energy*, Vol. 55, pp. 514–524.

Montecucco, A., Buckle, J., and Knox, A., (2012). "Solution to the 1-D Unsteady Heat Conduction Equation with Internal Joule Heat Generation for Thermoelectric Devices", *Applied Thermal Engineering*, Vol. 35, pp. 177–184.

Niebyl, D., (2018). *Spomenik Monument Database*, London, UK: FUEL Publishing.

Snyder, G., and Toberer, E., (2008). "Complex Thermoelectric Materials", *Nature Materials*, Vol. 7, pp. 105–114.

Stierli, M., and Kulic, V., eds., (2018). *Toward a Concrete Utopia: Architecture in Yugoslavia, 1948–1980*, New York: The Museum of Modern Art.

Wang, X., Kim, M., Love, P., and Kang, S.-C., (2013). "Augmented Reality in Built Environment: Classification and Implications for Future Research", *Automation in Construction*, Vol. 32, pp. 1–13.

Yilmazoglu, M., (2016). "Experimental and Numerical Investigation of a Prototype Thermoelectric Heating and Cooling Unit", *Energy and Buildings*, Vol. 113, pp. 51–60.

Zhao, D., and Tan, G., (2014). "A Review of Thermoelectric Cooling: Materials, Modeling and Applications", *Applied Thermal Engineering*, Vol. 66, pp. 15–24.

Index

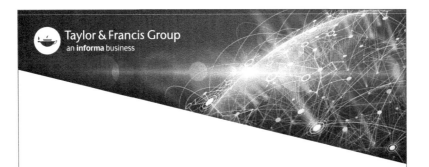

For Product Safety Concerns and Information please contact our EU representative GPSR@taylorandfrancis.com Taylor & Francis Verlag GmbH, Kaufingerstraße 24, 80331 München, Germany

T - #0211 - 090625 - C224 - 254/178/13 - PB - 9780367433963 - Matt Lamination